CREATING THE HUMAN ENVIRONMENT

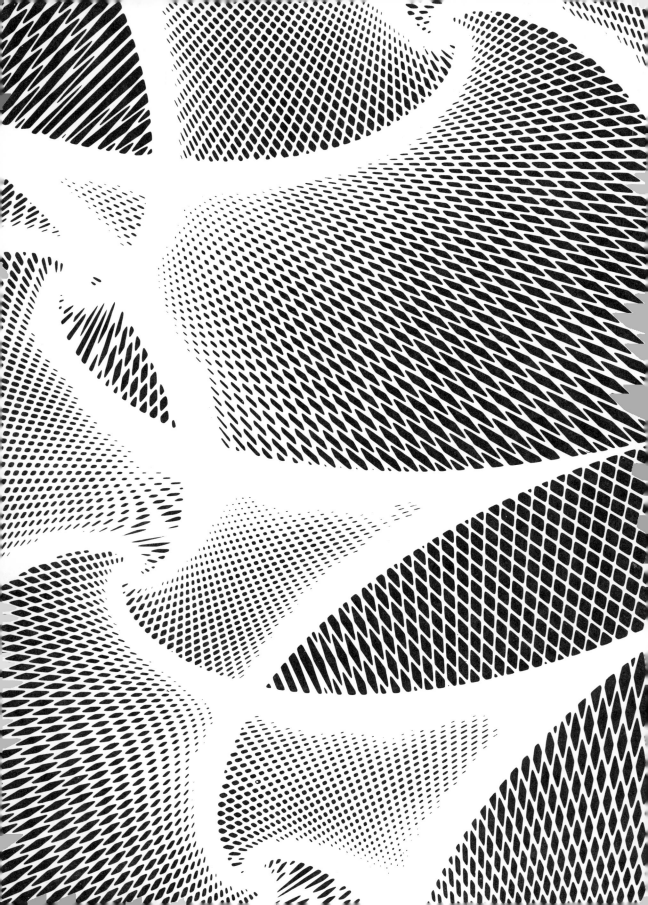

Creating
the
Human
Environment

A REPORT OF THE AMERICAN INSTITUTE OF ARCHITECTS
BY GERALD M. McCUE, WILLIAM R. EWALD, JR., AND
THE MIDWEST RESEARCH INSTITUTE

UNIVERSITY OF ILLINOIS PRESS
URBANA, CHICAGO, LONDON

Published with the assistance of a grant from The Graham Foundation for Advanced Studies in the Fine Arts.

"A NATIONAL — NOT AN URBAN CRISIS," states William R. Ewald, Jr. in his study of social influences on the future of the physical environment. This crisis embraces every person, institution, and segment in American society.

The American Institute of Architects commissioned Mr. Ewald and the Midwest Research Institute to examine the social and physical contexts of American life and to project them to the year 2000. The goal of the AIA was to define the possibilities and limitations of the architectural profession which would affect its future. The reports reveal that there are indeed severe constraints upon improving the environment, but that the present opportunities for the profession to become a leading force in revitalizing our society are unparalleled in the history of the profession, and perhaps of any profession.

The Committee for the Study of the Future of the Profession was constituted as a special committee of the Board of Directors of the American Institute of Architects at the recommendation of president Charles M. Nes, Jr. and held its initial meeting in September 1966 under the first chairman, Llewellyn W. Pitts. The purpose of the Committee, as described by Mr. Nes, was "to discuss and determine on a more factual basis the problems facing our profession not only today but insofar as is possible in the years ahead" and "to initiate fact-finding procedures which will enable the institute to plan more surely to meet the demands of the future, and to marshal a body of informed opinion for this purpose."

The work of the Committee included three main phases. The

first consisted of an exchange of views and speculation as to the meaning of current trends in the building industry and the profession. The second phase was a conference where those persons outside the profession identified the factors believed to be most significant in affecting the future of the profession.

In the fall of 1967, following Mr. Pitts' death, AIA president Robert L. Durham appointed Gerald McCue as chairman of the Committee. He and David C. Miller of the Communication Services Corporation prepared a *Summary Review and Recommendation for Further Work* and with the Committee recommended to the AIA Board of Directors that three studies be made for the reconnaissance and analysis for future projections in those areas which were deemed most important to the future of the profession. The studies proposed were: (1) U.S. society; (2) management and legal aspects of the U.S. building industry; and (3) technology in the U.S. building industry.

The third phase of the study began in 1968 when the AIA Board of Directors authorized the Committee to proceed with the studies. Abt Associates (Henry Bruck, project director) were retained as consultants for coordination of the two study modules. The first module, "A Summary Review of Current Research in Societal Trends Related to the Physical Environment," was awarded to William R. Ewald, Jr., Development Consultant of Washington, D.C. The second module, "Economic, Financial, Business, Management, and Technological Trends within the Building Industry," was awarded to Midwest Research Institute (Mssrs. Haney and Shoup, project managers).

The study of the Committee for the Future of the Profession has been conducted by the following members of the American Institute of Architects:

Rex W. Allen	George E. Kassabaum
Robert W. Cutler	David A. McKinley, Jr.
Louis De Moll	Charles M. Nes, Jr.
Robert L. Durham	Llewellyn W. Pitts
Samuel T. Hurst	William H. Scheick

Gerald M. McCue, Chairman

The work of this Committee achieved a uniquely progressive study for the AIA. For the first time, survey research methods have been used to project the future of the total creative process of building the human environment as a service to all of the design professions and the building industry.

William H. Scheick
Washington, D.C.

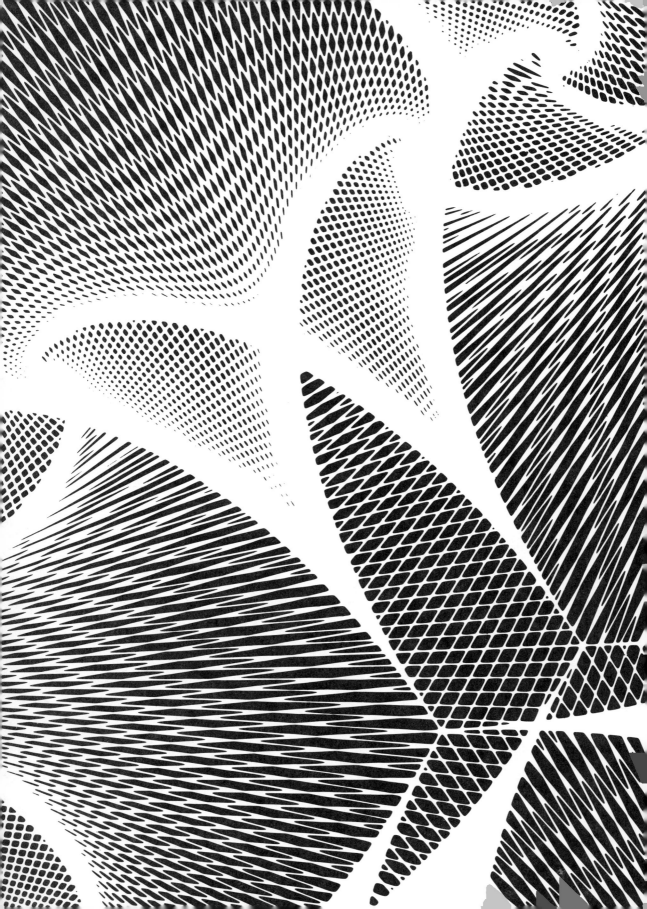

PART ONE

Reconnaissance of the Future
(1920-1985-2000)

WILLIAM R. EWALD, JR.

INTRODUCTION

We like to think of this nation as a youthful, open society that offers an equal chance "to anyone who wants to work for it." As prerequisites for rewarding participation, we establish a good education — not "too much" and not the "wrong kind" — hard work, self-discipline, an ingrained sense of the practical, keeping out of trouble, and getting along with others. Government per se and most intellects are considered suspect, to be closely watched. The test of all manner of things rational, irrational, or extrarational[1] is pragmatism — does it work? Thus, the door is "always open" to any idea and to anyone.

As to the future, our ongoing view has been mostly in terms of next week, next month, or the next year or so, even if we *do* have plans to send our children to college, have a little insurance set aside, "own" a house, make time payments on cars and other necessities, and have made a lifetime career commitment so long ago we've forgotten we did. "Live each day," "let tomorrow take care of itself," and "don't borrow trouble" are our philosophies for meeting the future.

Recently, however, H. G. Wells' futuristic visions from the early 1900's, *Astounding Stories,* and George Orwell's *1984,* have become, in a disquieting way, more real to us than the science fiction we first took them to be. It took an atomic bomb to open our eyes. Twenty years later, our minds were opened by the space probes, and now again by the moon shots. Most recently all media from RAND's scientific Delphic oracles, TV's "Star Trek," and the front page of the *Wall Street Journal* to Herman Kahn (a solid-state medium of a new sort) have been filling our receptive minds with the "certainties" of the technological future. In particular, talk about computers is becoming as pervasive as pollution and poverty.

We appear to believe that the technological future being described to us is contiguous or overlapping with our short-term personal view of the future. When we really think about that, it puts us in a temporary state of cultural shock, best treated by a long drive in the country and a return to our old reliable pragmatic personal philosophies. This home remedy is not going to work much longer. It has been failing us a little more each year since World War II, which was probably the last time Americans shared as a people a sense of purpose and mission. More individuals are richer, but we seem spiritually poorer as a nation. Given the modern communications network we have, it is difficult to state "we are poor but we didn't know it."[2] Morale is low and there is restlessness, not only among the young, the black, the scientists, and increasingly the professionals, but also for different reasons, the middle class and the right wing.

We seem to have reached a time when we need to stop and think and learn how to recognize the wisdom we need, wherever we can find it. But there is the danger it will only postpone to another decade serious attempts to grapple now with the opportunities of the future as well as the problems we have inherited from the past. At the rate today's world is changing, we are deceiving ourselves if we believe a problem or an opportunity postponed now will be the same when it better suits us to get to it. They have a history of transforming themselves. The way TV has exploded the vision of a new life for the black man alone should be enough to demolish this escapist thinking. We face numerous other examples in pollution, youth's dissatisfactions, transportation, population concentrations, and the threat of nuclear warfare. They are all interrelated.

"Ordering" the Future: Transition, Shock Front, and the Technological Age

Those who will design and build the environment for the next fifteen to thirty years should take time out now to order their perspective of the future. The moment is propitious. This report is intended as an aid to that process. Perhaps we could best begin by pointing out that it is most likely that between our personal, "immediate" (out to two-year) view of the future and most of the "technological future" that our minds are now being filled with, there is a "transitional future"

TABLE I-1. *"Ordering" the Future*[3]

	Future	Point of View	Time Span	Target Years	Deciding Generation	Relevant National Elections
	immediate	personal	next week, next month, next year or so	1969-70	this one	1970
	transitional	group	next 2-4 yrs	1971-73	this one	1972
		institutional	next 5-15 yrs	1974-84	this one	1976
	technological	societal	last 15 yrs of century	1985-2000	next one	1984
		global	21st century	2000+	third one	2000+

The Shock Front (leftmost vertical label)

(of fifteen years). We are aware of powerful technologies that will require fifteen more years to take full effect, and we can conceive of several more revolutionary ones that may be fifty years or more away. Their timetables will be determined by the social inventions.

We may be more inclined to think *beyond* our immediate personal two-year perspective if we understand that for the moment, concerning the evolution of the technological future, time is on our side. (The urban riots are here considered the result of our high order of one-way communication causing a violent confrontation with the believed affluence of society and its outdated social mores.) We still have time to learn how to take charge of the impending, much greater impacts of the technological future. If we start work now, first in groups, then through institutions — professional, government, private enterprise, and nonprofit including universities and churches — we can help assure that the societal and global use of technology after 1985 is for the purpose of creating a *human* future environment. We have time to turn onrushing technology to human purposes rather than permitting men to apathetically drift into the role of "breeding humans to tend machines." It isn't coming so fast that we need to give up, yet.

We have entered a new era. Most of those who have seriously studied history identify current times as a break with the past equivalent to the beginning of the Agricultural Revolution (4000 B.C.) and the Industrial Revolution (1600 A.D.). Even the most conservative acknowledge that we are in for an *accelerating* continuation of the Industrial Revolution. Special terms are being used to mark this time

5

of Technological Revolution like "Technotronic Age,"[4] "Technological Society,"[5] "The New Industrial State,"[6] "Post Industrial Society,"[7] "Age of Discontinuity."[8] It is to be a "Sensate Culture"[9] and "God Is Dead."[10]

The unsettled, riot torn, breaking-up, swept-along feeling of these times has perhaps been most accurately captured by the biophysicist John R. Platt. The rest of this century he likens to the "shock front" at the leading edge of an airplane's wing as it breaks the sound barrier, before the air flow smooths out again.[11] In pure physics terms there is, after all, a limit to how fast and how much change is possible. This is true for humans also. If mankind, as we understand it, is to survive on earth, it must pass not only through this shock front but also into a new condition in the history of man — "steady state" — in which the population is in dynamic ecological balance with earth. A potential of *two* epics in one lifetime! The behavioral scientist John B. Calhoun, famous for his rat experiments into density-communication and overcrowding, places the human psychological limit of population on earth at about 9 billion, versus the current 25 to 50 billion calculated by others in pure human animal feeding terms. Harrison Brown in 1957 put the feeding level at 7.7 billion.[12] At present growth rates the 9 billion world population will be reached in 2010. Calhoun expects we will overshoot it by 50 per cent before settling back. Donald Bogue predicts the world population is coming under control, that birth rate started to drop in 1965 and that by the year 2000 growth will be either zero or close to it.[13] Others foresee famines by 1975.

We sense and feel the break-up caused by the shock front, and perhaps attribute to our "natural enemies" — opposing groups, institutions, or nations — troubles that far supersede their malicious efforts. Through television we "participate" in the shock front — the Vietnam War; the Detroit Riots; the assassinations of John F. Kennedy, Martin Luther King, and Robert Kennedy; Resurrection City; walks in space; the Chicago Democratic Convention Police Riots; Berkeley and Columbia turmoil; Walter Cronkite pointing at new technological marvels; ABM's; SST's.

That there needs to be time and a place to think and understand in this tumultuous era cannot be emphasized enough; forethought in the comprehensive social, physical, and economic terms of environment is a prerequisite both for working out the urgent problems of today and for projecting the research and institution-building necessary to realize future human opportunities. We know that it can take twenty years for a defined concept to be implemented. The future begins today.

Furthermore, in the shock front we are entering, more unthinking action — the typical highway construction, OEO programs, Lake Erie, for example — is neither warranted nor justifiable. Often, doing *something,* even if it's wrong, is an accepted "reason" for action and is often resorted to. The feel of the last resort hangs heavy. As Schillebeeckx has said, "Fear of the future hangs over secular mankind."[14] It may be what is driving huge corporations and huge governments to make huge oversimplifications in order to take some sort of action in the "urban crisis."

We've gone so far as to act simultaneously as if the physical environment can be ignored as a trivial detail while claiming that a most urgent need is to build 26 million homes in the next ten years.[15] Perhaps only an environmental professional like the architect can make sense out of this. But even he will need time to think.

Historically, we have tended to overestimate change in the short run, and when it doesn't materialize quickly, we are lulled into a sense of complacency or frustration. This leads to foreseeable "crises" to which we respond by taking what we proudly call "action." Typically, we *react* rather than anticipate. We struggle with many present-day problems because we ignored them when they were future opportunities. Change in the long run is almost always *understated.* It simply outstrips our imagination. In the shock-front time of great technological and social change we are now into, we are confounded by the vast, seemingly endless predictability of new "unpredictables." But the "immediate" technological changes we may be anticipating, or dreading, are more part of our children's and grandchildren's future. They simply won't happen as fast as we seem to think.

We will feel impacts from new technology more and more as we move deeper into the shock front from 1971 to 1984. We may even be able to foresee now, with a useful degree of understanding, some of the basic technological changes which will occur in the next generation, 1985 to 2000. But our grip on the future really begins to slip over the last fifteen years of the century. Beyond the year 2000, we can't predict much more than that it is *then* the science-fiction technology we read about today will be in full operation — fuel cells, 3-dimensional TV, vacation trips to the moon, 100+ years of life, 150-IQ computers, robots, "smart pills," and more than we can imagine.

7

The Human and the Technological Future Environment

As designers of the present and future *human* environment, we should not fall into the trap that big private enterprise and big government seem tipped toward — oversimplification and nearly blind faith in the technologies of the future. Projections of the technological future are hopefully not the same as projections of the human future.

Technology is simply the vision of the future most easily communicated and most easily marketed. It is made up of "things" we can tabulate, draw pictures, and make models of. Our minds are swollen with information on futuristic gadgets. But what a human environment must be, we haven't begun to really understand. We have limited social and economic action programs for "instant" solutions, but we have no comprehensive social-economic-physical conception of the total future human environment, or of how to build it beginning now and phasing through the transitional period of the next two to fifteen years into the technological future. The human needs and the numbers involved are great, and there is a limit to resources. There is, therefore, a need for efficiency. This has brought forth cost-benefit ratios and program planning and budget systems. Cost-benefit ratios measure economic efficiency; as such they are constraints on the means, not the objectives. Designers of the future environment should assimilate and transcend these management tools so that we may proceed to human-benefit ratios.

Perhaps a human conception of the future environment that is more than personal (i.e., two years) and more than efficient (Program Planning Budgeting System) is the peculiar contribution only the environmental professions can make at this time. What other professions have defined for themselves the responsibility to design and build environments that contribute to the development of individual human beings and their society? Is the combining of art and spirit with science and technology to create the future urban environment the unique role of the architect? Is he prepared in the period of transition into the technological future to join with the other professionals such as the biologist, the systems analyst, the behavioral scientist, the anthropologist — as well as the planners and engineers he is already familiar with — to begin the evolution of a human concept of environment? Can the architect transcend the mastery of the building of single buildings and move on to sharing in the design of whole environments?

8

These are more than rhetorical questions. They require an affirmative answer by architects if the character and aesthetic design of the future human environment is not to be either ignored as inconsequential as it may be by many economists, sociologists, and some planners, or treated as a matter of pure technology by the behavioral scientists, engineers, and industrial production lines. The building of the future human environment must be both a human and a technological triumph. If this is to be so, we must see the future environmental design process as a unique meld of the two. We must deal in a way appropriate to our age in the realities of building with concrete, steel, glass, wood, aluminum, brick, and plastic to serve the activities and spirit of men. It is as Charles W. Moore, chairman of Yale's Architectural Department has put it, "Architecture is only properly teachable in terms of *use* in response to the people who are to inhabit buildings, their life styles, their concerns, their privacy and their public realm."[16]

Without totally ignoring the technological in this study, we shall emphasize the human aspect of the challenge. It is social inventions that are most needed now to facilitate the proper use of the technological ones. Too little has been said of the decisions that humans must make to determine what technology will be used and how; people have an impact on technology as well as technology having an impact on people.

This report's concentration on social inventions was determined by careful plumbing of the most knowledgeable technological judgment in this country over the past four years by this investigator. When pursued in depth, almost every imagined technological barrier to development was found ready to break if subjected to concentrated effort. The greater the effort, the sooner the breakthrough. The limit of what men can do is not *on* men, it is *in* them.

From industrialized housing and New Towns to avoiding world famines, it becomes clear now that the primary barrier to implementation are social inventions and the will of individuals and society to apply and fund already known technology and to get on with the research we "know" we need for shaping the future. There is a transcendent matter of communication involved here.

1.

TWO PERSPECTIVES INTO THE FUTURE

"THINKING ABOUT THE FUTURE is not only the mightiest lever of progress but also the condition of survival," said Pierre Bertaux, quoting F. L. Polak, at the 1967 American Institute of Planners Conference. There are those, however, who would not agree with this analysis of long-range planning — and with ample reason — ridiculing inaccuracies of past attempts to project the future.

For example, a report entitled *What About the Year 2000?* published in 1929, the work of the Committee on Basis of Sound Land Policy, a considerable body of professionals, projected a population for the year 2000 that we passed in 1962, because in 1927 they did not predict two system breaks: World War II and its subsequent "baby boom." As they saw it, "the preponderance of evidence set forth by recent authorities points to a population not in excess of 200 million by the year 2000. Perhaps the population will never exceed this number, and probably will fall 10 million or 15 million below it."[1]

Or consider the remarks of Martin Van Buren, who as governor of New York in 1829 wrote President Andrew Jackson that:

> The canal system of this country is being threatened by the spread of a new form of transportation known as "railroads." The Federal Government must preserve the canals for the following reasons:
>
> 1. If canal boats are supplanted by "railroads," serious unemployment will result. Captains, cooks, drivers, hostlers, repairmen, and lock tenders will be left without means of livelihood not to mention the numerous farmers now employed in growing hay for the horses.
> 2. Boat builders would suffer; and towline, whip and harness makers would be left destitute.

10

3. Canal boats are absolutely essential to the United States. In the event of the expected trouble with England, the Erie Canal would be the only means by which we could move supplies so vital to waging modern war.

For the above-mentioned reasons the government should create an Interstate Commerce Commission to protect the American people from "railroads" and to preserve the canals for posterity. As you may know, Mr. President, "railroad" carriages are pulled at the enormous speed of 15 miles per hour by "engines," which in addition to endangering life and limb of passengers, roar and snort their way through the countryside, setting fire to the crops, scaring the livestock, and frightening women and children. The Almighty certainly never intended that people should travel at such breakneck speed.[2]

As a leader, Van Buren certainly had the facilities of his day at his disposal for being informed, but his information was incomplete.

The same can be said of two great contemporaries of ours: David E. Lilienthal and Dr. Vannevar Bush. Lilienthal told this investigator that the TVA had not anticipated the great migration to the city; and that TVA had a multiple-use resource policy for rural development but no urban policy.[3] The migration from farm to city from 1920 to 1967 has been estimated at 37 million. It is considered one of the greatest migrations in the history of man.[4] No one in the United States in the early 1930's could have been more interested in being informed or more competent to inform himself on something like this than Lilienthal, but neither he nor any of the nation's leaders was aware of this major "system break."

In 1945, Dr. Bush told President Truman regarding the development of the atomic bomb, "This is the biggest fool thing we have ever done. . . . The bomb will never go off, and I speak as an expert in explosives."[5] (It went off July 16, 1945 at Almagordo, New Mexico; and August 5, 1945 at Hiroshima.)

With such experts misunderstanding the potentials of the future, who *can* understand the future? Of course there have been accurate predictions by H. G. Wells, Jules Verne, Arthur C. Clarke, and both Huxleys, but how does one know at the time who is to be proven right? Perhaps all the answer needed is what government and private enterprise have permitted in Lake Erie.[6] Day by day over fifteen years, the lake was killed. It wasn't that it wasn't predictable. It was just neither expedient *nor practical* to those directly involved to consider the consequences or to project to the public what was happening. The future fate of the great lake enjoyed by many was decided by a very few. There was no forum on the future of Lake Erie to discuss what was likely to happen in its future. Nobody knew they needed to be interested, but anybody could have understood if informed. So although we know we cannot predict the future, we can at least try to shape it.

Methodologies, System Breaks, and the Future

To try to study the future environment there are a number of methodologies that may be used, any of which may prove useful. Herman Kahn describes eight approaches derived from combinations called extrapolative, goal-seeking, synthetic, morphological, theoretical, intuitive.[7] Robert W. Prehoda concentrates on technological forecasting, "foreseeable inventions."

Kenneth Boulding's lucid explanation divides prediction into mechanical systems, pattern systems, equilibrium systems, and evolutionary systems.[8] He makes clear that "the main cause for failures in prediction is a sudden change in the characteristics of the system itself, like a door in a wall." Such a change has been called a "system break." Examples are death, bankruptcy, marriage, a new job, the outbreak of war, inventions, sudden changes in birth or death rates, rapid productivity shifts, etc. He cites the need for the educational system to "plan for surprise."[9]

So we admit to the fallacies possible in prediction and to the certainty of unforeseen "system breaks" but feel somehow stricken by the notion that we should not therefore be permitted an "image of the future."[10] According to Bertaux, ". . . Every culture has just the future that is contained in the dynamic force of its image of the future. The future of a culture can be predicted by the power of its thinking about the future. No culture can maintain itself for long without a positive and generally accepted image of the future. A culture which shuts itself up in the present or what amounts to the same thing, in a short-sighted perspective of the future, has no future."[11]

The Macrocosmic and Microcosmic Views

The abiding concern of the design professions is the construction of a more viable human environment. We therefore shall investigate the future human environment from two perspectives: the macrocosmic and the microcosmic — hereafter, "macro" and "micro." The macro perspective traces the great forces of change-at-work on and through society to the individual; micro examines the total force exerted by many millions of individuals upon society. Investigation shows that despite all the *potential* ascribed to futuristic technology, the decisive factor in deciding the future is the will of people, not the technology. And oversight, failure, or the exercise of will is common to both society and the individual.

So little has been communicated on the human future environment that it may be useful from the outset to attempt to list the basic factors to be considered in each of the two perspectives we will use.

BASIC FORCES OF CHANGE

MACRO Impacts		*MICRO Impacts*	
Environment → Individual		*Individual → Environment*	
population	time	physiological	cultural
	space	psychological	social
technology	expectations (free will)	spiritual (free will)	ecological

The combined interactions between the factors themselves and the individual in each grouping of impacts produces a result that is greater than would be expected from studying each in isolation; the effect is synergistic. The task is to understand this and to make use of this knowledge in human ways.

The expectations of society, the great growth and concentration of population, the application of technology — the meaning of all these over increasing increments of geographic space and time are the forces of change generally discussed when looking into the future. They are all beyond our individual control. They are the macro forces. They seem to beat down on us. Just thinking about them can be depressing because we seem so impotent to influence them. Although they *are* real forces, they are not the only ones.

If we would accept the projection of the past into the future as a smooth predictable curve or the uncontrollable impacts of society upon us, we would have no need for the projection of the individual's impact on the environment, both singly and in the aggregate. Nor would we be concerned with the likelihood or human meaning of technological system breaks to men. But we *don't* accept such a deterministic view. And as a result, we are left with the uncomfortable understanding that *we* as individuals and in groups have our own

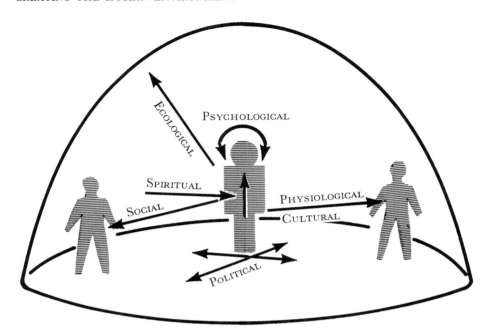

FIGURE I-1. *Micro Impacts of the Individual on the Environment*

impacts, and consequently our own responsibilities, concerning the creation of the future environment — physiologically, psychologically, ecologically, spiritually, socially, culturally, politically — and consequently have a need to know. The more aware, the more comprehensive this understanding, the greater the responsibility — and the greater the need to know. This may be the unique responsibility of the environmental design professions — in regard to both the urgent problems of today and the great opportunities of tomorrow.

In both of these perspectives concerning the forces of change, so enormously influenced by population and technology, there must be feedback (or "feed forward" as I. A. Richardson has put it) from the individual. According to Roger L. Schinn, cyberneticist Norbert Wiener underlined this necessity: "He insisted as a moral proposition that machines must be designed to pursue human goals, not machine-determined goals, and that in all moral and policy decisions the 'feedback' must be routed through persons."[12]

The micro perspective demands the establishment of meaningful participation for all who are both affected and interested from the bottom up. The macro perspective demands professionalism and full-scale efforts, not tokenism from the top down. There is conflict between the two views. It can be creative conflict. For that we must have dialogue to seek agreement as to the process and the facts both use. The micro perspective is micro also in regard to strategies, objectives, its time span of concern, and its scope. That does not make it less important. But the micro perspective *is* more intense, more emotionally involved, and more often than not more irrational, but hopefully extrarational as well. It after all argues most directly the human case and is therefore at the center of purpose. The micro viewpoint tends to insist on results immediately — unrealistically. The macro view seeks thorough professional, multidisciplinary investigation and understanding before taking action, however long that may take — unrealistically. Dialogue is needed over such differences; how do we achieve it?

The Conditions for Dialogue on the Future Human Environment

For dialogue in these circumstances to be meaningful there can be no suspicion that "the deck is stacked" or that the people involved are playing in "somebody else's ball park." To this end, both the public and private sectors in the future can be expected to modify their past mode of operations; but they will still own their own ball parks and set the rules.

Government may be forced to improve its management, decentralize more decisions to cities and states, formalize longer-range accountability of decisions, and develop "social indicators"[13] as well as fiscal ones. But it will take time. In addition to profits, private enterprise may devise ways to acknowledge serving public need as a measure of its capacity; but this may well take three generations of top management or eighteen years.[14] It can be expected that both government and private enterprise will modify their operations slowly, while our needs to comprehend and direct the forces of change grow exponentially. By way of example, "If we assume that the complexity of relations among one billion people is represented by an index of 1, then the figure for three billions would potentially be 18 and for six billions, 222."[15]

Besides these slow, hoped for improvements in government and private enterprise, part of the solution would appear to be in creating new "ball parks" — especially nonprofit ball parks, and public-private COMSAT-type corporations. The purpose would be to create new institutions prejudiced toward the long-run consequences of certain sensitive immediate issues, and unique large-scale ones as government and private enterprise are prejudiced towards short-run "safe" issues. In our society, both of our two great decision-making institutions, government and private enterprise, have been constructed to be responsive to the short term. A businessman must make money every year or go out of business. Similarly, a politician must be a hero every year or he won't be reelected.[16] Both, naturally enough, avoid the thankless difficult issues as long as possible.

Nonprofit problem-solving "environmental situation and outlook centers" funded through foundations, professional societies, civic associations, churches and universities (affiliated with universities but not dominated by their rigid departmentalization) could thrive on the big issues of concern for a human future environment and receive funds from both government and the private sector to help them. Public-private corporations would have a freer swing at operating roles in these same problem-opportunity areas.

Electric utilities may be the most natural catalyst for this purpose. They have a territorial understanding of place that is not circumscribed by political boundaries. They have a longer range operating perspective than most institutions — ten years.[17] They understand engineering and the professional approach. They deal with both the public and private sectors, considering themselves ideologically part of the private sector but concerned with public issues and public bureaucracy too. At the present time, the funds that they can contribute to another institution for environmental planning in their territories is restricted and most likely taken from their public relations budget (as required by law in forty-eight of the fifty states). Consequently, what funds do contribute most to community "forward looking" are small.

Electric utilities, and other utilities, throughout the country could contribute the seed money for the proposed new nonprofit centers for their specific regions. State laws would need to be changed so that these utilities could put major funds into environmental planning through those independent nonprofit situation and outlook centers.

Private enterprise is a potential source of funds for these centers. At present, private enterprise contributes only 1/80 of the 5 per cent charitable tax deductions it is allowed.[18] Large blocks of common stock, up to 50 per cent, are being held by mutual and pension funds

16

these days.[19] Perhaps this is enough of a concentration to make feasible a serious effort to win stockholder approval for more generous use of the 5 per cent deduction or for support of environmental design centers as a straight business expense. The argument would be that these contributions to the centers would help keep viable the environment in which corporations do their business.

Assuming such nonprofit centers are in existence to offer opportunity for the exploration of choice, goals, values, and consequences for executives, professionals, and the interested public — the time, place, and condition for dialogue on the development of the future human environment will have been created. Such centers would be needed at all levels from the neighborhood to the national. We need to agree on process used by these centers. A possible hierachy and system from philosophy to procedure is shown in Figure I-2.

For the development of a future environment that admits and enhances the rational-irrational-extrarational qualities of individuals, we need the scientific approach of observe, relate, abstract, distinguish, deduce — and more. We must start with an encompassing philosophy derived from our values and proceed straight through a whole (reconnaissance and research, analysis and design, decision and delivery) system to the construction procedures that complete the human projects.

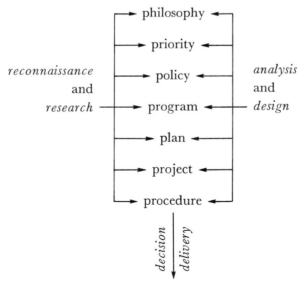

FIGURE I-2. *Process for Creating a Human Environment*

It is the balance of human intellect, emotion, and spirit that is critical. The process of creating the future social, economic, and physical environment will either steady or tip this balance. In the professions of architecture and planning, art and spirit are reputed to meet science and technology. Both professions are concerned ultimately with building real things in the here and now that last into the future. These things are built to serve people who are simultaneously rational-irrational-extrarational and changing. This is an enormous demand. In attempts to decide upon a course in these stressful days, we can and do oversimplify. We are sometimes told our choice for building the future environment is between practical technology (read "anthill") or spontaneous individual effort (read "anarchy"). The sensible human choice, of course, is to take neither. But something must be put in their place.

We nominate enlightened dialogue leading to specific action. But we need social inventions to make intelligent two-way dialogue possible now concerning the future we are headed into, the 200 million of us. That's the function of the proposed nonprofit situation and outlook centers.

It is proposed that to avoid becoming a planned society, we must become a planning society.[20] It is further suggested that to achieve a planning society, we need a dialogue assuming the good will of all parties in each situation and calling upon such techniques of factual exposition as the computer, graphic displays, and seminars.

It is not expected that lay people can contribute equally to the technical content of a situation, but certainly none in a democracy who are interested should be deprived of registering their ideas concerning philosophy, priority, or policies.

All advocates of government by an elite, from Plato to Hitler and Stalin, have ridiculed the competence of average citizens to form rational opinions upon complex issues. There is no doubt that many nineteenth-century utterances absurdly exalted rationality. Yet the best anthropological evidence, as Franz Boas pointed out, is that the judgment of the masses is sounder than the judgment of the classes on broad questions of policy where sentiments and values are concerned. This doctrine must not be perverted into a claim for the common man's expertness on technical or artistic matters. Nor does contemporary thought refer to the individual citizen's judgments. Rather, it refers to collective decisions arrived at in group interaction and dealing with "matters of common concern which depend upon estimates of probability."

As Carl Friedrich continues: "This concept of the common man salvages from the onslaught of the irrationalist revolt those elements in the older doctrine which are essential to democratic politics. It seeks a middle ground between the extreme rationalistic ideas of an earlier day and the denial of all rationality by those who were disappointed over its limitations. . . . Enough common men, when confronted with a problem, can be made to see the facts in a given situation to provide a working majority for a reasonable solution, and such majorities will in turn provide enough continuing support for a democratic government to enforce such common judgments concerning matters of common concern."[21]

The eminent biochemist Roger Williams points out that physiologically, individuals differ greatly and concludes, "if people react differently perhaps it's because they *are* different. If you are going to plan for people, you'd better plan for individuals because that's the only kind of people there are!"[22] Beyond that, as much as possible, we had better plan *with* people. That means those who are sincerely interested, and at first that may not be many, must have the means to take part — something denied them today.

We are now confronted with the worst mess this civilization has ever gotten into, and we have got[ten] into it mostly through the blundering ignorance of the people who exercise power in this country and the people who perform the technical operations in this country. If there is any remedy whatever for it, that remedy is to train men, whole men, full men, who have read enough different philosophies, enough different histories, enough different religions to begin to entertain a modest doubt of their own capabilities and their own convictions. We are cursed in this country with people who are sure of themselves but who have no background for their attitude."[23]

In these times, we find ourselves fighting a full-scale war without having first had full public discussion and a public declaration. We mount marches in order to change outmoded laws. We riot to be heard, and in our professionalism, we huddle in our separateness. It seems time to declare that communication has broken down. Rational men are put at an enormous disadvantage in society when a shout suffices for a concept, when private technical language is acceptable "one-upmanship" or when callous self-advantage is given as an apology for a "non-economic" human act. Under such conditions, aesthetics and beauty and all the extrarational aspects of environment become too delicate for the times. Only the irrational thrives.

The mechanisms we have inherited for participation don't work well enough in these changing, complex times. They need to be modified and supplemented but not so naively as to expose the machinery of society to the monkey-wrench throwers. For full participation of men — rational-irrational-extrarational — we need to invent the means for men and women of good will to talk over these changes and decide what cities, communities, homes, and lives are to be. We see nonprofit centers to restore communication in our society as one of the most needed social inventions of our time.[24]

2.

THE DIMENSIONS OF THE FUTURE

THE SHOCK FRONT we have entered is shaking society from the ghetto and the campuses to the blue-collar home and middle-class suburbia. Even people at their clubs are disturbed. Churches seem an island from another time. We are without a map, headed into a totally new kind of future. But many, perhaps most, have never had it so good and are loathe to see change. They are concerned by inflation and the upsets that minorities of the poor and the elite (especially students) are causing. Their patience is wearing thin. The Harris Poll shows they understand there are urban problems. On various issues, from 68 to 92 per cent are aware, but they vote 2 to 1 against more taxes for public programs to solve them.[1] Schools have been closed in Akron because the voters have refused to approve higher taxes. Newark has closed its libraries and museums to economize. Federal research and development funds have leveled off.

We have a national, not an urban, crisis. We call it urban because we are newly self-conscious about the large percentage of us that lives in cities and because that is where the riots are. We have entered the edge of the shock front. Its first blows are being felt within the cities where society is concentrated. We are called upon to make decisions, not only city by city but as a nation, that will contain and redirect the enormous shake-out the technological future promises as it builds up to full force over the next fifteen years. Technology is converting us from a fear-of-failure society to a pleasure-seeking society, but in the process nobody's happy.[2]

In the next 15 to 30 years, another America will be built. There will be 80 to 100 million more people — in bigger cities and new ones,

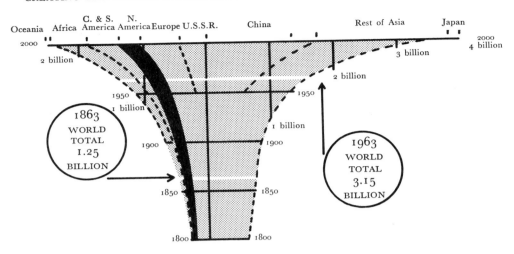

Source: adapted from *The Statesman's Year-Book,* 1963. New York: St. Martin's Press, Inc. Reprinted by permission.

FIGURE I-3.[3] *World Population Growth — 1800 to 2000 A.D.*
(Estimated World Population in 2000 A.D.: 6.5 billion)

more roads, more buildings, more gadgets, more wealth, and more leisure. But there is an overtone in the phrase "another America." Another America will be different. Will it be better? *Automatically?* The way we are going at it now?

This study is a reconnaissance of the future. It is an attempt to understand what is most valid, most likely, most overlooked, and of most concern about the future to those who will design and build it.

The driving factors which will decide the future are technology and future populations as they interact over various increments of time within expanding geographic space, according to peoples' expectations. Population growth is a world phenomenon (see FIGURE I-3). The world population is projected to double to 6 billion by the year 2000, and urban population is expected to quadruple. In the United States the best estimate of current trends is a total population of 308 million by the year 2000 with 73 per cent of these in urbanized areas of 100,000 or more; furthermore, two-thirds would be living in four super regions: 74 million in the Atlantic Region from Virginia to Maine,[4] 45 million in the California Region, 74 million in the Great Lakes Region from Milwaukee to Buffalo, and 15 million in the Florida region.[5]

Technology is a major factor in deciding where the population locates, at what rate, and how. It changes the meaning of time and space and creates unexpected expectations as well as those planned for. It changes the operation of society, its sense of itself, and the meaning and lives of the individuals in it. It is creating a whole new breed of men.

From now on, to master the technological future, account must be taken not only of traditional "territories" but the *parts* of these spaces and their context — expanding from room to building to neighborhood to community to region to nation to world region to total world.[6] Can successful manufacturing plants or new towns of the future be built with an understanding of the use of this spatial scale? Can anyone in the Ozarks with a hankering to manufacture portable radios do so successfully without knowing that the Japanese make transistors? Distance is collapsed by communication and transportation technology, and basic relationships change. Similarly new deliberations, extending over varying increments of time from months to years to decades, will be necessary in these days of great change.

Most important of all is what people expect. This is the basis for their decisions. "Vigorous societies harbour a certain extravagance of objectives"[7]; but what if its people are timorous compared to their capacities and "want" too little or are outrageous in their demands because of their ignorance? With television doing its "thing," how are extreme misconceptions to be brought to a reasoned anticipation of the future? In the end the people and society decide what is to be done with technology — whether the decision is taken deliberately or by default.

What orders of magnitude are we dealing with? To better understand the dimensions of the situation, we have selected, analyzed, and compared the three or four most far-reaching and comprehensive estimates of the future available (reprinted at length in the Projections to Part I, pp. 108 ff.). They have been ordered — consistent years, 1960 dollars, etc. — to the particular purpose of this report and provide a unique source document in their own right. For this part of the report, there is no need to do more than extract and summarize the best judgments. The purpose of this chapter is to provide a sense of scale. More discussion of alternatives follows in Chapters 4 and 5. (Where one number is given it is either the median, or the accepted figure at the time.)

The Gross National Product in Table I-2 was derived from an

TABLE I-2. *The Basic National Factors*[8]

	1955	1970	1985	2000
Population		207	265	336
(millions)	166	206	253	308
		205	242	283
		798	1570	3290
GNP	456	795	1513	2942
($ billion)		736	1193	2030
		124	255	590
Construction	54	93	155	281
($ billion)		67	86	119
	(% GNP)			
Goods	53%	49%	48%	46%
Services	35%	39%	40%	41%
Construction	12%	12%	12%	13%
Household income				
(after taxes — 1960 $)	6400	9000	13,500	24,700

annual growth rate of 3.7 per cent from 1955-1970, and 4.4-4.5 per cent from 1970-2000. This will not seem so abstract if it is realized that 1 per cent difference in GNP rate of growth, from 3-4 per cent, makes a total difference of $8000 billion between 1970 and the year 2000. The total GNP aggregated from 1970 to 2000 is in the order of $52 trillion. That, according to Lyle C. Fitch,[9] is enough to provide a dwelling unit for each added household, eliminate existing substandard housing, provide a second dwelling for 25 per cent of the year 2000 families, double education expenditures, improve pollution control, introduce new transportation devices, create generally higher standards of design for the entire urban environment, and permits 1 per cent of the GNP to be invested in overseas assistance (double present aid) as well as all normal ongoing public and private operations of this nation.

In these figures a steady 21 per cent of the GNP is allotted for direct government purchase of goods and services (federal, state, and local). This may be understated. Tax incentives actually cost government income but do not show as government expenditures. It can be expected that such devices may well be utilized more in the future.

24

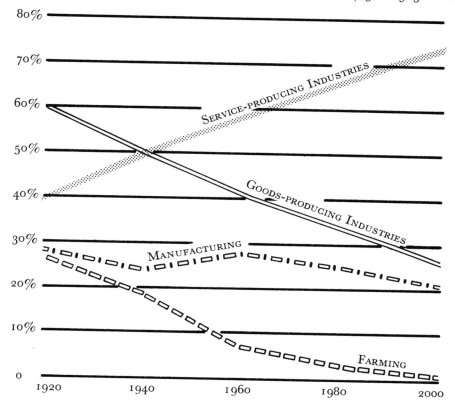

FIGURE I-4. *Who's Employed at What? U.S.*[10]

Whereas a high percentage of the people understands there are urban, pollution, and poverty needs, as previously noted they poll 2-1 against taxing themselves to meet them.[11] This can be either a national demonstration of "let George do it" or perhaps more likely, a vote of no confidence in having government do it. They might well prefer tax incentives for the private sector as well as new public-private corporations and nonprofit institutions if the machinery of Congress would encourage it.

Looking at services and goods as employers, a big "X," as is shown in the figure above, was made back in World War II (Figure I-4). Since then, services have been the primary employer and are projected to continue that way until nearly 70 per cent are employed in services by 1985, and 75 per cent by the year 2000. Manufacturing is expected to drop to 21 per cent by then, and farming to only 2-3 per cent. Industrial plants are no longer the critical factor they once were. Health and education, research and service facilities are becoming the key to quality of life and growth.

The Future People and What They Will Buy

With whom will we be sharing the next thirty years? The black population will increase only slightly from the current 12 to 13 per cent in 1985 to 15 per cent in the year 2000. (What we are discussing here are national projections, and they may not mean much to us where we live.) If blacks are to dominate the central cities of thirteen major metropolitan areas by 1985 (plus the school systems of eleven more), it is only an academic fact that blacks constitute merely 12-15 per cent of the total national population. Central city concentration is where 89 per cent of the nation's black population growth took place from 1960-1966, as an example of what makes local issues into national issues.[12] What a profound change to contemplate — in 1985 a predicted 20 million blacks in central cities rather than the 1966 total of 12 million. Is there the will to permit dispersal of some of the black population out into planned new metropolitan-area communities; or by national policy discouraging metropolitan and central cities growth?

The working age population (20-64) will increase from 106 million in 1970 to 136 million in 1985 to 169 million in 2000. The biggest growth in the population will be in the apartment dweller (age 25-34) from 1970-1985 — 26 million. They then become the wave of single-family dwellers of the future from 1985-2000.

From 1955 to the year 2000, those over 65 will have more than doubled to 31 million (they will total 20 million by 1970). Young people (below 25) constituted 43 per cent of the population in 1955. They are projected at 47 per cent in 1970, 45 per cent in 1985, and 41 per cent in 2000.[13] But is it the birthrate that can make the biggest difference in these projections. And some are predicting that it will; that the local population in the year 2000 might well be 280 million instead of today's popular 308 million figure. A few years ago 331 million was "the" figure.

How will people be spending their time and their money in the future? The two are closely related. Table I-3 (following) gives both total dollars and percentage of GNP for personal expenditures. It utilizes the Resources for the Future estimates for total time worked (including extra jobs) given here:[14]

26

	1955	1970	1985	2000
hours/year	2070	1950	1860	1790
weeks/year	49.6	49.2	48.9	48.6
hours/week	41.8	39.6	38.0	36.8

Work weeks of 21 hours by the year 2000 are predicted by some. National Planning Association sees 33.1 but that is for the basic job; Kahn and Wiener say 30.[15] Combinations of holidays, three-day weekends, more and longer vacations and sabbaticals have all been considered in various combinations. Some say professionals will still be working 60 to 70 hour weeks and the rest will be wondering what to do with themselves.[16] In any case, personal expenditures are given in Table I-3. As can be seen, it is believed that as incomes rise, people's interest in food and clothing, purchased transportation, vehicles and housing can be surfeited. Their interests and needs in recreation,

TABLE I-3. *Personal Expenditures* (billions of 1960 dollars, and per cent/GNP for median only)[17]

		1955	1970	1985	2000
1. Food tobacco, clothing, accessories, other household expenses		120.7 42.9%	176.0 33.3%	234.0 29.6%	393.3 26.6%
2. Auto purchases and operating expenses		35.6 12.7%	53.6 11.6%	92.0 11.6%	153.1 11.6%
	H		73.3	162.0	342.5
3. Housing	M	33.5 11.9%	60.5 13.1%	103.0 13.0%	171.6 13.0%
	L		54.7	82.0	123.1
4. Recreation, travel, education, and religion		22.9 8.1%	43.9 9.5%	86.0 10.9%	159.7 12.1%
5. Personal and medical care		22.0 7.8%	43.9 9.5%	83.0 10.8%	159.7 11.4%
6. Purchased local transportation, and personal business		17.7 6.3%	33.7 7.3%	66.0 8.4%	122.8 9.3%
7. Household furnishings and appliances		15.3 5.4%	25.9 5.6%	51.0 6.4%	92.4 7.0%
8. Household utilities		13.7 4.9%	24.5 5.3%	43.0 5.5%	77.9 5.9%

travel, education, religion, medical care, furnishings, new household utilities and purchased transportation increase. Housing holds at a steady percentage but its actual dollar amount increases vastly. A house can get too big, too lonely, too expensive to remain a want competing with travel, education, and better medical attention. Housing, especially types of housing, is one of the most difficult factors to project. The data base is very poor.

Future Construction

Future residential construction is derived from the basic factors and personal expenditures given in Tables I-2 and I-3. Working backwards from total population, using the median figures, we derived households, households by families, individuals, age of head of household to housing starts and, finally, building types (see Table I-4).

Whereas it is projected that construction will remain a steady 12 per cent, that percentage aggregates to huge amounts based even on the assumption of no major new public-works programs. This can be taken to be quite conservative. Higher or lower building-start possibilities can be estimated by halving or doubling the median. (Construction has always been a volatile industry.)

TABLE I-4. *Residential Construction and Households*[18]

	1955	1970	1985	2000
Total households (millions)	47.9	62.0	81.0	98.0
Families	41.7	51.0	67.0	80.0
Single	6.2	11.0	14.0	18.0
Under 25 (millions)	–	4.5	5.9	–
25-34	–	11.6	19.7	–
35-54	–	23.7	27.7	–
55-64	–	10.6	12.0	–
65+	–	12.1	15.9	–
Housing starts (millions/year)	1.58	2.4	3.2	4.3
Single-family	1.4	1.6	2.3	3.1
Multi-family total	.2	.5	.4	.6
garden or walkup	–	.4	.3	.5
high rise	–	.1	.1	.1
Mobile homes	–	.3	.5	.6

TABLE I-5. *Construction by Types* ($ million)[19]

	1955	*1970*	*1985*	*2000*
Total construction	51.8	91.0	150.0	264.0
Total private	38.0	64.0	102.0	180.0
residential	21.0	38.0	60.0	118.0
commerce and industry	6.7	10.8	18.5	23.2
utilities	5.5	7.4	11.5	18.7
other	4.4	7.4	12.2	19.4
Total public	13.8	27.1	48.0	84.1
education and health	3.3	4.1	5.6	7.4
highways	4.3	10.1	19.6	34.6
other	6.1	12.9	22.8	42.1

The basic figures given in this chapter and the gross projections for construction foretell the great power there is behind future construction. But they tell us only of the potential of our resources. What we will do with these resources *actually* is to be decided by the will of individuals and the society. Typically these are becoming decisions taken collectively as national decisions. Washington is where basic policy of this sort is made. In a sense, considering the impact of federal decisions and the manner in which we operate now, the total $52 trillion GNP (to the year 2000) will be taken through the Congressional authorization and appropriations budget procedure one year at a time. Each department of government presents its own case to the Administration in power. Senators and Congressmen have their own views. Years later, the Supreme Court is called upon to referee who was right. All of this affects private decisions, spending, and national goals.

But we have no operating, long-range conception of the future for this nation. Bold concepts like the push West of the railroads are not matched in scale or kind by separate technological and engineering feats which actively and creatively involve very few of us. The 8½ year, $24 billion goal of landing a man on the moon, or the 15 year, $56 billion, 42,500 miles of interstate expressway we can only watch happen. And there is no national concept of human and technological priorities or how they should all fit together. Still, more and more we have become a national community whose calendar is marked for the national elections (the reason for their inclusion in Table I-1). This sense of the national community — the community of interests and experience we share largely through television, and the fact that only 15 per cent live in the same county for a lifetime, 50 per cent in their native state and every year 20 per cent of us moves — is perhaps the most significant new dimension of the future.[20] In the midst of our present confusion, we have the opportunity to move into the future as a national community with great opportunities as well as great problems. The states are there but they don't have the funds to match their authority. Metropolitan areas have become the neighborhoods of the national community. Rural or urban we live through our cars in 100-mile "cities"[21] and reach across the continent or the oceans by plane more easily than we used to take a train from New York to Chicago.

We have now a sense of the basic dimensions of the future — the quantities involved — as derived by projecting trends into the future. What about the quality of the future? What about the surprises?

3.

BASIC ALTERNATIVE PATHS TO THE FUTURE

IN THE LAST FIFTEEN YEARS of this century, technology will have advanced to the stage where the people can have *anything* they want. That is not to say that they can have *everything* they want. Choices must be made, by omission or commission. What will the people want for themselves and for their children as they move from 1970 to 1985 — to 2000? And how will they make their decisions known?

President Eisenhower's *Goals for Americans,* commissioned to leading American intellectuals in 1960, called for a sense of national community, of national purpose and the necessity to establish and agree on national priorities.[1] Unfortunately, the National Planning Association's pricing of the goals showed that even the affluent and powerful United States could not afford all of those in 1970 or 1975. Only a sustained rate of growth in the nation's Gross National Product and a comprehensive coordinated effort well beyond anything in the nation's peacetime history could achieve them.[2]

If we cannot afford the future, how will the choices be made? By what priorities will we follow which paths to what future? Table I-6 was designed to help us consider the basic alternatives. Actually, we might expect the path to zig and zag, to combine a bit of all four of the possibilities. As we go along we will make decisions, or not, either of which may alter our course. Hopefully, we will avoid the extremes, but one thing seems certain: most of us will have to learn to tolerate increased frustrations.[3] For most, values, technology, politics, education, community will be either changing too fast or too slow. For very few will it be "just about right." For most of the privileged, the old, the small businessman, the middle class, the middle aged, change may be coming too fast. For many of the young, the disadvantaged, the black, the poor, the scientist, the professional, the humanist, change may be coming too slow. For those whose job is to manage change, to build for it, or to investigate it, the rate of change may be

TABLE I-6. *Four Paths to the Future* (looking at the future from different perspectives; author's comments in parentheses)

	1970	*1985*	*2000*
REVOLUTION (age of leaders 25-35)	→ *violence and anarchy* to bring down present corrupt institutions	→ *a people dictatorship* to restore the human values, rework national priorities	→ IDEAL, *a spontaneous society* (serendipity made "efficient" technology and all for 300 million people!)
REASON (age of leaders 40-50)	→ *anticipation* of choices and long-range consequences added to society's concentration on the short term	→ *a planning democracy* that encourages technology directed by national and community priorities determined by direct participation in policy planning	→ IDEAL, *scientific humanism* (a new order of civilization for rational-irrational-extrarational men; both planned and spontaneous)
RESPONSE (age of leaders 50-60)	→ *bargain* and balance of competing interests, responsive to current pressures which set priorities	→ *a traditional democracy* with minimum attempt to formalize national priorities, reliance on marketplace and ballot box	→ IDEAL, *corporate democracy* (efficient response to problems and opportunities determined to be a combination of big government and big corporations)
REACTION (age of leaders 55-65)	→ *violence and control* to bring to an end once and for all mollycoddling of present and future dissenters, violent and otherwise	→ *a paternalistic society* which looks out for people and protects property rights, provides security	→ IDEAL, *an elite society* (maintaining order, efficient production, society's leaders and institutions held to be paramount — a technological society)

more challenging than it is frustrating. What are the attitudes, institutions, and resources that will both limit and decide?

The Paths of Revolution and Reaction — Violence

Revolution or reaction, each is represented by minority groups taking an emotional initiative either outside the institutions of society or, in the case of reaction, by use of it. Here, they are considered the least likely paths that we would choose as a nation to take to the future. But they are not to be precluded as periodic aberrations. They lurk as the threatened response to insensitive, inept management of change by the leaders of our institutions and society at large. What is worse, one feeds the other and would create violent swings from one extreme to the other.

A history of past human injustice, a general comprehension of the great capacities of technology, and misunderstood estimates of the affluence of the society have generated great expectations directed at outmoded institutions. When instant gratification of those expectations "or else" is demanded at a national level, the situation for revolution is at hand.[4] When communication — dialogue — between the protagonists and society breaks down, the stage is set for violence. The step from there to violent revolution can be short.

It is unlikely such demands by radicals will, or can, be met or outmaneuvered by archaic institutions, thus sustaining the confrontation. Or if by some chance the demands should be met there is great psychological triumph as well as "progress." Demands may be for a more "equable" sharing of the nation's wealth and future opportunities or from a great fear of the inhuman misuse of modern technology. Visions of even greater technological capacities in the future intensifies both the demands and the fears, and shortens the period tolerated before immediate gratifications.

In recent years we have seen rebellions from Montgomery to Detroit, from Berkeley to Cambridge. It is possible that with the continued inept management by government, churches, universities, corporations, banks, and other institutions of these manifestations of the shock front we could see an attempt at national violent revolution in the future. Suppose neither violent radicals nor a considerable number of moderate people are satisfied with society's rate of progress. Revolutionaries feel that there will be no satisfactory progress dealing with the existing paternalistic institutions of the present corrupt

33

society. Their alternative is to work outside these institutions — to divert, disrupt, and destroy; to generate the sympathy, support, and participation of moderates; to organize, then confront and divide present leadership, turn prospective opponents apathetic, destroy existing institutions and take over — using any means at hand: violent revolution. That there would necessarily be a period of anarchy (perhaps from 1976 to 1984) followed by a dictatorship is not denied. But it is said this would be a "people's" dictatorship and would ultimately lead to the spontaneous society (after 2000) where everyone is himself, free, and making use of technology without being run by it. There would be no need for government, they say. Or if there were, it would be incorruptible. It would be totally different from the existing institutions which corrode men today.

Some go so far as to say it might be necessary to kill off 10 to 20 million people during the violence and people's dictatorship, but that the high purpose of the goals justifies the means and that they live by the ethics of the age to come, so "our" ethics do not apply to them. Rational thinking is considered a trick of the Establishment.

Revolutionaries generally take the initiative — sometimes in anticipation of violence by the reactionaries. *Or* their purpose can be to goad the rigid people attempting to hold onto the past into an overreaction so that radicals can win the sympathy and support of the moderates. Reactionaries, when careful about their response to revolutionaries, in turn also work to win over moderates. Each extreme, naturally enough, presents its case to win maximum moderate support.

In Chicago, during the 1968 Democratic Convention, the taunts of youth did not photograph like the policemen's clubbings. Still both sides "won." Over 60 per cent of the American people watching supported the action of Mayor Daley's police, and the Yippies drew into their folds the support of thousands of moderate students in Chicago and elsewhere.

The exasperation of the reactionary sector of the American people, with demands from the "spoiled darlings" (college and high school students) and the "lazy, shiftless" black, is hard to overestimate. Reactionaries are found at all levels of income and at all ages although most are over fifty, and the bulk are in the lower class or the lower middle class. If there is a fear of a takeover by revolutionaries, it is easy for the reactionaries to imagine policemen as "their" troops.

The reactionaries often represent the same sort of anarchic violence as the revolutionaries.[5] They also are likely to be self-righteous

34

about their actions and the repression of revolutionary violence. Once in charge, "security" leading to entrenched paternalism is likely; it would be run by an elite society of those who "think right."

The path of reaction is not anticipated. It is dependent on emotion and stupidity for success. Much more likely is the pressure of enough reactionaries disturbed by enough revolutionaries, rebellions, *or change* to cause those following the more moderate responsive paths to adopt repressive tactics.

Response as a Path to the Future

What we have now is responsive politics. Under the pressure of circumstance we respond, bargain, and pay off. Response is made to organized power. It does not spend its strength on weak, invisible causes. The pressure from all sides is continuous. The philosophy is pragmatism — will it work now? Pragmatism, with its own self-righting, short-term acting gyroscope, is built into our Constitution, something we are loathe to consider changing without good reason. It should be remembered there isn't any longer lived constitutional government in the world than that of the United States. For some, this helps make it current deficiencies more comfortable to think about living with than the unknown ones of an untried path, especially if these epic times are misread as "business as usual," only a little more so. To many, however, it is now apparent that we have problems our present mode of democracy doesn't meet. The marketplace democratic society is not managing pollution, traffic, housing, crime problems, education, or national purpose to our satisfaction these days. If this has become generally acknowledged, but we still don't trust government with enough funds to provide solutions — and we don't — new responses are called for. One might be either to contract out more of the responsibilities and problems of government to private enterprise as business opportunities, or to strengthen the nonprofit sector. Or both.

The business of contracting out the government's business is a natural to look for. "Once we are out of Vietnam," big corporations and big government can be expected to fall into each other's arms. It would become government's responsibility to "package and deliver" local problems as markets to big private enterprise. This would require corporations, Congress, and the nation to suddenly stretch their vision of the future to five years. In addition, the federal government would probably have to provide other new incentives and guarantees. Business is in business to make money, not just to solve the problems of government. Government inherits problems from society when society hasn't been able to solve them in the usual ways. One of the reasons society's problems aren't solved is the short-term view of little businessmen and little governments. Big government and big business combining with big universities to solve the nation's big problems without spending big public money would be the most progressive direction that the responsive paths might attempt.

However, the response path to the future, by indicating that political pressure is the practical way to dialogue, would invite accommodation to the one-year outlook of most small businessmen and social reformers. It would encourage pressures expressed in a variety of ways, violent as well as peaceful. There would be continued rebellion: more shouting confrontations by the social reformer working outside "the system" and more intense lobbying and backroom thumbscrews within it. There would grow up taxpayer as well as student rebellions. Reactionaries and ordinary citizens as well as frustrated liberals would join in spontaneous as well as planned demonstrations. The respected economist, Robert Heilbroner, has an explanation of the roadblocks we face. He believes even elementary improvements in the society are made slowly and painfully, and that the planning necessary to meliorate the plight of the cities is stymied because:

> it interferes with both the privilege and ideologies, not of big business, but of small business, whose representative, in a large way, Congress really is . . . the 10 or 12 million small businessmen, whose economic weight is just a feather on the scale, have an enormous political power. It is the attitudes of small business that permeate America today, just as the labor attitude did in the thirties.[6]

Small business can be expected to continue to oppose taking even a five-year look ahead, something the most progressive of the large corporations have accommodated in recent years. Small business would oppose big firms taking over the social problems and converting them into big business, leaving the small firms with only what bits and pieces they could pick up in subcontracts.

A mediating force between the big and small scales of enterprise and government — utilizing the scientist, the professional, and the interested citizen — could be a strengthened nonprofit sector. To maintain the right to be called responsive, rather than ultimately repressive, a democratic government must encourage dialogue rather than political pressure, physical confrontation, and force. The non-profit sector would be the most likely meeting ground for that. It could provide a place of dialogue between the response path and the path of reason (even including elements from the extremes of revolution and reaction). Strengthening — and professionalizing — the nonprofit sector with its army of citizens of goodwill is probably one of the few creative courses open to the response path. It could peacefully conciliate the effects of the short-term view which is so favorable to the status quo.

The response path to the future would be based on a thing-making, service-selling economy with quite limited federal controls at first. But the threat of environmental, societal, and global disaster would grow, and so would the controls. We would expect the response path to the future to be a low morale path. Its top priorities would probably be negative ones; to keep taxes low, avoid long-term commitments, minimize government spending, and stop inflation. We would be expected to learn to live with 5 per cent unemployment, "unavoidable" pollution, traffic, and riots rather than "borrow trouble from the future." The GNP rate of growth would undoubtedly slow to 2½-3 per cent[7] and our world financial position as well as our leadership would be undermined year by year until we faced calamities at home and abroad that required czars to solve them, thus removing from the realm of public discussion the big issue of creating a human technological environment.

The response (to the moment) path to the future would encourage irresponsibility and discourage participation. There would not be any sense of ongoing adventure for Americans as a whole. There would be no long-range objectives worth working for. Progress, such as it was, would be made in imperceptible increments providing small satisfactions. Major federal stimulus of needed civilian research and development would be withheld. Progress in space and defense technologies would continue to be as rapid and as progressive as civilian technologies would be slow. By way of example, contrast the evolution of NASA's technologies over the past seven years with how little automobiles have changed in the past twenty. H. G. Wells spotted this sort of contrast in the early 1900's.[8]

The greatest danger of the response path would be the cloak of respectability it could give to repression of individual liberties. Reaction and revolution as paths to the future, pursued through outright violence according to either a planned or a "do it as you go" conspiracy have been discarded by this investigation as unlikely because to be a successful path, they must enlist the majority of moderates in this country. The chance of the revolutionaries, given the circumstances of our society, achieving substantial moderate support for a violent course is considered unlikely. But under the guise of being responsive to the needs of the society, the difficulties of the times, and acting for the will of the majority, the responsive path, if adequately provoked, might deem the rights of minorities and individuals expendable. Reaction could be made respectable. It could meet the various disturbances of the next decade, which are likely, with full force and develop a police state in the process without being named one. By sustaining the circumstances for disorder, it could justify its "pragmatic" tactics. When one thinks of the power of the federal government's 3000 computers applied to "necessary" control of the situation, the possibility of a police state approach as a respectable response path is not to be dismissed. This potential is not likely if the openness required by a strong nonprofit sector is encouraged.

The strengthening of the nonprofit sector at this time is the best hope of opening up *two-way* channels of communication, involving the people in deciding their destiny in a time of great change. The nonprofit sector becomes the mediator between the extremes of reaction and revolution and the bridge to reason and investigation. It offers a bridge from inadequate programs and continued disturbance to the potentials of a high morale society. Most important of all, it limits the likelihood of the response path turning repressive as its primary response. It blocks the over-centralization of government.

Reason as a Path to the Future

Evolving naturally from our traditional democracy, reason as a path to the future would integrate into it the scope of science and anticipation. It would acknowledge the threats and promises of technology in the shock front we are now into. It would acknowledge the order of magnitude changes, the convergence of all disciplines, the communication breakdown and the need for devising new means for dialogue, and the constraints of the U.S. economy in the public and private sectors as well as their great potential. Its perspective would be in increments of time appropriate to particular issues.

Reason as a path to the future does not mean only rational processes — program planning, budgets and cost-benefit ratios — as the means of measuring the desired human results. Diversity is more expensive than monotony, but there is a human cost to monotony and efficient control that the path to reason would recognize and not be willing to pay in order to save dollars. For men recognized as rational-irrational-extrarational beings, it would be unreasonable to choose a path that was exclusively rational.

Full use of technology, full access to information about it, full participation in the creation of the future society, full employment and a high rate of economic growth with a low population growth would have high priorities. The necessity for turning Vietnam tax dollars into civilian tax dollars would be understood from the outset. Federal incentives for encouraging high-priority research and technological developments in housing, health, education, ecology, welfare, transportation, etc. would be matched by social inventions to keep these efforts responsive to the will of individuals and the society. The private sector would be deeply involved, both large and small businesses would have roles; and science and technology and their long-range impacts, along with concepts of national development policy and settlement patterns, would have a defined relationship to government at all levels rather than merely a lobbying one.

The ultimate aim of this path would be to transcend the purely responsive to realize a scientific-humanism that was both responsive and open to (and anticipating) full participation. It is seen as the way to a future in which the creative development of the society is the great "business" of the society.

Following such a path would call for long-range commitments while maintaining responsiveness, especially to local issues. Full employment would near 2 to 3 per cent[9] unemployed with guaranteed jobs for all even if only twenty hours per week. Everything possible would be done to discourage population growth in this country, and in the world, along with incentives to maintain annual GNP growth at 5 per cent[10] or above, and either an inflation of not more than 2 per cent or a compensatory automatic cost of living boost for retirement incomes. Productivity increases of 3 to 4 per cent[11] would be the aim as would population growth rate increases to 2000 of 1.3 per cent.[12]

GNP rates of growth are not necessarily the best way to measure progress in a society. It is the current yardstick, but either if people decided that more than 21 per cent of the GNP should be spent by government or if they wanted to take part of the productivity increase in *time* rather than money, the GNP growth rate would slow. This is not a bad thing if the society sees this as a better human use of its resources. But it raises the point that we need new capacities for dialogue. Critical value judgments have to be made, and we have only puny means at hand to arrive at consensus while maintaining diversity. A *high morale* dynamic society, with the full participation of its interested citizens, that measures, decides, and uses its capacity according to its highest values may not call for the highest possible annual rate of GNP growth. But it is unlikely that *vast* new amounts of leisure or a low rate of growth in GNP would be part of a high morale society in the next fifteen to thirty years. Rather we would expect to master an epic time of change in human terms. Such a challenge would probably call for more direction and more leisure — perhaps more or less direction than some want and more or less leisure than others desire. But it would be a national commitment that decided, a combination of the macro and the micro perspective.

In finding our way, avoiding the extremes of revolution and reaction, we would expect there to be great interplay between the paths of response and the paths of reason to avoid an elite technocracy and to encourage spontaneity in its place. The vehicle for achieving the high morale society is the same as is necessary to fathom its philosophy and formulate its priorities. It requires an independent, nonprofit, institutional base.

Possible Life Styles

As Sam Browne, 25-year-old student leader put it at a recent student power conference, ". . . it's fairly difficult to tell a worker making $9600 a year that he is all that deprived. The struggle of the working class seems to be to obtain a second car and pay off the mortgage."[13] Talk of violent revolution and attacking reactionaries is current, but there is no strong indication that it will be a vital force in the next 10 to 15 years. So we will dispense with an examination of those particular life styles.

As to the probable life styles, they will owe a debt to the revolutionary and reactionary. Ignoring the ways of the majority and living according to one's own tastes will be more popular. The tastes for most, moreover, are likely to gravitate toward an environment with many physical amenities built in. We will be seeing more of the California garden apartments for "swingers." Studies show that more and more apartment dwellers expect wall-to-wall carpets, air conditioning, a balcony, swimming pool, landscaping, community spaces and parking under cover to be built into the monthly rent.[14] The quality of single-family homes, offices, motels, college dormitories, etc. has also been upgraded in the past ten years. This can be expected to continue. With increase in the scale of environment conceived and built under one ownership, the opportunity for amenities *and security* can be expected to increase.

The increased quality, including the size of housing units,[15] we believe, can increase construction to more than compensate for the estimated 10 to 15 per cent population decrease. This increase in construction will be true, however, only if the value is there. Value will mean the right amenities at the right price. This will call for creative and technological efforts far beyond what the handcrafted building industry is now capable of. We consider most of the present construction estimates conservative if major design and technological improvements are taken into account. In addition, with each hour of new leisure time people get, their homes and general surroundings become more important. If they will also have time for continuing their education and vocational training, some of this will be done by preference in or near home. The community they live in will be of greater concern.

People will continue to locate where there is maximum "concentration of diversity."[16] This is one definition of *city*. The requirements for locations of manufacturing industry will loosen because of market growth, differential labor costs, and new technology. However, as a percentage of total employment, manufacturing industries are less and less important as employers. Health, education, and services are the big growth industries. Whereas it may be obvious that these are freer from constraints than a steel mill as to their location, they have their own requirements. These include access to amenities, people, and all the opportunities that become more and more important to the full life of rational-irrational-extrarational men as their time is freed from the domination of work. It is true that many amenities can be "designed in," and that many amenities are features of climate and topography already in place. (Climate "control" seems out, not only for 1985 but for 2000; but before 1985 good forecasting will be possible, and some weather modification may be possible by the year 2000.)[17]

Choice of location will not change as much as we might think until we develop national policies to strengthen existing smaller cities and to encourage building whole communities, more quickly and with higher design standards. We might learn this and demonstrate it over the next fifteen years (primarily in metropolitan areas), but as a way of living significant enough to be termed a new style of life, it will probably be towards the end of this century or the beginning of the next before the means are at hand if we follow the responsive path to the future. The New York State Development Policy Report, *Change/Challenge/Response,* saw development as it relates to location in three overlapping phases: Phase I — the extension of present metropolitan areas including developing nearby new towns and reserving open space; Phase II — the creation of new metropolitan areas in strategic open locations; and Phase III — the creation of scattered small cities at locations with particular amenities. It was assumed the simultaneous planning and development involved to realize all three would be properly coordinated and that the various technological developments of the sort that required federal incentives would be included.[18]

Sir Raymond Unwin, the great British planner, once said he was appalled how little people wanted of life. Private enterprise and advertising have altered that somewhat in this society as far as acquiring "things" is concerned. But many public wants of this society have yet to find their own means for communication or institutional bases. However, our list of public wants ("crisis") has now grown to such lengths that the Defense Department, NASA, and AEC may be prevented from taking to themselves the federal "fiscal bonuses" that will be growing to useful dimensions in the coming decades. These "bonuses," based on the projected growth of the GNP and federal income taxes beyond what is already earmarked for spending, are expected to grow from the present $2 to $100 billion *per year* by 1980.[19]

What are these public wants? The rich people in Los Angeles know that they themselves can buy only *indoor* fresh air. Solitary 3D-color-television and "remote" computer outlets and tons of gadgetry can by purchased by the individual in the future but not good schools and museums to browse in or a safe, beautiful, lively community to enjoy.

If we are not too long in realizing the limits of what we as individuals can buy for our own personal use, if we are not too long in realizing the nation's great technical and financial capacity as well as its real limitations, if we are not too long in realizing the precious nature of the sense of place to humans, we may yet create *the* great human-technological environment of man's history. But it will take dialogue to keep us from being too long. It will take independent, nonprofit institutions to effect much of the new effort needed to realize public wants. And it will take a high-morale society with commitment to a concept of why it is postponing some immediate personal satisfaction for future group and community enjoyments.

4.

SHIFTING FACTORS
OF GREATEST IMPORTANCE

THERE ARE ESPECIALLY IMPORTANT FACTORS affecting the future that should be examined separately or at least singled out. For the designers and builders of a future human environment, what *are* the most relevant, the most likely "systems breaks" or underlying factors that should be given special consideration for 1985? For the year 2000 and beyond?

It is not that here and now we are going to pick dates and define all the big environmental surprises; that clearly would be preposterous. But it seems equally preposterous to believe that we cannot think usefully about major "surprise" changes in the environment until they have happened to us. Here we can at least try to demonstrate this proposition. For instance, if research and development efforts into human concerns, from a comprehensive understanding of human environment to contemporary forms of mass transportation, are presently being weakly and simplistically conceived, can't it be responsibly assumed that *real* efforts would produce some surprises? Again, if, by comparison with other nations, we appear to be more like some of those whose birth rates are much lower than ours, much less like those which are higher, can we not deduce what the surprise here might be? Or if there is a growing national, poltically based interest in where and how people settle, must we dismiss the possibility of a surprise — a national development policy? Should we ignore trends that seem to be changing the racial character of our central cities? Can't we sense some surprises there?

In that 68 per cent of all U.S. deaths stem from two basic causes, isn't it likely that stepped-up research concentrated there would soon produce surprises in our general health and longevity? If the need for blacks and students to take part in decisions that directly affect their lives is so great and so unsatisfied that they have resorted to violence as a way to use the press and TV to communicate their complaints, can we doubt the need to invent some surprising new means of communication, not only for the minorities who riot but for those who don't — with surprising results? If government and private enterprise both separately and working together have been unable to devise programs to build low-cost housing in the past twenty years of efforts (since the Housing Act of 1949), will we dare surprise ourselves by devising other ways and new institutions, if necessary, to do so?

We have provided the best projections of future trends available. Those projections and the choices of alternate paths to the future might become more useful if the investigator's insight were now allowed enough autonomy to "test" for issues, surprises, and system breaks deserving the particular attention of environmental designers. A system break is a radical change unexpected even by the experts. A surprise in this case might be defined as something that in detail or kind may be beyond present common knowledge. A factor may already be evident. We cannot be exhaustive in this search but we can attempt to identify major possibilities. Each deserves from a million to a billion dollars of research in its own right.

People and What They Want

Population (Millions)	1955	1970	1985	2000
Census B series		207	265	336
Census C series	166	206	253	308
Census D series		205	242	283

A low birth rate could produce a national population of less than 280 million in the year 2000 versus the "most expected" 308 million (from Table I-2). It is a surprise we could work for with strong hopes for success.

Birth rates are the basic component of population growth. If migration and death rates hold steady and the U.S. maintains its 1968

45

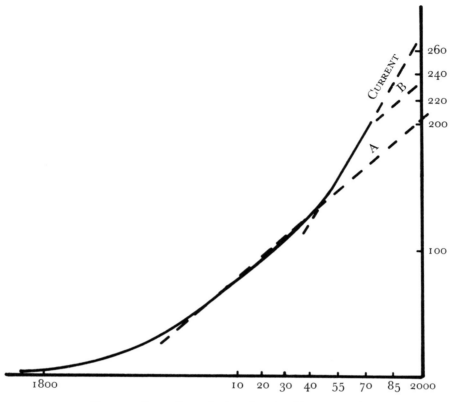

FIGURE I-5. *Population by the Year 2000*[1]

birth rate which is still above the depression low (based on a fertility rate of 86 per 1000, age 15 to 44), the population by 1985 would be 237 million. By the year 2000 it would be 279 million. If we maintain our present rate of growth based largely on a fertility rate of 86 per 1000 until 1985 and then drop to Sweden's 1965 rate (79 per 1000), the population in the year 2000 would reach 267 million. (Why this comparison with Sweden? To illustrate the feasibility of a lower population than we might be expecting.)[2]

Figure I-5 shows another possibility. By applying the U.S. historic rate of growth (line A), prior to the World War II baby boom, to the 1968 population (parallel line B), the year 2000 population result is 235 million, even lower than "Sweden's Way" after 1985.

What about another baby boom after the Vietnam War? It is likely that as many babies will be born then (1971-1975) per year as after World War II, but this would be the result of today's much lower fertility rate applied to a much larger number of fertile women — the World War II babies grown up. The World War II baby-boom birth rate was 123 per 1000 in 1957. Sweden's fertility rate in 1965 was 79; U.S.'s in 1968 was 86; Britain's in 1963 was 91. Such fertility rates applied after the Vietnam War would produce a small baby boom. This would result in a much smaller percentage of national growth than the World War II boom. In a large way this may be based on "The Pill" which has helped cut the U.S. fertility rate beginning in 1962. Furthermore, we had three times the troops in service in World War II than in Vietnam to date.

TABLE I-7. *Selected Nations Compared — 1968*[3]

	Births*	Pop.	Pop.	People	GNP
	1000	millions	% yr growth	square mile	person
Japan	13.7	101.0	1.1	706	$ 696
Sweden	15.8	7.9	0.8	45	2204
France	17.4	50.4	1.0	237	1436
West Germany	17.6	60.3	0.6	628	1447
Britain	17.8	55.8	0.5	594	1451
U.S.A.	18.4	201.3	1.1	56	2893
U.S.S.R.	18.2	239.0	1.1	28	928
Argentina	21.5	23.4	1.5	22	740
India	41.0	523.0	2.5	445	86
Brazil	41-43.0	88.3	3.2	27	217
Mexico	44.1	47.3	3.5	62	410
Indonesia	40-45.0	112.8	2.3	196	85

* Per 1000 *total* population, the U.S. 1933 low is 18 per 1000; the 1957 high, 26 per 1000.

Also, contrasting the 1968 birth rates, population, densities, and rates of growth of various nations in Table I-7, which nations are we most like? The USSR or Sweden? Is it more likely we will tend towards the USSR, the Western democracies, or the Asians and most Latin American nations?

The question leads to another. In 1968 a Gallup poll[4] found adults in various countries in favor of four or more children as an ideal number responding as follows:

United States	41%
The Netherlands	24
Britain	23
Norway	22
Uruguay	20
Greece	19
Finland	14
Sweden	11
Switzerland	11
Austria	7

Is the United States opinion likely to remain at a level of two to four times those of the nations listed? Or is it more likely to drop to its 1936 or 1966 levels on that same question when the poll showed 34 per cent — or will it be less? Even in 1968, considerably fewer higher-income families favored four children or more. Since average household incomes are expected to be $13,500 in 1985 and $24,700 in the year 2000, what effect might this have? Lower birth rates than the experts use may be the trend, especially if we look beyond 1985.

Consider also this additional bit of evidence. For the first time in its history, the 23,000-member American Public Health Association at its 1968 annual meeting passed a resolution 2-1 urging "that safe, legal abortions be made available to all women as a 'personal right' — even for family planning purposes. . . . Such laws have existed in Japan since 1948, in the Soviet Union and European countries since 1950. The incidence of legal abortions in the U.S. today is about two or three per 1000 pregnancies. In Japan, the incidence of legal abortions is about 300 per 1000 pregnancies, and in Scandinavia the incidence is about 80 per 1000 pregnancies."[5]

HEALTHY OLD AGE AND EXTENDED LIFE SPAN

If by the end of this century people commonly live to be 80 with the vigor of 45 to 50 year olds, *that* would be a surprise.

Thirty years ago life expectancy was 70 (to the year 2010). As it is now, a baby born in 1970 can be expected to live 76 years (to the year 2046). Some experts are willing to add another 5 to 7 years to the life expectancy of a baby born before 2000 (others only 3 or 4 years) — but these extensions do not speak of the human concern for added *healthy* years.[6] Until as late as the early 1950's, lengthened life expectancy was still primarily due to the cut in death rates at birth and in early childhood. There is still some gain to be made there, particularly with the blacks. But as Rene Dubos has said, "A large part of the increased life expectancy in the older age groups represents merely prolongation of survival through complex and costly medical procedures, rather than healthy years gained from the onslaught of disease. It corresponds to what has been called medicated survival."[7]

There are several good reasons for expecting the surprise of healthy old age.

1) The causes of death are concentrated, 52 per cent in cardiovascular-renal diseases and 16 per cent in malignancies. Discoveries related to these — whether in regard to cells, pollution, stress, or diet — would have dramatic effects in health immediately and in population totals within ten years.

2) There seem to be several promising research potentials deserving support which, if adequately funded, might well produce major results in five to ten years.[8]

3) Current research efforts into aging could not be more minimal. There is now no sustained, comprehensive long-range effort. Modest new federal expenditures could have major import.[9]

4) Politically, retirees are becoming a new force. Growth in number of people over 65 is striking (as is their steadily improving education). In 1970 people over 65 will total 20 million. In 1900 there were 3 million, by 1930 that had doubled. By the year 2000 there will be at least 28 million. By the year 2000 instead of having a grade school education, over 50 per cent will have been to college.[10]

5) Transplants.

6) Right now 30 per cent of the people over 65 are below the poverty line ($3000). Their median income is $3645 versus a 1970 U.S. median of $9000.[11] With creeping inflation and fixed pension incomes, this situation, without public intervention, will not improve. The poverty line in 1985 may well be $5000. The burden of lifetime's heaviest medical expense for these and other old families will fall on their largely middle class children. This gives this "minority" problem a majority political vote.

7) The earlier, healthier, and better educated people are when they are retired (all three can be anticipated), the more vigorous they

can be expected to be in working as a group to improve their health, their roleless status in society, and their standard of living.[12]

The issues listed above should work to change political priorities in the direction indicated by the White House Conference on Aging in 1960 (and by current Senate Bill S 870 and the campaign statements of President Nixon). If they do, it can be anticipated that the institutions and funding needed to utilize existing breakthroughs and to find new ones will be in operation by the early 1970's, with results for application before 1980. And healthy life to 80 conceivably could be commonplace by the year 2000.

Man's life span is considered 90 to 100 years today. It is not very likely there will be change enough in that by the year 2000 to be relevant to those reading this. But extending healthy life to 100 years, 200 years, or more, is a system break to look for after the year 2000. It would take at least a generation to attempt to assimilate what this will mean to the individual. It is worth considering now because of the tremendous impact it would have; the whole purpose and style of life would back up to decisions to be made in this century.

Nobel Laureate Linus Pauling has said:[13]

"Death is unnatural . . . theoretically, man is quite immortal. His body tissues replace themselves. He is a self-repairing machine. And yet, he gets old and dies, and the reasons for this are still a mystery. When once a real understanding of the physiological activity of chemical substances is obtained, medical progress will be swift. The medical research man will be a molecular architect. He will be able to draw the atomic blueprints for promising pharmacological compounds. Chemists may then synthesize them and biologists test them. He will be able to analyze and interpret the structure of enzymes, tissues and viruses to learn the mechanisms of disease, and then the way of combating diseases. When this time comes — and it is coming — medicine will indeed have become an exact science."

Many other scientists agree. Others like Rene Dubos are concerned especially with the environmental impacts on the health of man.[14]

Robert W. Prehoda's book, *Extended Youth,* begins an exploration of what may be feasible. Figure I-6 is reproduced from it. If all major illnesses (including heart disease, stroke, and cancer) were eliminated, the human life span would be extended into the grey area of Envelope One. Control of the aging process itself would extend life into Envelope Two to 200 years old or more! Then at last we would have

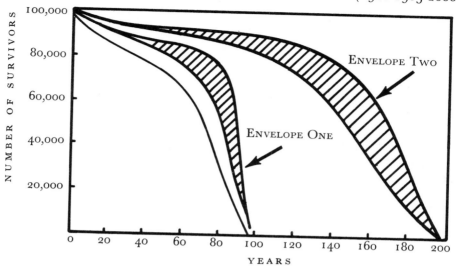

FIGURE I-6. *Extended Life — 200 Years + ?*[15]

the thirty years it may take, with accelerated education facilities, to transcend the constraints in the multidisciplinary approach and create the holistic approach.[16] Other questions arise. How many marriages if one lives 100 to 200 years? (In Christ's time 30 to 50 years was normal.) Just the two Margaret Mead is already advocating? Or communal marriages?[17]

The study of body protein and DNA has gone too far to dismiss the surprise of greatly extended life. After 2000, just when we may have gained control of the world birth rate at the 7 to 9 billion level, we may have invented a century-long problem of another way to the double population by greatly extending the life span. It is not too soon to think and prepare for this. On our way to a life span of 100 to 200 years, we will no doubt pass through a period of prejudice termed "ageism" similar to present-day "racism."[18] All the old bodies around in a youth-cult age possibly will be resented. Furthermore, old people asserting their rights in "unreasonable" ways will probably create as much social dissension as the black has in the world of today.

BETTER EDUCATION

There would appear to be several surprises in education, a crucial factor in both American culture and economic productivity. The first

51

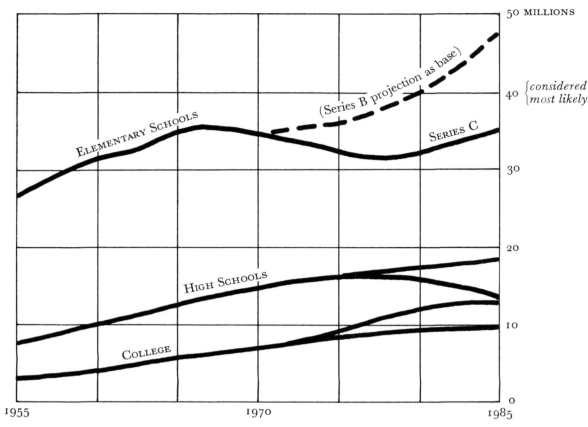

FIGURE I-7. *School Enrollment*[19]

surprise may be that from 1970 to 1985, when the GNP will be doubling and population increasing from 20 to 25 per cent, elementary
and secondary school enrollment will be about the same or less than
it is now. We are so used to all lines on all graphs for the future soaring upwards that just the directions of the ones below are surprises.
College enrollment may gain by 40 per cent but probably not more
unless fourteen years of schooling becomes compulsory and subsidized.
That is nothing like the tripling of college enrollment in the past
fifteen years.

It is conceivable that by 1975 to 1980, we will have a compulsory
fourteen years of school — through two years of college. We may
make tuition free or start paying people to go to college to make this
possible. Premier Joseph R. Smallwood instituted such a plan for

Memorial University (4500) in St. Johns, Newfoundland, in 1965 to stimulate the province's development. Tuition is free and junior and senior year students receive $100 a month income if they come from out in the Province, $50 if their families live in St. Johns.[20] This principle might also be applied for ghetto children in the lower grades with a matching bonus to the schools to upgrade the quality of their education.

Another surprise to come before the year 2000 is the anticipation that most people in their work career of forty years or so will be learning three different jobs.[21] Even if that is not a surprise, it is too significant a factor to be passed by without special notice. The costs and the number of people involved, the facilities and buildings to be built, the changes in peoples' lives will be tremendous. It might be that the minimum wage could be paid to those in college or institutes for special courses. The recognition that education and training is serious work requiring motivation by the individual might make it another vehicle for implementing the Full Employment Act of 1946 if private enterprise, government, and community service jobs are not available.

Americans have shown by poll that 79 per cent want a guaranteed job, not welfare or a guaranteed income.[22] They already evidence concern for education, with the 60 per cent of their local taxes allocated for education and the added amounts they put into higher education. Few Congressional bills have ever been more welcomed than the G.I. Bill of Rights, the Fulbright Scholarships and the Merit Scholarships. We already have the precedents. Paying all people to make the considerable personal effort it takes to study fits the future after the year 2000 when we anticipate more limited job opportunities and a need "to get money to people." When more productive facilities are automated, they won't be able to work as much as they might want to. But continuing their education and personal development, as well as training for all those jobs in a lifetime of 100 years, will require that they study more. Perhaps the first 30 years will be study in one form or another as previously mentioned.

At present there is a growing dissatisfaction with the way elementary and high schools and universities teach in these changing times — or fail to. At present there is vigorous dissatisfaction with the priorities of our society and the young people's role. In the Yankelovich survey published in *Fortune*, January 1969, 40 per cent of the college students registered firm dissents and were named the forerunner

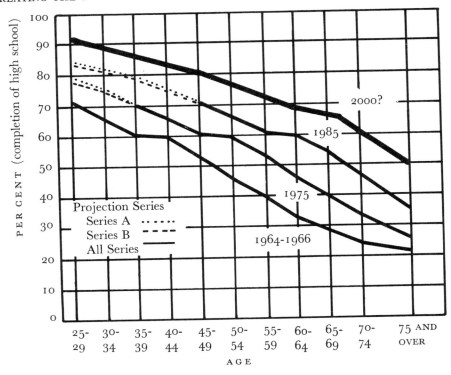

FIGURE I-8. *More and Better Educated*[23]

group.[24] In the Harris poll of high schools, 50 to 60 per cent of the students expressed strong demand for more student participation in school policy-making.[25] The point is that the dissatisfaction is not from a small percentage of troublemakers. Small wonder that there is exasperation when teaching methods are in one century and the students, television, and the computer in another.

Educator Anthony B. Oettinger has condemned the rigidity of educational institutions (only 1 per cent of the budget goes into teaching research) and seriously questions whether there will be any serious changes in teaching methods utilizing the computer and other technology[26] within the next 10 years. Broader understanding of GNP growth and of the contribution of education to it might change that. Then too, perhaps modern teaching technology will be more quickly adopted outside the basic educational system where its utility can be conclusively demonstrated faster. The necessity to upgrade adults in their jobs and help them learn new jobs just might be the needed wedge for innovation in education.

Once it is understood that we must accelerate GNP growth through individual productivity if the surplus needed to meet national goals is to be generated, and that education is part of the key to that, education may have the opportunity to modernize. The quality and quantity of those who will complete high school (and college) can be expected to increase. (See Figure I-8.) It would seem a thorough airing of national priorities could arrive at no other conclusion. A large impact of this sort, if the subject were thoroughly explored in the next 2 to 5 years, might begin to be felt before 1980. Figure I-8 gives the percentage of those completing high school.

MORE LEISURE

Of all the projections into the future, there is none more expressive of future life styles or more uncertain than future hours of leisure. The surprise we would predict here is in contrast to the prevalent understanding that there will be many additional hours of leisure by 1985 and 2000. We believe time spent at work on the major job will decrease noticeably, expressed in various combinations of shorter work hours per day, more three-day weekends, and longer vacations. But the concept that by 1985 or 2000 we will be staring at huge blocks of free time to do with exactly as we choose, we believe is fallacious for at least five reasons:

1) The recent and projected boom in leisure-oriented industry may be more a function of income for the masses than great changes in leisure time (i.e., time on the job dropped 5 per cent from 1950 to 1960, incomes increased by 15 per cent, and boating increased 94 per cent).[27]

2) Most people, given the choice, have chosen work and more income over time off because there are many things like travel, outboards, education for the children, better homes, second homes, and other material items to buy and pay for. It is true many of these new wants require time away from work to enjoy, but they have to be paid for too so there will probably be a mixture of more time spent working and more income.

3) There is much that needs to be done in this society and when people comprehend what they can do, no doubt they'll use part of

55

their new free time to do it. Organizations will either contribute employees' time away from the major job for nonprofit pursuits, or people will hold second part-time jobs.

4) Keeping up with the job and learning four different occupations in a lifetime will require nearly continuous study 4 to 12 hours every week, at home or at special adult centers, and periodic returns for extended concentrated periods of study.

5) Traffic congestion will probably get much worse over the next fifteen years before we adequately begin to cope with it. Combined with more long weekends and the lack of adequate planning, commuting will take a sizeable bite out of potential leisure as people locate further and further in time from their changing places of employment.

As Sebastian de Grazia has pointed out, the decline in the hours worked each week since 1870 did not greatly increase free-choice time. These hours off the job were filled with duties or chores, everything from do-it-yourself home maintenance and PTA to commuting time.[28] But even he concedes that the next few hours gained off the job may be qualitatively different in that they may offer genuine leisure. And the Outdoor Recreation Resources Review Commission studies show time as the major barrier to more indulgence in favorite outdoor activities — not money, health, or old age.[29]

What will higher incomes, a three-week vacation, and a 38-hour work week in 1985 and further reductions by the year 2000 to a four-week vacation and a 36½-hour work week mean in future life styles?

The ORRRC studies attempt to provide the basis for answers to that question. By analogy, up to a point, it can be expected that people will do what today's higher income people do: take more vacations in a year in more seasons, take more outings or side trips, and spend more money. They will spend more time with friends and relatives, do more reading (and less TV watching), participate in more club, organization, and church work; go to more concerts, plays, lectures, and museums, and spend more time in active sports and hobbies (less time driving their cars for pleasure).[30]

By the year 2000, outdoor recreation demand is expected to triple, much of it within a four-hour drive of peoples' homes or the homes of their friends and relatives since that is by far the greatest (51 per cent over the next highest, 12 per cent) of all reasons given for choice of vacation place.[31] The distance traveled and length of stay doesn't vary significantly by income (below $15,000). Averaging vacation and weekend jaunts together, the typical roundtrip is 250 miles and the time away from home 2½ days.[32] Weekends are the busy times. By some having "weekends" also on Tuesdays and Wednesdays, the burden on facilities could be spread.

The predominant use of leisure is inside — inside the person's own home and his friends' homes first of all, but also in the buildings required for many of the facilities (listed below in Table I-8) in his immediate community and in his 100-mile radius city.

TABLE I-8. *Leisure — the People's Choice*[33]

Activity	Per Cent
Looking at TV	41
Active sports	30
Reading	24
Gardening, work in the yard	20
Workshop or homemaking hobbies	19
Visiting with friends, relatives	17
Participating in clubs, organizations, church work	13
Spectator sports	10
Playing bridge, cards, chess, etc.	7
Going to movies	6
Pleasure driving	6
Going to plays, concerts, lectures, museums	2
Photography	1
Specific Sports:	
Fishing	18
Competitive outdoor sports (football, baseball, golf, tennis, etc.)	12
Outdoor swimming or going to a beach	10
Indoor sports (including those both indoor and outdoor)	10
Hunting	9
Boating and canoeing	3
Skiing and other winter sports	2
Camping	2
Horseback riding	1
Hiking	1
Going for walks	1

It can be expected that a people who have demanded continual up-grading of the total physical environment will continue to do so as their incomes increase. Even small increases in leisure will intensify this demand much further.

Henry Clark's examination of a non-nervous view of more leisure time identifies three major schools of thought: 1) service to others, 2) contemplation, 3) playfulness and spontaneity.[34] We might better understand the wide range of possibilities of greater free time and the "desanctification" of work by relating it to these.

It should be recognized also that the amount of leisure time is not uniform for all types of employment. An electrician working in New York may put in a full week at 25 hours (since 1962) and earn $10 to 15,000 per year, while typical doctors and businessmen may seldom work less than 60 hours and earn $30 to 40,000 on up. What people in different occupations have time to consume, what they can afford, and what they want can be quite different. But the majority will be more like the electricians than the doctors. Professionals, managers, and technicians are expected to increase, but only from 22 per cent in 1970 to 25 per cent in 1985 and 27 per cent in 2000. On them will fall the same long hours.[35]

One of the greatest impacts of leisure will be how it frees people to explore and discover a new order of quality — in all parts of their lives. With more time to explore themselves and their environment — in a lifetime, each year, each week — new standards of life will be established. Telecommunications will spread these patterns across the land. The impact of just a few hours more leisure per week, a week or so more per year, ultimately the three-day weekend will have profound effect even as they *start* to be realized.

It is important that the concept of quality, defined in subjective human terms as well as scientific terms, be incorporated into thinking about the future. Quantitative measures alone, such as GNP, automobiles, and population will not express the most important changes of the future. Perhaps the qualitative effect of more healthy old people who are better educated, with more free time but not so mobile as those younger is one way of illustrating why the quality of our living environment will be in for much closer examination.

BETTER HOMES

The construction priority being most seriously discussed in this country today is to "rationalize" home construction so as to reduce costs to make decent housing available for the poor at prices they can afford. Six million such homes in the next ten years was the Johnson Administration goal.[36] The surprises we anticipate from this are: 1) there will be some housing construction breakthroughs; the present concern over housing has existed for 16 to 29 years now, long enough to make it hopeful that the social inventions needed to permit the technological ones will be made over the next 5 to 10 years; 2) although technological construction breakthroughs will be forthcoming, it is obvious that a comprehensive systems approach is necessary because only 33 per cent of the cost of housing is in the building and utilities. Forty-three per cent is in financing and 25 per cent in land and taxes — both these factors must be considered also. A 20 per cent cut in building costs (about the maximum reduction to be expected) only reduces the total consumer's cost 12 per cent (7 per cent construction, 5 per cent in financing);[37] 3) the 10-year goal of 26 million new and rehabilitated units (including the 6 million low cost) set by the Johnson Administration will be met within 12 to 15 years.

"Look for the weak point in society as the place to innovate," says Jacob Bakema, co-architect and planner for the rebuilding of the center of bombed-out Rotterdam. He was referring also to the American ghetto.[38] Though generally innovation is conceived for a specific purpose, actual application turns out to be much broader: thoughtful architectural details for the elderly or the disabled, for instance, turn out to be advantageous for many others. Finding the situation where there is freedom enough to innovate is the crucial matter in an over-developed (overregulated) country like the United States.

Another surprise about the social and technological innovations, aimed at and justified by the need for low-cost housing, is that they are the only way to better homes. "Better," in the case of homes, means also bigger and more homes per family as well as better design and more appliances and facilities built into it. Bigger homes, 750 square feet per person by 1985, nearly double what they were in 1940, is one of the surprises we would predict that seems to be being overlooked. It will take new technology to deliver this space. Actually, to hold its share of the GNP or improve, the homebuilding industry in the face of increasing land costs, taxes, and financing costs must increase its efficiency. It must also offer more quality as well as build in much greater quantities, even though enough skilled craftsmen equal to the job do not exist.

Mobile homes are the best current success story in factory methods applied to shelter. They have virtually taken over the low-cost market increasing from 90,000 units in 1961 to 317,000 units in 1968.[39] The industry calls them horizontal apartments. The mobile home concept can be expected to be encouraged by HUD. Paul Rudolph refers to the 12' x 8' x 60' unit that rolls down the highway to the site where it is lifted into place in a high rise, or stacked in low rise or town houses as the "20th century brick" — designed as a modular unit with walls that fold out, all utilities, etc., built in.[40]

If human needs are not forgotten in the rush to cut costs and the proper social inventions as well as technological ones are made, there is every reason to expect significant breakthroughs and savings in home construction. There are certain human considerations that must come first. One, we should admit we have experimented very little and know very little about *desirable* human environment. Science knows only what is bad for people. Second, there are human costs to increasing densities we need to study and consider. Some of those associated with high rise apartments, which is one way to reduce the per unit cost of land, we do know and should be forewarned about — as far as families are concerned. (Another way to reduce the cost per unit of land is not to build in expensive large metropolitan regions.) Careful site planning and higher densities can reduce land costs and at the same time provide social benefits. More good design, changes in building codes, markets, financing, zoning, housing codes, union practices (avoided by mobile homes), and taxing, as well as land planning are among the social inventions that can contribute savings — and benefits.

With more time for leisure and learning, more time will be spent at home and in its environs. Sophisticated equipment like computer remote consoles, 3D-color-TV, and technologically advanced appliances might well be modularized for easy service and replacement — as a concept of the original design — and built in or added on. A home study hall and entertainment center will add new space and functional requirements to the home. Taken together with the larger homes that seem to come with larger incomes, these are additional pressures for larger homes, more equipped homes, and more second homes. And this is already the trend. Low income families ($5915 per year or less) have 1013 square foot homes. Those with higher incomes ($12,549 or more) have 1934 square feet if renting, 2374 square feet if buying.[41] Homes have been growing in size, including mobile

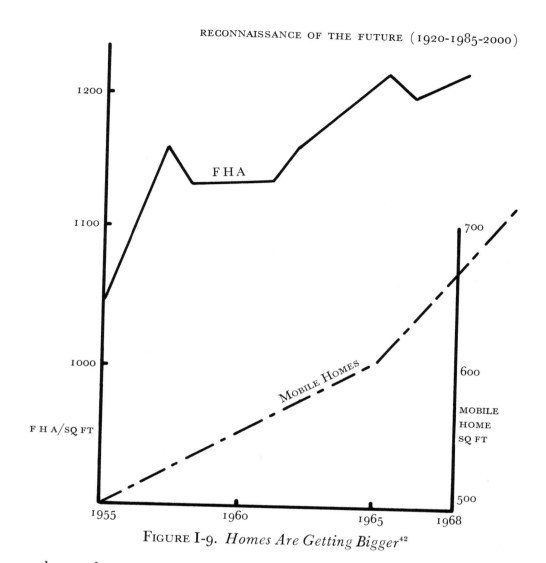

FIGURE I-9. *Homes Are Getting Bigger*[42]

homes from 500 to 720 square feet in the past thirteen years.[43] In addition, there is an interesting figure available from Manhattan. Residential area per person has gone from 250 square feet to 500 square feet from 1900 to 1963. This has been caused by a steady residential area supply and a decrease in population; family size has dipped from 4.8 people per family to 2.9 people. Square feet per person is expected to go to 600 by 1985.[44]

It is recognized that a great view, or special design, or psychological space (as occurs with second home or travel) can reduce floor area or volume per person, but even allowing for that possibility it is our estimate that future Americans will average 750 square feet per person, making 2000 to 2325 square feet in 1985 the basic home (presently the U.S. average house is 1600 square feet, about 485 square feet per person).[45] Over 25 per cent are expected to have second homes by 1985 — which would average 400 to 600 square feet. If all this is true, the construction costs of a fewer number of new households predicted by this study in 2000 (90 million versus the median 98 million) will be compensated for by their size and the dollar value of construction.

An Operable Sense of National Community

It would take a system break, a really big surprise, to turn off the migration from the small towns and farms to the big city and instead to encourage migration away from the metropolitan area. In Chapter 3 we gave the accepted best estimate: concentrating the next 80 to 100 million people where most people already are. Here we are saying this need not be accepted as final if we choose otherwise. Where people settle (along with unexpectedly low birth rates and institutional changes that would permit speed-up in the application of technology) is among the biggest possible changes to look out for.

We all know the factors that have pushed and pulled people by the millions into the big metropolitan areas. This all adds up to "nothing succeeds like success," referring to the concentration of opportunity for ordinary people — and for those who manage the opportunities. They are headquartered in the big cities. Eighty per cent of the GNP is a matter of private decisions that are only secondarily guided by governmental incentives and whatever leverage there is in government's 20 per cent of GNP expenditures.

This concentration of decisions in private hands pretty well states the basic reasons why most people who are seeking to keep the shine on their "hard nose" reputation project the past into the future when it comes to forecasting *where* people will locate. This tends to perpetuate present patterns helping prove, in time, how right the forecasters were. It's all a matter of being "practical." People aren't asking themselves what is good for people, or what the people really want.

To destroy totally the notion that a nation's settlement patterns can be significantly influenced by public policy, the case is made both of the uncontrolled growth of Moscow and the so-called failure of the British New Towns because they have syphoned off only 10 per cent of the growth of London. Somehow certain other examples are left out of this sort of argument, like the U.S. Homestead Act, the current Russian development of Siberia, and the present movement of 20 million Chinese to the hinterlands. And the lack of relevance of Britain's New Towns to our circumstances is ignored. Their New Towns are intended as free standing communities outside easy commuting to London and are largely based on industrial jobs. Hardly the case of a Columbia or a Reston or a Foster City.

It would be helpful not to be deluded by entangling ourselves in the wrong issues when the possibility of a national policy for settlement is discussed. We need not argue "back to the farm" or for free standing New Towns as *the* basis for national settlement policy. Considering deliberate public policy for settlement in the United States at this time need claim no more than that political, social, economic, technological, and institutional factors might be combined now in such a way as to offer a significant number of people the access to opportunity they want without being part of a metropolis.

We should look at the incentive to move caused by the inequities in welfare payments as shown in Figure I-10. It can be argued that people move to realize hoped for opportunities — jobs — not for welfare; but the disparity in welfare, if not an expression of opportunity, is at least good "insurance." Actually the contrast of other social services like health and education is equally great between rural and urban states. Taken together, we encourage people to move to the big cities. The pull is stronger the larger and more diverse a city is — whether or not it offers the healthiest life.

Through a national policy that attempted to put human and technological, including economic, costs in balance we might discover that not only will we be better off with a lower national population growth, but that the same slowdown might best be applied also to many of the largest metropolitan regions. Consider such large urban-area disadvantages as pollution, psychological overcowding, crime, poor education, insurance rates, sense of alienation, tripling land costs, people continually polling 70 to 80 per cent in favor of single family homes,[46] demonstrably higher costs per person for basic public services in cities over 250,000,[47] and generally higher costs of living.[48] Consider smaller city advantages such as improved access to opportunity provided by telecommunications and transportation, underutilized

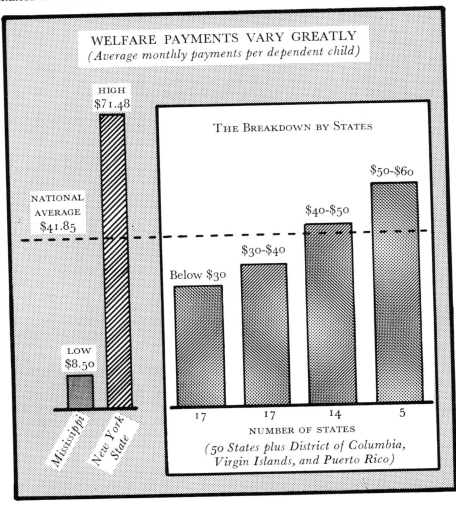

Source: ©1969 by The New York Times Company. Reprinted by permission.

FIGURE I-10. *The Difference in Welfare*[49]

public facilities, easier access to outdoor recreation, more personal identity, lower costs of land, few pollution problems, etc.

Some will argue a city must keep growing or die. This argument works up to a point, but world population cannot keep growing *without* human life dying. Control of the birth and growth rates must be anticipated. If human life expectancy is to double after the year 2000, we now should be planning to keep vacant areas around major cities and plan city centers for the future at the higher density growth that will be appropriate for the many more couples without children. To do so, needless to say, would take some social inventions, expecially an objective national dialogue that examined with both feeling and scientific skill the human costs and benefits of our choices for locating our homes. What might these social inventions be? What is the likelihood of their success against the forces we have readily acknowledged?

Jack Howard, Head of MIT's Department of City and Regional Planning, proposes not a back to the farm movement but a back to the city movement. He would like to see public policies which would:

1) Limit U.S. population growth.

2) Limit the maximum size of cities by:
   a. strongly discouraging further population growth of areas already beyond 5 million;
   b. discouraging much growth beyond 2 million (The 12 metropolitan areas of 2 million or over now grew only 20 per cent from 1950–1960, the U.S. average, whereas all the other metropolitan areas grew by 32 per cent);
   c. remaining neutral toward growth between 600,000 and 2 million, but in all size ranges, discouraging rapid growth — more than 2 to 3 per cent per year (doubling in 24 to 35 years);
   d. strongly encouraging growth up to 600,000 of metropolitan areas (or regional "cities") now over 100,000 and of a few others of especially favorable potential. (Item d. is especially concerned with 150 metropolitan areas, housing about 30 million people in 1960.)

3) Offer government assistance to transfer populations from the overpopulated central cities of the dozen largest metropolitan areas to new job opportunities in the 150 growth-stimulated smaller metropolitan (or regional cities).[50]

To these recommendations, deliberate encouragement could be added for starting New Towns of 20,000 to 50,000 in metropolitan areas and free standing New Towns and metropolitan areas.

The following table from the Economic Development Administration confirms the sense of Howard's statement.

TABLE I-9. *County Size and Future Jobs 1960-1975*[51]
(Assumes 4% national unemployment)

1960 Counties or local gov'ts population	No. of counties	% with projected job growth less than U.S. av.
Less than 10,000	823	82
10,000 – 50,000	1652	71
50,000 – 100,000	292	28
100,000 – 500,000	239	25
500,000 – 1 million	49	65
Over 1 million	16	87

Growth is projected here in counties of 50,000 to 500,000 population by EDA about where Jack Howard proposes it ought to go. Looking more closely at the urban complexes of over 1 million which contain a total of 96.6 million population, EDA then asked itself this question: "Assuming no migration occurred into or out of major complexes of over 1 million population, what could be the relationship between future jobs and future population both for major metropolitan complexes and within these complexes?" The data developed led to the conclusion that these major urban complexes face a serious problem of providing enough new jobs for their natural increase in population, even assuming no in-migration. "Indeed, the estimates indicate that in order to achieve an unemployment rate of 4 per cent, there must be a net out-migration of population of 6.3 per cent from our ten largest urban complexes and 4.8 per cent from our 29 largest complexes, over the period 1960-1975. This substantial imbalance exists even while taking into account the offsetting growth of jobs in the suburbs of these cities."[52]

The National Commission on Rural Poverty's investigation led to other proposed social inventions. It pointed out that the rate of rural unemployment is 18 per cent versus the nation's 4 per cent; that underemployment of farm workers runs as high as 37 per cent.[53] The result is disease, malnutrition, poor family planning, etc. Statistics, for instance, in 1960 showed that throughout the nation women 40 to 44 had produced an average 2.5 children; while in farm families with less than $2000 (70 per cent of all rural families), white families produced 3.7 and nonwhites, 6.4.[54] The Commission's report defined

66

a new right: "Every citizen of the United States must have equal access to opportunities for economic and social advancement without discrimination because of race, religion, national origin, or *place of residence.*"[55]

TABLE I-10. *Where the Poor Are*[56]

	Total (millions)	Poor (millions)	Poor %
Rural (total)	55.3	13.8	25.0
farm	13.3	3.9	29.3
nonfarm	42.0	9.9	23.6
urban (total)	134.6	19.9	14.8
small city	27.1	6.4	23.6
metropolitan area (total)	107.5	13.5	12.6
central city	58.6	10.2	17.4
suburbs	48.9	3.3	6.7

The Commission questions "the wisdom of massive public efforts to improve the lot of the poor in our central cities without comparable efforts to meet the needs of the poor in rural America. There is danger that programs limited to the needs of our central cities will be self-defeating. If economic and social conditions are greatly improved in our central cities without comparable improvement in rural areas, additional incentives will be created for migration to the cities."[57] Of the 13.8 million rural poor representing 40 per cent of the nation's poor in 1965, 11 million were white.[58] In 1967, for the entire United States, 71 per cent of the poor families were white.[59] The Negro feels poverty most keenly as a race because three out of ten Negro families are below the $3000 per year poverty level, while only one out of ten white families fall below the poverty level.[60] City immigrants from rural areas without good education, training, and skills are at the core of the urban-central city problem.

The center of major American cities is where the urban-crisis programs are focused, and that is where the Negro poor is concentrated. But no less a man than Gunnar Myrdal (whose views twenty years ago in *American Dilemma* were ignored) has recently said that in America there cannot be a program for the poor black; we must have a program for all the poor.[61] We believe there is even more to consider than that. The poor and the disadvantaged, measured by whatever criterion, are a minority in our democratic society. The poor must have the interest and support of the huge mass of Americans who consider themselves middle class to establish national priorities for assistance. (The top 5 per cent of our population earns 20 per cent of the national income, the bottom 20 per cent earns 5 per cent; those who earn the other 75 per cent make the ultimate decisions.) To assure the support of the middle class for programs of truly national scope, undoubtedly there must be the explicit understanding that everyone will take part and move "forward together." As this happens, it seems much more likely that there can be special assistance for the disadvantaged minorities whoever and wherever they may be.

The Advisory Commission on Intergovernmental Relations has proposed: "(1) development of a national policy to deal with urban growth, (2) a re-examination of multi-state regional planning areas and agencies, and (3) a new and expanding role for state governments through the development of state urban development plans."[62] Their proposals explicitly link the responsibilities of the Housing Act of 1949 with Full Employment Act of 1946. With the traditional thirty-year lead time for full implementation of social inventions, that puts us into 1976 to 1979. The Commission's proposals in a report entitled *Urban and Rural America: Policies for Future Growth*[63] (and being incorporated into legislation for Congress) consider everything from Executive Office responsibilities to practical incentives for locating industries; resettlement allowances for relocating people from labor surplus areas; job training support; elimination of present state, city, and federal incentives to big-city migration; New Towns; etc. The U.S. Chamber of Commerce has prepared a similar statement.[64]

The American Institute of Planners developed a complete statement on the basis for encouraging New Towns.[65] In addition its regional conference in Arkansas, July 1968, generated a National Policy Statement which made a coherent set of proposals for:

1. *Long-range national policies* for the development of both urban and rural America including the institutions needed for research, development and planning, meaningful participation, guaranteed jobs, decentralizing decision-making, national transportation policy, and financial incentives;

2. *Improvements in the federal executive* requiring a long-range national development policy statement by the President, a new Long-

Range Research and Development Office reporting to the President, interdepartmental monitoring of long-range priority; and, in conjunction with the states, the regionalization of the nation, the preservation of the unique qualities of each region and the strengthening of the states;

3. *Proposals for managing change* through the establishment of multidisciplinary policy research institutions free of political domination with ready access to all channels of public communication; encouragement of competing centers of knowledge and planning to avoid a governmental monopoly;

4. *Specific improvements in the state executive* and the state legislatures establishing multipurpose-multicounty regions within the states, restricting state government pay scales and the functions of executive offices, new semi-independent research and development application centers for technology.[66]

The above documents on national policies for development are all dated 1967 or later. There is no reason to suppose without national dialogue that they will be made operational and meaningful. On the other hand, there is no reason to assume that with dialogue they won't be. The possibility is to shift present trends away from a few megalopolitan complexes by the double combination of a national population reduction to a year 2000 population of 280 million or less, and a national policy for redistribution of decentralizing the major centers from 20 to 60 million people. There are a number of our most significant public and private organizations studying this now.

Decisions regarding national patterns for settlement are political decisions. It is interesting, in that regard, to relate the problems and the power of the thirty-four less populated states (less than 110 people/square mile). Among their problems they have 90 per cent of the critical hunger counties in the United States, 90 per cent of the redevelopment areas designated for financial assistance by EDA, and 90 per cent of the states whose average annual income falls below the poverty line. These thirty-four states can count in their power 100 per cent of the chairmen of the Senate Standing Committees, 66 per cent of the chairmen of the House Standing Committees, 66 per cent of the nation's governors, and 84 per cent of the nation's land area.[67]

The previous section has been devoted to national settlement patterns. A part of this strategy needing national stimulus and state authority is the encouragement of the use of eminent domain (or the pooling of single ownerships) to provide the large sites needed to create whole communities whether out in the states or in metropolitan areas. Both private enterprise and government might be given this power if used in a manner consistent with a public purpose.[68] Without such power, the assembling of large tracts in strategic places can be considered nearly unworkable. This is among the most needed of social inventions to provide the means for creating whole human environments.

The exercise of eminent domain, and a public writedown of the cost of land, similar to that of urban renewal, is probably the only way to a national strategy for developing new cities. This is especially true in large metropolitan regions. Well-planned new communities in metropolitan regions may be one of the only effective ways to help blacks move outside the confines of the central city. Another suggestion, by Anthony Downs, are ghetto-ettes — small enclaves of housing for low income groups, 40 or so people at a time, so small that the suburbs cannot feel they are being threatened but large enough to provide a sense of identity for the families moving out to the suburbs.

With the passage of the Full Employment Act of 1946, guaranteed jobs for all who are able to work became an official responsibility of the federal government. From 1954 to 1965, however, there was substantial and persistent unemployment at times double the normal pre-war rate in the United States of 3 per cent. For eight of those eleven years, unemployment was at 5 per cent or more — 5 million people did not find work.[69] It is doubtful that such a level of unemployment will be tolerated again. Translated, 5 per cent of the nation unemployed means 15 per cent of the white teenagers and 30 per cent of the black teenagers, concentrated mostly in big-city ghettos.[70] For the latter it meant depression-years circumstances in the midst of plenty, brought home to them with the irony of viewing TV's suburban family situation comedies.

It wasn't until 1961 that the Council of Economic Advisors, created with the 1946 Full Employment Act, had both a President's ear and his full attention. With President Kennedy, Walter Heller & Company set out and sold to Congress the target of 4 per cent unemployment based on the concept of a GNP annual increase of $4\frac{1}{2}$ per cent,[71] closing the $50 billion gap between actual and potential production. By 1966, GNP rate of growth had risen to $5\frac{1}{2}$ per cent and 7 million jobs were created. Employment dropped to 4 per cent. True to form for social inventions, Keynesian economics was applied in the United States thirty years after its invention.[72] It was reported that Milton Friedman, advisor to Presidential candidate Senator Goldwater, said "We are all Keynesians now" and the economists of the United States said "Amen."[73] U.S. economics came of age.

The responsibility of the federal government to manage the economy to assure full employment and economic stability has arrived. It's one of the keys to continuity the nation has needed to mature to the point of being able to formulate concepts for national (necessarily long-range) development. Full employment doesn't mean 5 per cent unemployed in the nation and 30 per cent in the ghetto any longer. It probably means 3½ to 4 per cent unemployment plus concerted programs to reduce it further. Guaranteed jobs are becoming established as a topic. Somehow Congress, the President, and the voters of the nation must continue to examine and grapple with it, vexed as they may be by the 5 per cent annual inflation we are experiencing today versus the 1.7 per cent from 1948 to 1967.[74]

As a nation, we haven't as yet arrived at the guaranteed-job stage. We might well start with changes in the welfare program[75] and proceed to tighten the definition of full employment to 2 or 3 per cent unemployed and conceivably to add specific government-paid jobs in community public works and services, paid education, and retraining. Theobald has argued for the guaranteed income but 62 per cent of the people polled in January 1969 were against it.[76] Americans want a guaranteed job now. In another century, perhaps, the guaranteed income will be seen as a necessity. Friedman's negative income tax is another way. Five such income maintenance propositions have been compared and priced at $11 billion to $38 billion per year.[77]

By taking seriously its full-employment responsibility at all levels, from retraining or resettling people to guaranteed incomes, the federal government has a powerful new *locational* tool to use if that is what people want.

The rate of growth of the Gross National Product is a combination of three basic factors: labor force, hours worked, and productivity. Adding them up as they are currently, *Fortune* figures it this way: the annual GNP growth for the next five years is based on a 1.7 per cent increase in the labor force, less 0.4 per cent decrease in average hours per worker plus 2.7 per cent gain in productivity per worker — a total of 4 per cent.[78]

The second Council of Economic Advisors chairman, Leon Keyserling, sees no reason why, with skilled handling (tight controls), the

GNP can't gain at 5 per cent or better per year without serious inflation.[79] For four years in World War II, GNP growth averaged 9 per cent (without runaway inflation). Walter Heller estimates 4 to 4½ per cent is more likely what we *will* do.[80] The National Commission on Technology, Automation and Economic Progress points out the GNP must grow at the rate of 4 per cent, at least, when the labor force is growing at 1.9 per cent per year if unemployment is to be held at 4 per cent.[81] Gerhard Colm picked somewhat more than 4 per cent for the next 5 to 10 years — with a figure of 5½ per cent needed if we are to realize by 1975 the National Goals set by the Eisenhower Commission in its *Goals for America*.[82]

The figures used in Chapter 3 predict an annual GNP growth rate of 4 to 4½ per cent from 1970 to 2000. But we should acknowledge here that some say the U.S. economy "has seldom, if ever, sustained a rate faster than 3½ per cent for any extended length of time."[83] Yet from 1869 to 1918 it did average 3.8 per cent.[84] For the past five years, we have been moving along at 5.4 per cent[85] (with inflation growing from 3.3 to 4, now 5 per cent). It will take deliberate priority emphasis to realize the 4 to 4½ per cent annual growth in GNP with inflation at no more than 2 per cent per year and unemployment at 4 per cent or less. If people throughout the nation understand the social and economic rewards of full employment and sustained national growth, the financial capacity and the social climate can be created to build a future human environment.

The experience in Europe after World War II illustrates this in Table I-11. The drop in unemployment coupled with high productivity produced growth in the GNP in West Germany of 109 per cent, in Italy 78 per cent, and France 53 per cent even though populations were relatively stable in that period (they grew only 8 per cent in the entire ten years).[86]

The 4 to 4½ per cent rate proposed, it is believed, upsets no international trade relations and would require a minimum of Federal restraints to avoid inflation. Encouragement of initiative, education, and technology would be the generators of this growth, applied to the increased labor force. Sustaining a higher than 5 per cent rate of growth without inflation, from most judgments surveyed, would require controls tighter than seems to be the mood of this nation for the foreseeable future. Reducing annual inflation from 2 per cent to zero might require a severe trade-off in unemployment which would seriously undercut the growth in GNP and the nation's capacity for re-

TABLE I-11. *Productivity and Unemployment*[87]

Country	Per cent rate of productivity change		Per cent unemployed		
			1951-1962 Trend		
West Germany	4		9.0	0.7	Down
Italy	4	above average	8.8	3.0	"
France	4		?	?	"
Netherlands	3		2.3	0.8	"
Belgium	3	average	9.8	4.0	"
Norway	3		1.1	1.4	Up
United States	2		3.3	5.6	"
Canada	2	below average	2.4	5.9	"
United Kingdom	2		1.3	2.1	"

building its sense of purpose as expressed by President Nixon. It is the kind of judgment, however, that could be made. Nothing is certain except maybe the social unrest this would set loose.

An operable sense of national community is based on what people want and what resources they have for achieving it. A previous section of this chapter has emphasized what people want; the resources of the economy, including our labor force and the GNP rate of growth, are covered here.

To realize an operable sense of national community, there needs to be wide understanding of the great economic resource the U.S. economy truly is. Professional men, especially the designers of the huge technological environment we are looking into — dependent in so many ways on political decisions — need a working understanding of their nation's economy.

Lyle Fitch stated that the relationship of GNP to people is not a constant.[88] More people does *not* necessarily mean a GNP that does as well per person as a lesser population would. Increased productivity with a slowed population growth greatly increases the chances for greater personal and public disposable income. This makes a greater likelihood of more funds available for creative community, national, and international purposes while forestalling more pollution of the environment, overcrowding, and a generally lower quality of service and standard of life. Fitch summarizes by stating "there are reasons for supposing that the total GNP for a population as large as 360 million would be little larger than for a population of 280 million."

Accelerated Civilian Research and Development

At present 83 per cent of the federal outlays for research and development go to Department of Defense, Atomic Energy Commission, National Aeronautics and Space Administration for defense purposes, but we rate a new emphasis on civilian research and development as a surprise to be watched for. It is said that half the research scientists in the United States are "employed" by DOD. Since the federal government now accounts for 60 per cent of all research and development (R&D), clearly civilian needs are undernourished (see Table I-12 below).[89]

TABLE I-12. *Federally Supported Research and Development, Present Style*

A. Federal R&D Expenditures (1967)[90]

	$ millions	% of total	
Dept. of Defense	$ 7,113	45	response to
NASA	5,310	34	exterior
AEC	1,275	9	challenge 83%
HEW	1,012	6	
Dept. of Transportation	267	2	
Dept. of Agriculture	262	2	response to
NSF	196	—	internal
FAA	155	—	challenge 17%
Dept. of Interior	126	—	
Others	239	—	
	$15,763	100%	(figures rounded; won't add)

B. Federal Research by Field of Science (1967)[91]

	total 1967 $ millions	%
All Federal Sponsored	$5,623	100
Life Sciences	1,430	25
Psychological Sciences	107	2
Physical Sciences	3,817	68
Social Sciences	178	3
Other Sciences	90	1

TABLE I-12. (*Continued*)

C. Where Scientists and Engineers Are Employed (1954–1965)[92]

	1954	*1965*
Federal Government	37,600	69,000
Industry	164,100	351,200
Universities & Colleges	30,000	66,000
Nonprofit Institutions	5,300	17,400
Total	237,000	503,600

A balanced national research program would bring up the R&D expenditures in response to internal challenges. It would aim at increasing productivity, improving human health and the quality of human lives, as well as defense. We need to begin this by recognizing our internal and external goals may be more than we can afford. In so doing, we increase the pressure for increasing all research since some economists say 50 to 80 per cent of the annual growth in GNP is gained from new technology.[93] One economist is said to put it at 90 per cent.[94] If the population component of GNP increase is held down and we want to maximize GNP growth, we must both increase productivity *and* minimize leisure (ultimately conflicting goals).

Within the past 25 years, firms have grown into the top rank or strengthened their hold there through innovations such as television, electrostatic copying, computers, synthetic fibers, and jet engines. It is said that 90 per cent of all R&D is carried on by under 400 major corporations.[95]

Basic (creative) research is about 14 per cent of the R&D total, applied (innovative) research 15 per cent, and over three-fifths is for development. Federal support for research has increased 225-fold[96] in the past 30 years but the growth has leveled off since 1966, which is really a cut in this time of inflation. Total U.S. R&D stood at $6 billion in 1955 increasing to $20 billion by 1965 after the Russians launched Sputnik in 1957. Congress has done some of its fastest, crudest budget trimming in this most sensitive area. Research and development is incapable of promising short-term results and is difficult to explain, so it lacks political sex appeal. Former Presidential science advisor Jerome B. Wiesner warns that we will be a "sick country technologically" if the present sort of R&D funding continues another 5 to 10 years.[97] Sick also financially, socially, and ecologically, it should be added.

Research, development, and education are strategic decisions for sustained growth. These bootstrap means to continue the expansion of the nation's economy come into the purview of modern federal policy if full employment, the elimination of poverty, and a more healthy, human future environment are long-term national priorities in deed as well as in word.

The financial support that is needed for a balanced R&D effort is relatively small in relation to other federal expenditures (3.6 per cent of the GNP),[98] but that would support a significant extension into the civilian sector of federal R&D stimulus. It can be expected that this extension will be contested by existing establishments, public and private. Existing establishments need proof of results before research begins, and they conceive of the future as the next two years. The "joke" for years has been that the Department of Agriculture spent more on research about the potato bug than the total research into human housing and urban environment through HHFA. At present HUD has only $11 million for such experimentation, and the National Science Foundation seems unprepared to recognize the social sciences as more than a token scientific responsibility in its pitiful 1 per cent of the nation's R&D budget.

The emphasis of this investigation has been and remains on the social inventions needed to clear the way for the application of technological inventions. In restating that here, it is worth pointing to Table I-12 where it can be seen that at present only 3 per cent of the federal R&D money is going into this social science area now, and probably only a portion of that for social problem-solving purposes. Of the total federal R&D budget, 83 per cent is for response to external challenge. As to who does the research, only 3 per cent of the researchers are now in the nonprofit sector where touchy social-problem situations can really be tackled.

It is true that foundations attack these problems, but probably not more than $15 million per year of their grants[99] could be assigned to this purpose, which is only 0.06 per cent of the total U.S. R&D budget of $25 billion. Foundations are now under attack by Texas Congressman Wright Patman for alleged indiscretions of all sorts. Their support of "quick results" programs in some of society's major social-problem areas has brought them into the political arena for "indecent exposure." This threat to one of the great innovative forces of society can become serious. If the people do not understand and permit Congress to overreact, controls might be instituted that would seriously curtail the freedom and creativity that the foundations and the entire nonprofit sector can contribute, especially in politically sensitive areas. Such a situation would leave *only* the bureaucracy and the marketplace to raise and evaluate alternative decisions. The problem is that each is fully capable of eliminating those issues considered to be in conflict with vested interests or issues where a longer-range outlook differs with current understanding of what best serves existing institutions and their leaders. RAND-type corporations, foundations, church efforts, various civic associations, and certain university-based investigators are probably the most objective and believable means for undertaking social-problem investigations.

We have singled out here for further study both broad fields and specific items as being of particular importance to the designers and builders of the future environment: telecommunications, transportation, health, housing, waste disposal, inexpensive tunneling. The discussion thus far is intended to incorporate our emphasis on R&D for the social inventions needed.

TELECOMMUNICATIONS

"Surprise" is the correct term for the whole area of telecommunications. This is one of the few places where the external challenge (defense and space) has financed research and development that overlaps with the internal challenge. (Atomic power is another.) Television, lasers, electronic video recording, improved transistors, more efficient electric generation and distribution, and continuing increases in computer capacities combined with the social inventions needed can only create surprises. No area of technology today is in as advanced a stage of development prior to full application as telecommunications.

When we speak of the impact of technology on society in the short range, propelling it into change, telecommunication technology looms larger than all the rest. It is involved in both expectations of people and their potential for understanding and control of their environment — human and technological. In telecommunications we have proven hardware ready for broad application with many of the institutions for implementation already in place. Social inventions needed for the positive application to assure a human-technological environment are needed, to be sure, but they are discernible and reported elsewhere in this reconnaissance.

The expected impacts of communication technology are perhaps most dramatically symbolized by the forthcoming use of the computer for personal two-way communication.[100] Putting knowledge and the processing of programs at the fingertips of researchers is already an accepted practice through computer remote-control consoles sharing the same computer. The groundwork for the widespread use of this service has already been laid.

An individual's personal capacity to perform will be augmented many times through his personal "dialogue" with computers. It is difficult, adding graphic display and other equipment to computers, to conceive just where their remarkable impact will end. Perhaps the best measure of a nation's capacity for change — and its control of change — is in its computers:

Computers — June 1967[101]

United States	32,500	Italy	1,300
West Germany	3,300	Australia	530
Great Britain	2,200	The Netherlands	500
France	1,950	Switzerland	500
USSR	1,400	Sweden	430

The computer has increased its capacity and performance 1 million times since it was invented in the 1940's. It is to increase at least another 100,000 times by the year 2000 — compare that with the 5 to 10 factor of improvement that heretofore meant a "serious invention."[102] When computers become accessible for *personal* communication use, the innovations (shopping, studying, entertainment, work, research, etc.) and impacts (on the home, location of population, urban form) will be profound.

It has been freely predicted by many that 3-D TV and computer consoles with graphic display and print-out devices will be available in the home. This is an ultimate statement. No doubt schools, universities, research organizations, service and manufacturing corporations, governments, hospitals, churches, etc., will use them first. Their acquision of computer capacity may take the next 10 to 15 years. It would be after that before the broader home-market applications begin to develop. Working at home, avoiding commuting, is not likely for the middle-aged who already have a physiological living pattern that calls for going off to work. But studying at home is another matter, and much of the keeping up with the technology and learning new jobs could take place at home, beginning within the next ten years.

By means of new telecommunications, the whole potential for a national policy for settlement becomes much more realistic than it is considered today. The Establishment has its own revolution — telecommunications — which *can* rationalize and restimulate the whole forward thrust of the nation in positive directions.

Effective cross-communication between the professions and non-profit institutions, universities, government, private enterprise and interested laymen is not possible without new applications of telecommunications.

The role of telecommunications in defining and realizing long-range community and national priorities has yet to be defined. That is the purpose of the dialogue center, the situation and outlook facility utilizing a nonprofit institutional base referred to throughout this investigation.

Think also about the potential of 20 to 30 TV channels to choose from, of neighborhood use of television and two-way communication utilizing the telephone wires that already run into almost every home. What does this portend when combined with selecting what one *wants* to see on television at any particular time either by selective video recording in the home or on command to a computer-TV center?

Much broader and longer range are the effects on politics. The present political world is created by the fact that most citizens see or read the top news story of the day and very little else. But in the coming atomized society, the information the citizen gets will arise from his own specific concerns, whether they relate to the traffic problem in his community, legislation dealing with his business, or draft policy. Today people do read things which affect them personally when they happen to crop up in the press, but they are not in a position to ask for that particular information. When everyone can select his own fund of information, the political problem of gathering an effective body of support behind a particular rational issue or a candidate will become very different and very much more difficult.

At a much more specialized level, the communication revolution might send scientists back to the literature. Interpersonal communication will hardly be displaced, but if one can query an inanimate data base with the same flexibility, there'll be more of that.

Throughout business and industry, computerized information systems will spur decentralization and dispersion of power. Many decisions, in a contemporary firm, must be made at headquarters because that is where the information is. In a computerized environment, information is no bottleneck, and more decisions can be made on the spot.

Advertising will lose the captive audience the mass media now provide, and it may develop toward an information service in which the customer takes the initiative in asking for help on a purchase. Such a change would have its costs. Advertising would become less of a stimulant to action; it would better serve immediate wants, but advertisers would find it more difficult to create new wants.

The whole concept of space, of distance, takes on less significance as communication gains in ease and richness. Already, the people in a particular profession or institution tend to become a single community, more meaningful than the geographic community. Communication satellites make it less and less sensible to link the cost of communication to the distance covered. Picture-phones, conference calls, and computer-mediated connections of the sort Licklider and Taylor predict will make it less and less important to travel. There is a unique quality to personal contact which will continue to draw people together for that informal process of testing and probing for hours or days by which men come to trust and understand each other. But the sort of travel which brings people together for an hour or two of intense focused conversation may be replaced by long-distance discussions that accomplish as much or more without wasting hours in getting back and forth.

Indeed the whole shape of our cities and homes may change as people increasingly work at home and communicate to all the world from there.

A picture begins to emerge of a society ever more individualized in its interests and tastes. Certainly no one any longer need fear that 1984 will see a nation of helots cast from a single mold. But the consequences of such individualization will not be completely good. In the 21st Century, the sort of critic who now attacks conformity in society may be complaining of an atomized society. He may look back with nostalgia to the days when a movie star had millions of avid followers and gave unity and content to the life of the nation — whereas in his day every little clique of creative people makes its own movies incorporating its own idiosyncratic point of view. Modern technology, he'll assert, has destroyed our common cultural base and has left us each living in a little world of his own."[103]

TRANSPORTATION

Another surprise would be an adequately funded R&D program for intracity public transportation, something on the order of $200 million per year[104] to make up for lost time versus the automobile companies' $100 million.[105] At present the total *market* for public transit equipment is $100 million per year.[106] No wonder that since the FDR Administration remodeled the street car in 1933, there have been no innovations in public transit systems and equipment.

Intercity transportation would have its surprises too, if highspeed ground transportation were to receive the sort of attention here the Japanese gave their Tokaido Express. They poured $1.4 billion into their 320 mile, 125 mph special-designed trains and roadbed. (It is completely fenced in and the rails leveled daily by a crew of 400.) We have put only $20-50 million into the East Coast Metroliner which cannot cruise much faster than 100 mph without large additional costs for new roadbeds, straightening, new grade separations, and additional security.

Since a large enough quick payoff market doesn't exist for a public transit breakthrough and it is too costly a venture for any city or state level of government to undertake, technological inventions and their application will need federal stimulus. There is reason to question *when* such public transportation R&D might be expected. Perhaps it will take 5 to 15 years to develop and begin applying satisfactory prototypes for both intercity and intracity ground transportation. The inventions needed here appear to be both technological and social. Who can make the decisions if the tough questions are asked? Who will formulate the questions?

Discussion is reaching the serious stage regarding means to finance a $1 billion per year trust fund for the development of modern public transportation systems.[107] (The interstate highway program trust fund is $4 billion per year.) Some cities are at the stage of implementing new subway systems and need assistance. Others warrant improved bus service and should not be held off. But the test and refinement of the 500 mph underground gravity vacuum tube train, the 300 mph air cushion monorail, linear induction trains, slow moving walkways or minirails, dial-a-bus, and computer-guided cars all need trial applications to test their feasibility and best usage. Adequate R&D funds for this do not exist — but could if that is what people want. Of course, they can't want what they don't know about.

The computer-guided vehicle — initially gasoline powered, ultimately by electricity or fuel cell — requires a special right-of-way, so it takes on, at least in part, the characteristics of public transportation. A vehicle that could be ambidextrous enough to be controlled both by a driver on city streets or country lanes and by a guiding system in special rights-of-way would seem to be the "personal-mass" transit that the American would prefer. By this means he would not give up the goal of point-to-point transportation in one vehicle. Nor would the driver have to leave his preferred low-density neighborhood or have the work and nervous strain of driving. Guideway systems, it is said, would increase existing expressway capacities 5 to 10 times.[108]

General Motors has said the legal question of liability for equipment failure is at present unsolved, but they have not attacked control by computers as a difficulty. It would seem that the most familiar of our complex technologies — the automobile — coupled with the as yet unfamiliar but proven capacity of computers is a natural.

When enough cars are electrically propelled, they can go underground. At this time that appears unlikely until well after 1985.

Aircushion machines may make sense over water sooner than anywhere else. When the noise and spray of these vehicles is conquered, they will turn rivers in metropolitan areas into public-transit use, thus solving the difficult right-of-way problem. Hydrofoils and turbine jets offer short-run commercial possibilities. Super cargo ships of 60 feet draft and submarines towing containers may haul most of the freight commerce after 1985. Containerization of freight will make possible automated handling for all modes of transportation.

A surprise freely predicted is for major metropolitan area application of VTOL's and STOL's in the next 5 to 10 years. When only 20 to 30 per cent of the air travelers originate in downtown and over 50 per cent of the flights are under 200 miles[109] — the true nature of efficient service is apparent. Beginning equipment for such service is becoming available — access by beltways and expressways is nearly in place. It remains to locate the sites and develop the social inventions for acquiring sites and to implement new methods of air traffic control.

The jumbo jet has had its maiden flight. Whereas runways in many places are prepared to handle the new 400-passenger monsters, there aren't more than a handful of terminals that can. In addition, access to the terminals will be the next bottleneck. This is as yet unattacked. The outlook of the FAA, limited to ten years ahead and strictly to air transportation, is another example of the limitations of the sort of public agencies that are currently making the decisions.

As to the SST, there is still a controversial battle to be fought to keep them from flying at supersonic speeds except between continents. This is one challenge to designers they should be required to face. By 1975, supersonic service will be in effect between continents. If it is held to that, this is a further impetus to concentrate people at the rims of continents. Hypersonics (double to triple SST's) avoid the boom problem by taking the boom up to their operating altitude of 100,000 feet. Hypersonic service will probably appear after 1985 at the earliest.[110]

Personal air transportation by rocket belt or small platform for work or pleasure is not so far-fetched for the year 2000 in low-density areas. Miniaturized computers with increased capacity coupled with radar might solve the collision problem. Right now there is a one-man do-it-yourself helicopter kit available for the price of $3000. Private planes and helicopters steadily increasing in number and requiring separate landing facilities from transport aviation fields is no surprise except it may continue not to grow as much as had been predicted. VTOL's and STOL's would increase the density of planes in the air, restricting the use of private planes.[111]

Following both transportation and telecommunications is perhaps the most appropriate place in this section to refer to electric energy. Major aspects of both are dependent on electricity as is true of new technology in health, for example. We expect that the electric utilities will keep pace with the enormous demand of doubling their output every ten years.[112] We take that too much for granted. In no other area of technology are we so confident about our competence, leaving problems of thermal, water, and visual pollution aside — which of course we can't.

HEALTH

Surprises should be sought and expected in four underfunded areas concerning health:

1) virtual elimination of the two big killers (68 per cent of all deaths), cardiovascular-renal diseases and malignancy — initially a greater R&D effort;

2) a reduction of deaths caused by poverty, especially Negro infants under one year — a greater application effort;

3) the realization of healthy old age — initially a greater R&D effort;

4) adoption as federal policy of a more comprehensive research and preventative approach to health concerned with the whole man, his total environment, and the meaning of a "good day" for him in it — R&D and application.

It is necessary to look at a cause of death table (Table I-13) to be convinced that research efforts concentrated here would make startling differences both in the rate at which people die and subsequently in the increased number of healthier old people in the environment. It has been estimated that ten healthier years would be added to life if there were "total" cures in the basic two causes of death — cardiovascular-renal diseases and malignancy. Recognizing the great mysteries and the great varieties of these diseases but anticipating that much greater research efforts than at present will be made on a world-coordinated basis, we would look for the "surprise" of real breakthroughs in adding substantially to both the length and health of people's lives.

TABLE I-13. *Rate and Causes of Death*[113]

Cause of death	Deaths (1,000)	Deaths per 100,000 population
	1965	*1965 est.*
Tuberculosis, all forms	8	4.1
Malignant neoplasms	296	152.9
Diabetes mellitus	33	17.1
Major cardiovascular-renal diseases	1,000	515.9
Pneumonia	59	30.6
Ulcer of stomach and duodenum	11	5.4
Cirrhosis of liver	24	12.5
Infections of kidney	10	4.9
Accidents	107	55.2
Suicide	23	11.6
Homicide	10	5.3
All causes	1,825	941.6

One has to be over 65 before he again reaches the same chance of death as in the period from childbirth to his first year. The U.S. death rate for infants (under 1 year) in 1966 was 23 per 1000 population. For the black in poverty, the infant death rate is double that. The death rate of the black poor at all ages is nearly double. It is also high for all the poor. In fact, it is now being estimated that by concentrating on improving the health of the poor through better housing and nutrition, the total U.S. death rate would be reduced from the present 9.6 per 1000 to 7.3 per 1000 — the synthesis of the best experience elsewhere in the world.[114]

When people understand these facts about other humans, the surprise expected is that the needed funds will be voted. This is a matter for direct public stimulus.

Expecting the surprise of healthy old age has been discussed elsewhere (page 48). Anticipated breakthroughs in the causes of cardiovascular-renal diseases and malignancies are the foundation for such cheerful hopes. But a look at the pitiful resources presently being put into gerontological research today is enough to convince one that we have every reason to expect improvement there.

Not more than $14 million per year in federal money is going into the research on aging.[115] It is as if no one is seriously interested. Yet we are all going to be old and we know we would all like to be healthy when we are! This may be another evidence of the phenomena of our time of living exclusively in the here and now. Or it may simply be an example of very poor administration and neglect — a dramatization of the "impossibility" of directing aging research in the diffuse Department of Health, Education, and Welfare (HEW). It seems the old and sick, unlike the poor or the student, haven't had their riot yet. Supposedly, they are part of the National Institutes of Health under Child Care and Human Development. But there they are allotted only 10 per cent of the NICHD's budget, only a tiny fraction of the federal government's $1 billion plus for medical research.

There are a number of approaches to living longer and healthier. One is not to live in the city. A study by Hardin Jones shows people in rural areas live five years longer than those who don't.[116] In biochemistry one emphasis is in understanding and mastering the regenerative power of cells in the human body. An approach through another sort of research is worth noting also. Dr. John Olwin at Presbyterian-St. Luke's Hospital in Chicago is among those who are studying the aging effect on the circulatory system of salt water fish as they swim up fresh water rivers to spawn. Apparently steelhead trout and salmon pass tracer metal elements through their gills and age very quickly. The salmon die "of old age," but the steelhead trout swim back to salt water and recover their youth! Dr. Olwin's multidisciplinary team studying these effects and relating them to tracer elements clogging the human circulatory systems has been disbanded due to federal budget cuts. He estimates it may take five

85

years to reassemble his effort but that for $500,000 a year for five years, he would be able to add significant useful knowledge to the search for healthy old age.[117]

It has been said that the doctor-patient relationship has contributed only a negligible part of the drop in U.S. death rate from 17 to 11 per 1000 in the first thirty-five years of this century. Most of the credit is given to the public health authorities. "The cleanup of water supplies, sewage disposal, food inspection, the installation of indoor plumbing and other master urban technology . . . a wide range of professional capacities were responsible." In 1900, 25 per cent of the total death rate was attributable to diarrhea and pneumonia in infants. Antibiotics and other victories from 1935-1955 dropped the rate from 11 to 9.6. It is the degenerative diseases associated with the aging of organisms that are the causes now, i.e., cardiovascular-renal and malignancy.[118]

The total man is the next direction and concern for "Optimum Environment with Man as the Measure." To conceive such an approach means first to acknowledge that knowledge concerning man in his environment is at a low level and that there is no comprehensive scientific approach planned to reduce the human costs of this ignorance.[119]

The subject is enormous, complex, abstract but as real as a cough or a heart beat. The public already knows that they want and will pay for fresh air and fresh water. The human environment begins with fresh air and fresh water but doesn't end with them. After discovering the means for the various disciplines concerned with creating the future environment and the interested public to work together to assess this situation, there are some surprises to expect. The first surprise would be medicine and public health, combined with architects-planners-engineers, leading the way to a great comprehensive new program not only for prevention of the bad societal conditions, but for the creation of the good ones. The second surprise, as leisure increases and as the percentage of educated people grows, would be to observe the evolution of societal attitudes until, after the year 2000, their primary concern becomes the creation of the future human environment.

HOUSING

Technological surprises in housing await social inventions to permit their development. The systems approach makes possible designs

86

that are judged for speed of erection, total livability, easy maintenance, flexibility, and protection as well as installed price and amenities. Funds for housing R&D has never been serious money to Congress nor has there been recognition of the need for long-range continuity in such programs.

The surprise is that this may well change within the next 2 to 10 years as public disgust grows. We have concentrated on housing technology because housing uses 60 to 70 per cent of the land area of our cities, shelters all our people, and constitutes 33 per cent of the construction dollar. Also the other elements of the construction industry can be expected to continue their modernization and as such do not rate as a surprise. Besides streets and utilities, schools and community shopping centers are closely related and will in turn be more affected by housing technology than by commercial and industrial construction.

WASTE DISPOSAL

The surprise to look for is realization of the principle of autonomous waste disposal in Buckminster Fuller's Dymaxion House (conceived 1927 — prototype built in Wichita, Kansas in 1945). Several major corporations are now experimenting with "Goldfinger machines" — grinders combined with furnaces that reduce waste to ashes and a fraction of its original volume. Applied to single buildings, subdivisions or entire communities, the effect on community design would be substantial.

We are at present disposing of 3.5 billion tons of solid waste in this country per year, primarily by dumping and land fill: by 1980 it is expected to be double that. The economies and ecology of waste disposal for 200 to 300 million Americans concentrated in large urban areas is enough to encourage further research and development. Atomic wastes, growing from the present to over 80 million gallons of boiling, high-level radioactive material, represent another sort of problem altogether.[120]

Waste disposal conceived in a systems context would go all the way back to the design and production of disposable containers that deteriorate either naturally or were readily and economically converted.

INEXPENSIVE TUNNELING

At present OECD (Organization for Economic Cooperation and

Development) is attempting to make an estimate on the quantities, types, purposes, costs of tunneling. Du Pont is investigating methods. Constantinos Doxiadis has been a strong proponent for tunneling highways for the past several years. Apparently the laser beam used as an efficient communication medium requires protection from the weather which calls for tunneling. The most dramatic use of tunnels appears to be in high-speed public transportation, the 3000 foot deep inclining tubes for the 500 mph gravity vacuum train. But the subject has not been on many peoples' minds long enough to expect early results.

A surprise worth looking for is a breakthrough in inexpensive tunneling for all sorts of technologies — even high voltage electricity in time. Electric power transmission, public transit, communication, waste, commodities and goods may all be moved underground sooner than we think. With concentrated efforts, new applications might begin to be made within five years. It is more likely it will take 10 to 15 years. After 1985, application might begin in earnest. After 2000 there is every chance we will learn not to sacrifice human amenities and space to technology the way we do now.

5.

ORGANIZING KNOWLEDGE TO CREATE
A HUMAN FUTURE ENVIRONMENT

To date, just where has this exercise taken us? No further perhaps than to say that conceptional thinking before deciding, designing, and delivering the future environment — the human future environment versus the strictly technological future environment — is complex.[1] Further, there are no facts for the future, no single accepted exploratory methodology for it, no standard definitions.

It is important that this be made clear before futuristic mumbo-jumbo about predictions, projections, parameters and paradigms becomes too awe-inspiring and thereby becomes another intimidating technological macro-force. It would be good to establish, before the art of futurist thinking pronounces itself a science, that the future belongs to every one of us who chooses to consider it. It is not the exclusive property of experts, useful as they may be in aiding us. To establish and keep it that way, and to avoid stupid action without human design, we need to probe deeper. We need to organize our thinking. The reason is that our concern here is with a future *human* environment — not the future technological environment.

A human is a rational-irrational-extrarational being. He is a compound of intellect, emotion, and spirit. His needs and his understanding of his environment are not precisely quantifiable, and at this time there is no accepted comprehensive definition of *human environment* nor even any accepted ordering of knowledge, thought, or wisdom concerning it. Even so, we can discuss this situation sensibly here and to some purpose. We must or we will fall into the deterministic-technological trap that makes neat and simple that which is not. If we should do that, we will be contributing with others to the construction of an inhuman future environment.[2]

To do this we must somehow invent an understanding of the relation of the total rational-irrational-extrarational man to his environment.[3] With the help of others, perhaps a useful intellectual framework can be made workable. Environment in this context is at once physical, social, and economic with whatever sub-categories each of those three categories may need to make them comprehensive and open enough for society and human free will.

The intellectual framework developed should confine environment neither to technology nor to terms related to man either as God, as a robot, or as an animal in a society of animals. It need not accept the various government, university, library, newspaper, or working professional office indexes, including that of the Committee on Scientific Information (COSATI) of the Federal Council on Science and Technology in the Executive Office of the President. All of these are technical filing systems without a human philosophy adequate to the task of helping to organize all disciplines to build a human environment. They have not won general acceptance.

The COSATI Subject Category list

As an example, take the COSATI Subject Category list. It was established "as a uniform subject arrangement for 1) the announcement and distribution of scientific and technical reports which are issued or sponsored by Executive Branch Agencies and 2) for management reporting."[4] As revised in October 1965, the COSATI list divides knowledge in 22 broad fields, subdivided into 188 groups, which cover approximately 5000 subjects. The list was created with representatives from the Atomic Energy Commission, Department of Agriculture, Department of Commerce, Department of Defense, Department of Health Education and Welfare, and the National Aeronautics and Space Administration. It professes to be all-encompassing, yet it is apparent that it is derived from a military and engineering understanding of the Executive Branch. The list of the 22 broad fields it covers are:

Aeronautics
Agriculture

Atmosphere Sciences
Behavioral and Social Sciences
Biological and Medical Sciences
Chemistry
Earth Sciences and Oceanography
Electronic and Electrical Engineering
Energy Conversion
Materials
Mathematical Sciences
Mechanical, Industrial, Civil, and Marine Engineering
Methods and Equipment
Military Sciences
Missile Technology
Navigation, Communications, Detection and Correction Measures
Nuclear Science and Technology
Ordinance
Physics
Propulsion and Fuels
Space Technology

Efforts to organize and direct the recent American Institute of Planners' four-year consultation into "The Next Fifty Years — The Future Environment of a Democracy," called forth the creation of a comprehensive index and bibliography in 16 groupings which corresponded roughly to the commissioned investigations of the consultation: [5]

Philosophy
Science and Technology
Education for a Full Life
Housing — Good Homes for All
Health — For Our Span of Life
Recreation — Leisure, Psychology, and Reflection
Morals Concerning Minorities — Mental Health and Identity
Transportation (& Communication) — an Equal Opportunity
    for Access
Urban Form — Its Potential Contribution to a "Good Day"
The Arts — and Their Lively Contribution to Living
Natural Resources — Proper Use of a Chance-in-a-Lifetime
    Inheritance
National Development Policy

New Incentives and New Controls
New Institutions to Serve the Individual
Research for Choice
The Manpower Needed

When the 300 categories of this consultation index for AIP are contrasted with COSATI's 5000 subjects, the following were found to be omitted from the COSATI listing, clearly revealing a bias against the humanities and the social sciences:

anthropology	intellectual
art	intellectual life
attitude	interest
birth control	Judaism
causation	Keynesian
civilization	Keynesian economics
change	leadership
character	leisure
Christianity	liberalism
church	liberty
city	man
college student	metropolitan areas
communication	minorities
community development	national characteristics
competition	Negroes
decision-making	persuasion
entrepreneurs	poor
equality	poverty
eugenics	prediction
evolution	programs
family	prophecies
family size	public interest
foundation	real property
grants-in-aid	regionalism
gold	regional planning
heredity	social values
human genetics	state
ideology	taxation
immobility	underdeveloped area
individualism	unemployed
individuality	university

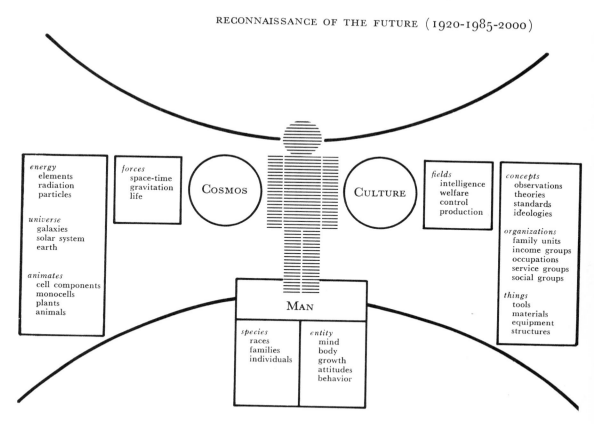

FIGURE I-11. *Development Index*[6]

urban renewal	world politics
utopias	worth
work	youth

If this is how the President's Science Office understands the organization of knowledge, no wonder we have complaints that this is a purely utilitarian society.

The Development Index

In the process of this current investigation for AIA, the Development Index devised in 1953 by K. Lundberg-Holm and C. D. Larson has been unearthed.[7] It is the most comprehensive, *human and technological* index for environmental development yet seen.[8] In that its basic form was first conceived in 1940, perhaps its 16 to 29 years has aged it

93

sufficiently now to make the opening paragraphs of the preface written then by W. H. Scheick accurate today: "That giant segment of American Economy, the Building Industry, has awakened to the fact that its progress depends upon a *science of building*. Practitioners of the arts and technologies of building are seeking information in their own and other fields of specialization. Their curiosity extends into the human and social sciences, now recognized as a source of facts truly fundamental to building technology. Naturally, the social scientists show equivalent needs for technical data."

The Development Index discusses Development Goals (new needs, new means, new forms), the Development Cycle (research, design, production, distribution, utilization, elimination), and defines Development Means as the environmental resources which man has available for development purposes grouped into three main categories:

1. cosmos — forms and forces which exist independent of man
2. human — attributes that characterize man
3. culture — fields of activity and forms created by man

Undoubtedly, the Development Index could be refined as its authors have invited, but there seems to be no difficulty in adapting the 16 categories and 300 subjects of the AIP index to it. The ekistic hierarchy of communities and all the rest of ekistics is easily absorbed into it. There doesn't seem to be another environment index so well developed that is comprehensive enough to swallow both COSATI and the humanities.

Other environment matrices have been proposed, however;[9] and John Calhoun's sensitive matrix does include as functions of the environment: survival, gratification, adaptability, diversity, options, complexity, creativity; and as levels of environment: compassionate, educational, cultural, social, affective, biological, physiological, and physical.[10]

Towards Integrating Knowledge

If we are to think of building the future environment in comprehensive *human* terms, we need a way for the different sciences, professions, and interested layman to converge — to organize their thinking and communicate with each other. A framework of organization would help use our plentiful communication technology to make the fullest use of our few scattered environment-skilled human resources. They need a common intellectual order for knowledge concerning development of the human environment, and common access to it, to accelerate their work during the critical shock-front phase. There is no accepted index of knowledge today that has a consistent internal philosophy; that is both flexible and comprehensive; and that is oriented toward ordering knowledge for thinking, decision-making, design, and production of the future environment.

The need has become so obvious that a random sample poll of high school principals showed 67 per cent of suburban students dissatisfied not just with the operations in the high school but with the sort of education they are receiving for the society that will be confronting them.[11] Among the very brightest, 40 per cent of the university students have registered an articulate dissent to the values of society today in an in-depth poll published for *Fortune,* January 1969.[12] Statements from some of these students, and from others as diverse as Dr. Martin Luther King and H. Rap Brown, call for a radical redistribution of income; they mean *national* income — GNP. This report will not pass judgment on who has gone too far and who is perceptive and justified, but it will point out a significant schism that is relevant. In its extreme, there is the "feel don't think" approach of Norman Mailer[13] which strikes a responsive cord among humanists on campuses and in the streets, but not among graduate students in business schools or the nascent scientists and engineers who are off in their labs, "minding their own business." It is significant that throughout the world the campus "troublemakers" have been the humanists. At their best they are asking legitimate questions no one seems prepared to answer. At their worst they are deliberately bent on destroying the freest institutions of society. Meanwhile, scientists continue their work which seems primarily to ask themselves questions which they know how to answer.[14] They seem unprepared to relate to the human needs of the society today. Two-thirds of the research scientists and engineers in the United States today are at work for NASA, DOD, and AEC.[15]

As Jacob Bronowski has warned humanists, "We live in a world which is penetrated through and through by science — the dream of H. G. Wells, in which the tall elegant engineers rule with perfect benevolence a humanity which has no business except to be happy, is the picture of a slave society; it should make us shiver whenever we hear a man of sensibility discuss science as someone else's concern. The world is made, is powered by science; and for any man to abdicate an interest in science is to walk with eyes open towards slavery."[16]

Will the humanists take heed on behalf of rational-irrational-extrarational man or merely rail against the rational?

Concurrently a host of warnings are being posted for scientists:

"It [science] is mostly new; it has not been digested; it is not part of man's common knowledge; it has become the property of specialized communities" (Robert Oppenheimer).[17]

"As a biologist, I have reached this conclusion: we have come to a turning point in the human habitation of the earth . . . I believe that continued pollution of the earth, if unchecked, will eventually destroy the fitness of this planet as a place for human life. . . . If the scientist, directly or by inferences from his actions, lays claim to a special responsibility for the resolution of the policy issues which relate to technology, he may, in effect, prevent others from performing their own political duties. If the scientist fails in his duty to inform citizens, they are precluded from the gravest acts of citizenship and lose their right of conscience.

Science can reveal the depth of this crisis, but only social action can resolve it. Science can now serve society by exposing the crisis of modern technology to the judgment of all mankind. Only this judgment can determine whether the knowledge that science has given us shall destroy humanity or advance the welfare of man" (Barry Commoner).[18]

". . . If the bills for pollution were handed back to the *sources* of pollution, we might see some surprising improvements in the quality of our air. But such a system of social accounting, I hasten to point out, involves political and ethical decisions rather than purely technological ones. Meanwhile, we are on a collision course with disaster!" (Lamont C. Cole).[19]

"We claim we live in a scientific era, but the truth is that, as presently managed, the scientific enterprise is too lopsided to allow science to be of much use in the conduct of human affairs. Scientists shy away from the problems posed by human life because these are not readily amenable to study by the orthodox methods of the natural sciences" (Rene Dubos).[20]

96

AFTERWORD AND RECOMMENDATIONS

Looking Backward over the Future

THIS RECONNAISSANCE of the future is not a definitive weighing of all possibilities. It is a preliminary search for fact, sound judgment, and direction, relying in strong measure on the professional insights that have shaped it.

The basic tenet of this investigation was declared early. The direction followed thereafter was to explore the relatively unexplored, seeking definitions of *social inventions* and their impacts rather than technological inventions. It is fast becoming the consensus of serious students of our rapidly changing world that the limiting and deciding factors are the will of society and its individuals — particularly as expressed through our institutions.

Technology is not ignored by this study but the technology that will have impact over the next 15 years has already been invented. The technology we will want to use after 1985 needs to be invented now. In both cases we have decisions to make — national decisions. For example, new transportation technology or new housing technology is too expensive to be developed and applied without federal stimulus. We have 20 to 50 years experience to prove this. We are back to social inventions and the sense of priority we need to achieve what we want to achieve. How do we make $24 billion moon-shot decisions for civilian space? It will take social inventions.

This Afterword pulls together those aspects of particular import to rational-irrational-extrarational men that are the unique responsibility of the designers of the future environment. At present the designer is approaching sites that are already overridden with the

97

constraints of planning commissions, zoning ordinances, financing institutions, building codes, and union practices. He is expected to competently follow the program of his client with taste, economy, and safety — on time. Actually his building may be almost designed by the constraints except for the details, or even including some of the details.

Even if the quantity of construction were not to increase in the order of magnitude outlined in this report, we would see the need for much greater quality and consequently for a greater capacity — to design whole environments not just single buildings. As it is, we shall have demands for both quantity and quality at the same time — plus a more meaningful involvement of those most directly concerned with how the buildings are to be used. Art, spirit, science, and technology are the total scope of our concern if we are to build a human versus a technological future environment.

"Perhaps the art which comes closest, not to a compromise, but to an integral acceptance of rationalization, is architecture. Nor could it well be otherwise, for it is the function of architecture to express the temper of the times, to accept its technological demands, its rationalized procedure, and its organized "modular co-ordination."[1]

We have attempted to order into a system the factors discussed in this report. Here we will touch briefly only the philosophy, belief, need, change, and efforts of that system on which recommendations to the American Institute of Architects are grounded. The factors numbered in Figure I-11 have been discussed in some length in Chapter 5. Put all together into a system, they make an argument for the "path of reason." The summary statements here attempt to come to conclusions drawn from the possibilities of this investigation.

Dialogue is the means by which the people of a democracy take personal charge of their destiny. It is where the macro forces of change meet the micro forces and the individual meets and revolutionizes his society peacefully. It is the means by which the various sciences and professions develop their greatest concepts. Without improved capacity for dialogue in this time of great change — the shock front — the potential for calamities and for misreading possibilities and motives is enormous. Without intelligent dialogue the extremes of revolution, reaction, and a noxious physical environment are nearly inevitable. Table I-14 attempts to show that to realize the full potential of our time, a comprehensive-integrated level of dialogue

TABLE I-14. *Factors, Surprises, and System Breaks of Particular Relevance to the Creation of a Human Future Environment*

Philosophy	Priority	Policy	Program
Basic belief. Equal access to opportunity for all which includes:	*Basic need.* A comprehensive concept for national development which includes:	*Basic change.* The invention of new forms of enterprise as needed which includes:	*Basic efforts.* The sharing of a new spirit and new order of human amenities which includes:
↑	↑	↑	↑
THROUGH DIALOGUE			
↓	↓	↓	↓
1. participation for those who seek it 2. national scale efforts 3. special attention to the disadvantaged minorities of all kinds	1. low birth rate 2. high GNP growth rate 3. guaranteed jobs 4. national settlement strategy	1. expanded civilian R&D 2. updated and continuing education 3. preventative health measures 4. eminent domain for development according to public purpose 5. professionalization of the nonprofit sector	1. healthy old age 2. extended life 3. more leisure 4. larger homes and second ones 5. telecommunications breakthrough 6. mass transit breakthrough 7. waste disposal breakthrough 8. cheap tunneling

is at one and the same time the cement and the lubricant between society, technology, and the individual. It is assumed as the primary means for an open society to understand and master its changing situation and its technology. The environmental designer, with an understanding of human beings and technology, has a major role to play in making this dialogue possible.

A Framework for Social and Technological Inventions

We all believe in Motherhood and Apple Pie and are against Sin. But if that is the extent of American philosophy today, we will never make it through the shock front to a human-technological future environment. We will get no further than the technological. "The deciding factor will be the extent to which Americans feel a personal responsibility. This, in turn, depends upon an intangible: their total philosophic attitude."[2]

From our whole history, however, it seems clear we are disposed to believe in equal access to opportunity for all, letting each individual make the most of the opportunity as he chooses. Our difficulty is in the disparity between what the Bill of Rights, the Constitution and Sunday sermons say we believe in and what we actually believe is "practical" to believe in as evidenced by the way we live. The design of the physical environment in itself contributes to or detracts from this access to opportunity as surely as do race, color, creed, income, and place of residence.

The basic tenet of our philosophy is personal responsibility, but personal responsibility is developed through participation by those who seek it. The one-way communication of the public media, and within most institutions, too often replaces personal responsibility either with fear or with outdated priorities. Meaningful personal participation in the important decisions that affect the individual is therefore given here as an explicit requirement of a working philosophy for creating the future human environment. It defines new relationships between the designer, manufacturer, financial institution, government and the client.

We have a basic need to admit we are a national community with major metropolitan areas, states, and regions as are our neighborhoods. If we can come to that understanding, we can more easily comprehend the priority we should give to establishing national objectives derived from our stated basic philosophy.

There have been valuable recent attempts to state this philosophy. In the closing Eisenhower years in 1960, we had the remarkable *Goals for Americans,* the product of a study led by Henry Merritt Wriston.[3] That was followed in 1961 by the Rockefeller Brothers reports, *Prospect for America.*[4] The Commission for the Year 2000 of the American Academy of Arts and Sciences began its closed seminars in 1965.[5] Independently, the American Institute of Planners' national consultation on the Future Environment of a Democracy, from 1965 to 1969, attempted to broaden and deepen the nation's concept of the relation of science and environment, philosophy and policies for the future.[6] There has been outstanding work by other institutions, especially the Committee for Economic Development,[7] Resources for the Future,[8] the National Planning Association, and lately the U.S. Chamber of Commerce.[9] John Gardner,[10] Buckminster Fuller,[11] Bayard Rustin,[12] and Paul Goodman[13] are among the private individuals who have developed as national resources in their own right. The American Institute of Planners' recent consultation on "The Next Fifty Years — The Future Environment of a Democracy," was also aimed in this positive direction: "To assure the primary importance of the individual, his freedom, his widest possible choice, his access to joy and opportunity, his impetus to self-development, his responsible relation to his society, the growth of his inner life and his capacity to love"[14] and recognized "the need to make it intellectually respectable to be both aware of the future and optimistic about coping with it."[15] (It should be noted that none of these were government-directed efforts.)

A "stream-of-time perspective was deliberately included in the AIA committee charge to each author to foreclose any leaping to unchallengeable recommendations concerning what should be done *beginning* fifty years from now. It also was intended to avoid short-term expedients that did not have the seeds of the future in them."[16] But just using the next fifty years in the theme was subject to misinterpretation by the short-term operators, as well as the congenital cynics and medicine men who never read into the consultation papers. We are dealing with the future that begins tomorrow, not fifteen or thirty years from now, and we hope to be responsible enough about the big issues not to promise results in two or three years if it will take a generation or two to deliver.[17]

Since the National Resources Board was abolished in 1943 after only ten years life, there has been no ongoing federal effort to develop national policies for the future other than the notable spadework of the Advisory Commission on Intergovernmental Relations.[18] Primarily, we have attempted national policy studies through the device of prestigious Presidential Commissions which meet periodically over their staff's work and then disband after making a report on one special subject.

We must expect and prepare for much greater future changes. This is a pragmatic society. If it is also a future-oriented pragmatic society, it can be expected that what we hold as our philosophy and set as our priorities will change in the future. However, certain human requirements will not change, and we must be held accountable for any irreversible decisions we make now that are deleterious to the development and enjoyment of ourselves and our grandchildren and their grandchildren in future years. Fresh air, fresh water, beauty, access to opportunity, privacy, freedom for self-development — these are in the legacy we say we would like to create. Through improvements in the motivations and capacities of private enterprise and government, we can help realize many of them. But we should not limit ourselves just to those institutions. There is a danger that either of them might become a "religion" rather than simply performing their function free of self-righteousness.

Government might safely go as far as William James' "Moral Equivalent of War" (1910) — two years of compulsory community service for youth.[19]

> The military ideals of hardihood and discipline would be wrought into the growing fibre of the people; no one would remain blind, as the luxurious classes now are blind, to man's real relations to the globe he lives on, and to the permanently sour and hard foundations of his higher life. To coal and iron mines, to freight trains, to fishing fleets in December, to dish-washing, clothes-washing, to road-building and tunnel-making, to foundries and stoke-holes, and to the frames of skyscrapers, would our gilded youths be drafted off, according to their choice, to get the childishness knocked out of them, and to come back into society with healthier sympathies and soberer ideas. They would have paid their blood-tax, done their own part in the immemorial human warfare against nature, they would tread the earth more proudly, the women would value them more highly, they would be better fathers and teachers of the following generation.

> Such a conscription, with the state of public opinion that would have required it, and the many moral fruits it would bear, would preserve in the midst of a pacific civilization the manly virtues which the military party is so afraid of seeing disappear in peace. We should get toughness without callousness, authority with as little criminal cruelty as possible, and painful work done cheerily because the duty is temporary, and threatens not, as now, to degrade the whole remainder of one's life. I spoke of the "moral equivalent" of war. So far, war has been the only force that can discipline

a whole community, and until an equivalent discipline is organized, I believe that war must have its way. But I have no serious doubt that the ordinary prides and shames of social man, once developed to a certain intensity, are capable of organizing such a moral equivalent as I have sketched, or some other just as effective for preserving manliness of type.

. . . It would be simply preposterous if the only force that could work ideals of honour and standards of efficiency into English or American natures should be the fear of being killed by the Germans or the Japanese. Great indeed is fear; but it is not, as our military enthusiasts believe and try to make us believe, the only stimulus known for awakening the higher ranges of men's spiritual energy.

But we must also be aware of the truth in Thoreau's statement:[20]

There will never be a really free and enlightened State, until the State comes to recognize the individual as a higher and independent power, from which all its own power and authority are derived, and treats him accordingly.

Private enterprise might go safely as far as to 1) set up nonprofit subsidiaries to perform certain functions atypical of its normal function, 2) loan staff to nonprofit institutions and, 3) take full advantage of its 5 per cent tax deduction to support them.

It was said that "each generation must redream its own dream"[21] and "the inhabitants of a city are both the participants and the audience in an on-going work of creation, of creating the city. . . . Once you associate people in the job of planning you associate them in a job in which you are co-mingling both the creation of form in terms of physical form, form in terms of social justice and form in terms of practical convenience and half a dozen other basic dimensions.[22]

For this to be possible within the traditions of this open society, we would look to a professionalization of one of the greatest traditions of the American society — the nonprofit association. What de Tocqueville said in 1830 is valid still today:[23]

Americans of all ages, all stations in life, and all types of disposition are forever forming associations. There are not only commercial and industrial associations in which all take part, but others of a thousand different types — religious, moral, serious, futile, very general and very limited, immensely large and very minute. Americans combine to give fetes, found seminaries, build churches, distribute books, and send missionaries to the antipodes. Hospitals, prisons, and schools take shape in that way. Finally if they want to proclaim a truth or propagate some feeling by encouragement of a great example, they form an association. In every case, at the head of any new undertaking, where in France you would find the government or in England some territorial magnate, in the United States you are sure to find an Association.

Associations, as de Tocqueville saw them, are at the core of our great traditions. Professionalized to meet the new technological era, they might become the new form of enterprise most needed — a third force for civilian problem-solving. They serve especially well in politically sensitive areas as has been espoused by RAND, Systems Development Corporation,[24] long testimony before the Space and Astronautics Committee,[25] by this investigator[26] and many others. They would be the American independent sector, updated.

The concept of great new responsibilities for nongovernment, nonprofit enterprise is an important concern of the Nixon Administration. One short speech by HEW Secretary Robert H. Finch is germane to this report.[27]

> In the first third of the twentieth century, we relied most on commerce and industry — the private sector. In the second third we turned to the federal government — the "public sector."
>
> In my judgment, the last third of this century will see a revitalization of the other great dimension of American society (what Dick Cornuelle calls the "independent sector") — the wealth of voluntary, non-governmental associations, including churches, labor unions, service organizations, fraternal orders and community groups. Historically they have been the instinctive American response to problem-solving since the days of the frontier.
>
> As we enter the new era of politics, this "independent sector" is becoming the great third force in American life.
>
> The political dialogue of the next thirty years will respond to the question: What kind of social and governmental environment can we create, within which the individual can make the most of his life? How can he maximize his free choice, his opportunity to live, achieve and serve as he chooses?
>
> When it comes to issues about the quality of our individual lives — the schools our children attend, the parks they play in, the air we breathe, the safety of the streets we walk on, the beauty or ugliness of our environment, the facilities for use in our leisure or retirement — the government cannot put together programs without dictating the terms of our private lives. The end result can only be a drab uniformity and loss of individual identity and free choice which is intolerable to a free people.

To participation — the essential reason for the strength in voluntary associations — should be added a needed new strength to cope with the technological future — competent staff of different disciplines working together as a team, specifically focused on problems and in a dialogue situation responsive to the people.

It is no secret that the spirit seems to have gone out of America. It's not only foreigners who notice this. We all feel it. The possibility of creating a human future environment is plain. With high morale we can do what we want to do, and show the way for the rest of the world which is not yet into the shock front but will be. The low morale or violent way, we choose not to contemplate.

Undoubtedly, it will not be nice bridge club ladies from the suburbs who will solve the ghetto problem (although they might help solve the suburban problem by opening it to low income families). Such national issues as a full scale housing program, supertransportation, human retirement, adequate health and welfare programs, and the full development of telecommunications for creating an active, needed means of dialogue will demand greater use of government at all levels, not simply the work of volunteer groups. But the opportunities ahead are enormous and neither government nor private enterprise, with their traditional orientations, can be permitted the responsibility for it all. Volunteer associations and professionally staffed nonprofit institutions have their place. Quoting Finch again:

> . . . Responsible Americans will demand a role in the great issues of the times, to make a difference in the history of this period. The Party which dominates the political landscape during the balance of this century will be the one which demonstrates its ability to focus private resources on demanding public needs.

> As we move into the last third of the century, America seems to face two contradictory problems: a growing agenda of increasingly stubborn, complex public business, and an "involvement crisis," a feeling by more and more people that they have a less and less significant role to play in the modern world.

> We seem to have too much and too little to do at the same time. We are coming to believe that America has more to do than it can — that we face more and more intolerable public problems that are moving farther and farther beyond the reach of our present and potential resources.

> On the other hand, more and more Americans, particularly the younger ones, feel under-challenged and under-involved. People say we face a

participation crisis, like the economic crisis of the thirties — a building tide of human concern with no suitable outlet.

The question is whether we can make these two "problems" solve each other, whether by building a society in which more people participate more fully, we can get acceptable if not utopian social results.

Recommendations to the American Institute of Architects

It is proposed that the American Institute of Architects, in recognition of the potential of its unique and vital contribution to the creation of a future human-technological environment, give consideration to the following recommendations:

One — broaden the appreciation and understanding of the significance of the physical environment to rational-irrational-extrarational men in the activities of their society and in their private lives.

Two — develop support for more research and development that deepens the understanding of the human environment, to be carried out jointly with kindred professions.

Three — insist on recognition of the human dignity involved for individuals of all incomes — especially low income — to take an active part in the physical design and creation of their homes and their community.

Four — call attention to the necessity for the strongest possible population control measures consistent with human dignity as the foundation for an effective concern for the creation of a human future environment in this nation and throughout the world.

Five — to help this nation realize the "extravagant objectives" of a great society, take public stands that help declaim those mechanistic "rational" interpretations of "first things first" that relegate charm, beauty, and serendipity to limbo when it comes to creating the future environment.

Six — actively support state and national policies that encourage maximum economic growth consistent with controlled inflation and a human utilization of the environment.

Seven — admit the difficulty and failure there is today in communicating many important aspects of a future human environment and seek to develop full utilization of the technology becoming available, making possible meaningful participation among the professions and between professions and lay people through the creation of environmental "situation and outlook centers" that utilize electronics, graphics, and computerization for two-way communication on any environmental issue; these centers should be designed to be interconnected and ultimately to be compatible for hook-up from the neighborhood to the international scale with full access to information for all who are responsible and concerned.

Eight — encourage change and modification in current governmental and private organizational operations concerning the environment, recognize also the natural short-term bias of these institutions, and lead the way for the creation of nonprofit environmental institutes associated with universities but not dominated by their discipline-oriented departments; these problem solving and design centers to be funded by government, utilities, private enterprise, universities, churches, foundations, professions, and individuals in such a way that they will not be dependent on any one sector and restricted to the mission of researching, demonstrating, and communicating alternatives of importance to the creation of the future human environment considering long-range as well as immediate consequences.

Nine — undertake the study of the Development Index, COSATI subject list, AIP/WRE Bibliographic Index, WRE matrix, John Calhoun matrix, New York Times' Thesaurus, Smithsonian Science Information Exchange, URBANDOC, university indexes, the Ekistics grid, Buckminster Fuller's principle of world design, and other professional office indexes to assure that a master environmental development index is proposed and adopted suited to all the professions concerned.

Ten — join with other professions and institutions to encourage the development of education through the graduate level that integrates science with the humanities as well as fosters an increased degree of specialized training in the design and technology of construction.

Eleven — support the concept that the next 2 to 4 years of the shock front be used to establish the basis and means for dialogue that can create the attitudes, institutions, and resources for the subsequent ten years of experimental building, research, and institution building for the fullest possible use of technology consistent with a truly human definition of environment, the needs of our day, and the future.

PROJECTIONS*

* The eleven tables included here were selected and developed in consultation with Leonard Fischman, president of Economic Associates, Inc., whose office compiled and annotated them.

TABLE I. *Population*
(millions)

Authority		1955	1960	1965	1970	1985	2000
A. U.S. Bureau of the Census							
Series	D				205	242	283
	C*	165.9	180.7	194.6	206	253	308
	B				207	265	336
	A				209	275	361
B. Scripps Foundation for Research in Population							
Problems	L			192.8	203	235	x
	M	165.9	180.7	194.7	209	258	x
	H			196.5	215	286	x
C. Social Security Admin.							
High-cost projection						257	301
Average projection		x	x	202.1	214	261	312
Low-cost projection						265	323
D. National Planning Association		165.9	180.7	194.6	(207)	259	322
E. Pickard		165.1	180.0	193.8	206	(257)	314
F. Kahn & Wiener	L				(207)	246	290
	M	165.9	180.7	195	(208)	258	318
	H				(212)	274	362
G. U.S. Forest Service		165.9	180.7	(194)	208	(260)	325
H. Resources for the Future, Inc.							
	L			(191)	202	(237)	268
	M	165.3	179.9	(193)	208	(265)	331
	H			(200)	223	(312)	433

Symbols: * Judged to be the single best projection at this time among those shown.
L — Low   M — Medium   H — High
( ) — Interpolated; not shown in original source.
x — Not given in source, and not considered useful to extrapolate.

Notes on Population Projections

GENERAL

With three exceptions, the series projected are official population estimates of the United States, covering the fifty states and the District of Columbia as well as Armed Forces stationed abroad. The RFF projections, which are one exception, differ only in their omission of Alaska and Hawaii, which between them had about 977,000 people in mid-1965. The Pickard series also omits Alaska and Hawaii, as well as Armed Forces abroad, but Alaska and Hawaii have been added back in from figures given elsewhere in Pickard's monograph.

The official population estimates understate the actual population (recently by about 2½ per cent), but are consistent with the 1960 census. The Social Security Administration series (see Authority "C," below) corrects for this undercount.

AUTHORITY "A" (U.S. BUREAU OF THE CENSUS)

The source — *Current Population Reports,* Series P-25, No. 381 (December 18, 1967) — includes copious explanatory notes and comparisons with earlier Census Bureau projections. The projections shown take off from "benchmark" estimates of the population as of July 1, 1966 — already slightly revised. Except for the low projection (Series D), they represent only very slight change from the last preceding full-scale set of projections made by the Bureau in 1964; the Series D projection is only modestly lower.

The Census Bureau is careful to say that "these figures are to be considered 'projections,' not 'forecasts,' since no one series is offered as a prediction of future population size." Unofficially, it is known currently to favor the "C" projection, as do at least some other authorities.[1] We also consider this to be the best present bet among the four series.

The "C" projection is keyed to a "completed fertility" assumption (total number of children ever born) similar to that recorded by women who were born just after World War I and who did most of their childbearing during the 'forties. This fertility rate is a little lower than the stated expectations of women 18 to 39 who have been sampled in recent surveys. It equates to an average of something over three children per "married, fecund" woman.

The amount of effort that census puts into its projections tends to make the best census projection the best available projection. Right now, the census projections also have the advantage of recency.

---

[1] E.g., Patricia L. Hodge and Philip M. Hauser, who give reasons for this opinion in a report prepared for the National Commission on Urban Problems (Research Report No. 3, 1968).

AUTHORITY "B" (SCRIPPS FOUNDATION)

These projections were published in P. K. Whelpton, A. A. Campbell, and John E. Patterson, *Fertility and Family Planning in the United States* (Princeton, N.J.: Princeton University Press, 1966); they may also be found, along with summary description of assumptions and methodology, in U.S. Bureau of the Census, *Current Population Reports,* Series P-25, No. 286 (July 1964).

The Scripps projections are very similar to the census projections shown in "A," except for the fact that they use an earlier base date (July 1, 1960) and hew more closely to the fertility expectations (size of completed family) reported by married women in 1955 and 1960 sample surveys (Growth of American Families Studies). The three projection levels utilize different sets of assumptions regarding the percentage of women who will ever marry, the size of completed family, and the distribution of births over the childbearing span.

AUTHORITY "C" (SOCIAL SECURITY ADMINISTRATION)

These projections, published in *United States Population Projections for OASDHI Cost Estimates,* SSA Actuarial Study No. 62 (December 1966), were prepared by the Office of the Actuary as part of planning for the long-range financing of the Social Security System, and extend as far forward as 2050. Taking off from July 1, 1965, estimates of actual population, they employ direct assumptions on the overall course of birth rates over future periods ("period fertility"), rather than deriving these from completed-fertility assumptions, as census has done. The low-cost projection combines a high fertility assumption with a high mortality assumption; the high-cost projection, vice-versa. The middle projection averages the low and high projections. All three series contain an allowance for net census undercount.

AUTHORITY "D" (NATIONAL PLANNING ASSOCIATION)

These series are essentially an averaging of the two middle census projections shown in "A," except that they were taken from an advance publication, Series P-25, No. 359 (February 20, 1967).

AUTHORITY "E" (PICKARD)

Refers to projections by Jerome P. Pickard, in *Dimensions of Metropolitanism* (Urban Land Institute Research Monographs 14 and 14A, 1967). These overall U.S. projections were made as a base

111

for the metropolitan area projections which were the study's main interest. They were derived from 1966 Census Bureau projections which went through 1985 (*Current Population Reports,* Series P-25, No. 329), using the Census B series through 1980 and a lower fertility assumption (midway between the B and C series) for 1980-2000.

AUTHORITY "F" (KAHN AND WIENER)

This refers to Herman Kahn and Anthony J. Wiener, of the Hudson Institute, Inc., and to projections published in their book: *The Year 2000 — A Framework for Speculation on the Next Thirty-three years* (New York: Macmillan Co., 1967). The projections were adapted by them from those of the Bureau of the Census published in *Current Population Reports,* Series P-25, No. 286 (July 1964), since superseded by the ones cited in "A." For the medium, Kahn and Wiener struck a point about two-thirds of the way from the then Census Series B to the Series C projection.

AUTHORITY "G" (U.S. FOREST SERVICE)

Published in *Timber Trends in the United States,* Forest Resource Report No. 17 (February 1965). These series, too, were adapted from the Census projections of 1964 (see "F"), but are closer to Series B than to Series C.

AUTHORITY "H" (RESOURCES FOR THE FUTURE, INC.)

Published in Hans H. Landsberg, Leonard L. Fischman, and Joseph L. Fisher, *Resources in America's Future* (Baltimore: Johns Hopkins, 1963). The projections were adapted from census projections to the year 1980 published in *Current Population Reports,* Series P-25, No. 187 (November 10, 1958) and unpublished census projections to the year 2000 then in process of being prepared. The principal adjustment made by RFF was to assume lower fertility rates, for the low projection, than those which had been assumed by the Census Bureau, and a spread in immigration and mortality rates, which affected both the low and the high. The census assumptions, at that time, were on a "period fertility" basis (see "A" and "C" above).

PROJECTIONS NOT SHOWN

Not shown in the table are population projections used by a number of other authorities,[2] which are adoptions of census projections unchanged or barely changed. Also not shown are projections of the Outdoor Recreation Resources Review Commission, *Study Report 23* (1962), which are by now somewhat outdated and have the added disadvantage of referring only to the years 1976 and 2000.

Of current interest, though not worked up as a set of projections, is the interview opinion given by Dr. Donald J. Bogue, past president of the Population Association of America and currently director of the University of Chicago's Community and Family Center, that "not within the next hundred years," let alone by the year 2000, would the United States reach a population of 300 million (*U.S. News & World Report*, March 11, 1968, p. 60). Dr. Bogue believes it possible that the population level may reach stability at about 220 million — a point which even according to the lowest census projection would be attained by 1980.

Although great surprises are always possible in the matter of population growth, the evolution of a stable population in the United States before the end of this century (if at all) implies such a radical departure from the whole previous history of fertility in the United States that it appears of too low an order of probability to be worth considering at this time as a guide to action. Even at the lowest recorded levels, registered during the Great Depression, births were high enough to maintain an increasing population.[3]

On the other hand, the possibility of a 2000 population level lower than 300 million is quite large enough to merit being taken into account. The Census Series D projection, which produces a figure of 283 million for 2000, assumes completed-fertility rates (children per woman) which are lower than for any cohorts other than those who had their prime childbearing years during the Great Depression and well below the already-achieved average levels of living females between the ages of 30 and 45 (as of July 1, 1965). Nonetheless, a lower ultimate population level than that of Census Series D (e.g., the RFF low of 268 million for 2000 — see item "H") is well within the realm of possibility.

[2] E.g., the U.S. Water Resources Council, the McGraw-Hill Economics Department, and population experts Patricia L. Hodge and Philip M. Hauser, in their report to the National Commission on Urban Problems.

[3] It is interesting to note, however, that of those women still alive who have completed their childbearing period, those with a high school education or better have not borne enough children to replace themselves.

TABLE 2. *Gross National Product*
(billions of 1960 dollars)

Authority		1955	1960	1965	1970	1985	2000
A. National Planning Association*		456	504	637	(795)	1,513	2,942
B. Water Resources Council		456	504	637	(781)	(1,435)	2,561
C. Kahn & Wiener	L	456	504	636	(736)	1,198	2,030
	H				(791)	1,597	3,384
D. U.S. Forest Service		456	505	(597)	702	(1,150)	1,890
E. Resources for the Future, Inc.	L	449	504	(599)	710	(1,100)	1,680
	M			(613)	746	(1,270)	2,200
	H			(634)	798	(1,570)	3,290

Symbols: * Judged to be the single best projection at this time among those shown.
  L — Low   M — Medium   H — High
  (   ) — Interpolated; not shown in original source.

Notes on GNP Projections

AUTHORITY "A" (NATIONAL PLANNING ASSOCIATION)

NPA projections are published in its National Economic Projections Series (NEPS), a subscription service, and revised annually; the last revision was in 1967. In addition to thus having the advantage of recency, the NPA projections probably utilize the most sophisticated techniques, in terms of reconciliation and integrated model-building, of any of those shown. GNP is built up from the output side, as the sum of gross product originating in government, agriculture, manufacturing, and nonmanufacturing industry. These sectoral outputs, in turn, are based on labor force projections (related to population through Bureau of Labor Statistics participation-rate factors), and assumption about rate of unemployment, and projections of average weekly hours and man-hour productivity. The output projections are matched against and reconciled with demand projections developed (through various subcalculations) for consumer expenditures, government expenditures, residential construction, and business investment.

The NPA projections are given in 1966 dollars and have been

transposed by us, for comparability, to 1960 dollars. Historical data have been made similarly comparable.

Because of its probably too-high projection of population growth and a tendency toward upward bias for other reasons, the NPA projections are probably a little on the high side. The combination of recency and methods used, however, gives reason to select them as the most reliable of those shown in the table.

AUTHORITY "B" (U.S. WATER RESOURCES COUNCIL)

The projections presented here were prepared for the U.S. Water Resources Council by the Office of Business Economics, U.S. Department of Commerce. The data will appear in a paper entitled "National Projections" to be published in the proceedings of the *Conference on Economic Analysis in Comprehensive River Basin Planning*. Starting from official historical data, GNP was projected in four parts: gross private product (on the basis of projected annual man-hours $\times$ projected gross product per man-hour), civilian government product, government enterprise product, and military product (each of the last three on the basis of projected employment $\times$ assumed constant average output per worker, using the 1965-level per-worker output in each case). Employment levels were derived by applying labor-force participation rates to the Census "C" population projections (presented in Table 1 herein). The data were presented in 1958 dollars and have been transposed by us to 1960 dollars. Figures for 1970 and 1985 were interpolated by us between those provided in the source for 1965-1980 and 1980-2000, respectively.

The assumption of constant productivity per government worker is consistent with that used in calculating historical GNP on a constant-dollar basis and is also used (explicitly or implicitly) in the other projections.

AUTHORITY "C" (KAHN AND WIENER)

The data are taken or derived from Kahn and Wiener, *The Year 2000*, Table XVIII, p. 168 (see notes to Table 1, Authority "F"). Kahn and Wiener's projections take off from a 1965 GNP figure which was evidently preliminary and is slightly lower than the more recent official figure. The projection method was to apply high and low assumptions of increased productivity per man-hour to the labor force derived from the medium population projection presented by the same authority in Table 1. Basic assumptions are: an increased labor force participation rate, from 56.9 per cent in 1965 to 59.8 per cent in the year 2000; an employment level of 96 per cent of the labor force; a decline of about 20 per cent in annual hours worked; and an assumed annual increase in productivity per man-hour of 2.5 per cent for the low projection and 4 per cent for the high. The low productivity increase rate reflects long-term U.S. performance; the high rate is a judgment based on possible impact of technological advances.

Data appear in the source in 1965 dollars and have been adjusted by us to 1960 dollars, with comparable data for 1955 and 1960 (not shown in source) being added.

AUTHORITY "D" (U.S. FOREST SERVICE)

Projections are from *Timber Trends in the United States,* p. 8 (see notes to Table 1, Authority "G"). Starting from official GNP figures for 1960 and 1962, GNP has been projected at an implied annual growth rate of 3.4 per cent to the year 2000. This compares with historical rates of 3.9 per cent between 1940 and 1960, and 3.2 per cent between 1920 and 1960. The projection assumes 4 per cent unemployment, in a peacetime economy with high military preparedness. Annual increase in output per man-hour has been assumed to be about 2.4 per cent throughout the projection period — less than the 2.7 per cent which obtained between 1950 and 1960. The data are derived, in part, from those published by the Outdoor Recreation Resources Review Commission in 1962 (*ORRRC Study Report 23*). Data appear in the source in 1961 dollars and have been adjusted by us to 1960 dollars. Data for 1965 and 1985 were interpolated by us, using the indicated annual growth rate.

AUTHORITY "E" (RESOURCES FOR THE FUTURE, INC.)

These projections, published in *Resources in America's Future,* are in some respects similar to those of the National Planning Association (Authority "A"), in that they use the same basic techniques of matching GNP output projections with GNP demand projections. The output projections were based on projections of labor force (derived by applying participation rates to population of labor-force age) and annual productivity per member of the labor force, without taking specific account of unemployment rates or of weekly and annual hours.

However, unemployment and work-time projections were made as a supplementary item and applied as a test of the plausibility of the implied man-hour productivity trends.

The initial demand-side projections included a consumer-expenditure projection which was independent of the output projections in that it assumed the continuation of per capita consumption trends. Reconciliation of these independent projections with the GNP projections automatically insured a plausible income-expenditure relationship.

TABLE 3. *Average Annual Rates of Growth of GNP*
(per cent)

Authority		1955-70	1970-85	1985-2000
A. National Planning Association		3.7	4.4	4.5
B. Water Resources Council		3.7	4.1	3.9
C. Kahn & Wiener	L	3.3	3.3	3.6
	H	3.7	4.8	5.1
D. U.S. Forest Service		2.9	3.4	3.4
E. Resources for the Future, Inc.				
	L	3.1	3.0	2.9
	M	3.4	3.6	3.8
	H	3.9	4.6	5.1

Note on GNP Growth Rates

These are the explicit or implied growth rates, as stated by the various authorities or calculated by us, of the GNP projections shown in Table 2.

TABLE 4. *GNP, by Kinds of Output*
(billions of 1960 dollars)

		1955	1960	1965	1970	1985	2000
Goods	L			(292)	330	(477)	692
	M	239	258	(306)	363	(608)	1019
	H			(322)	401	(776)	1502
Services	L			(224)	266	(445)	746
	M	156	189	(230)	280	(505)	909
	H			(239)	302	(611)	1234
Construction	L			(62)	67	(86)	119
	M	54	57	(73)	93	(155)	281
	H			(84)	124	(255)	590
Private	L			(44)	48	(61)	84
	M	40.6	40.6	(52)	66	(107)	197
	H			(60)	88	(175)	403
Public	L			(18)	19	(25)	35
	M	13.8	16.0	(21)	27	(48)	84
	H			(24)	35	(81)	187
Total GNP	L			(599)	710	(1100)	1680
	M	449	504	(613)	746	(1270)	2200
	H			(634)	798	(1570)	3290

Symbol: ( ) — Interpolated; not shown in original source.

Note on GNP Projections by Kinds of Output

Resources for the Future (Authority "E" in Table 2) is the only source providing the above type of breakdown. The projections shown were built up from more detailed projections on purchases of goods, services, and construction by consumers, business (for investment), and government. As in the case of the demand components of GNP, the detail will not add up to total GNP because of the independent projection of each series. In the medium, the discrepancy is only "statistical error"; in the high and low, it also reflects the fact that, in actuality, all of the lows (highs) could not co-exist — i.e., one or more of them would have to be higher (lower) by the amount of the discrepancy with total GNP.

TABLE 5. *Personal Consumption Expenditures, by Selected Type*

		1955	1960	1965	1970	1985	2000
				billions of 1960 dollars			
A. Housing	L			(50)	54.7	(82)	123.1
	M	33.5	42.2	(50)	60.5	(103)	171.6
	H			(52)	73.3	(162)	342.5
B. Household furnishings and appliances	L			(20)	18.9	(25)	72.4
	M	15.3	16.7	(21)	25.9	(51)	92.4
	H			(21)	31.7	(76)	173.0
C. Household utilities	L			(20)	21.0	(30)	43.9
	M	13.7	17.2	(21)	24.5	(43)	77.9
	H			(21)	35.7	(91)	211.0
D. Auto purchase and operating expenses	L			(44)	50.7	(76)	111.3
	M	35.6	37.2	(45)	53.6	(92)	153.1
	H			(47)	62.3	(134)	282.0
E. Personal and medical care	L			(35)	38.5	(61)	92.0
	M	22.0	28.6	(36)	43.9	(83)	150.5
	H			(37)	52.5	(124)	276.8
F. Recreation, travel, education, and religion	L			(35)	38.1	(60)	91.0
	M	22.9	28.6	(36)	43.9	(86)	159.7
	H			(37)	52.0	(111)	233.6
G. Food, tobacco, clothing, accessories, other household expenses	L			(152)	164.0	(185)	273.9
	M	120.7	135.8	(172)	176.0	(234)	393.3
	H			(160)	213.4	(363)	778.6
H. Purchased local transportation, and personal business	L			(27)	28.7	(45)	68.5
	M	17.7	22.6	(27)	33.7	(66)	122.8
	H			(29)	40.6	(101)	235.3

TABLE 5. (*Continued*)

		1955	1960	1965	1970	1985	2000
				percentage distribution			
A. Housing	L				12.2	(11.6)	11.5
	M	11.9	12.8	(12.9)	13.1	(13.0)	13.0
	H				14.8	(17.4)	19.8
B. Household furnishings and appliances	L				4.2	(3.6)	3.3
	M	5.4	5.1	(5.3)	5.6	(6.4)	7.0
	H				5.6	(8.2)	10.0
C. Household utilities	L				4.7	(4.3)	4.1
	M	4.9	5.2	(5.3)	5.3	(5.5)	5.9
	H				7.2	(9.8)	12.2
D. Auto purchase and operating expenses	L				11.3	(10.8)	10.4
	M	12.7	11.3	(11.5)	11.6	(11.6)	11.6
	H				12.6	(14.4)	16.3
E. Personal and medical care	M				8.6	(8.6)	8.6
	L	7.8	8.7	(9.1)	9.5	(10.8)	11.4
	H				10.6	(13.3)	16.0
F. Recreation, travel, education, and religion	L				8.5	(8.5)	8.5
	M	8.1	8.7	(9.1)	9.5	(10.9)	12.1
	H				10.5	(12.0)	13.5
G. Food, tobacco, clothing, accessories, other household expenses	L				31.7	(26.2)	21.6
	M	42.9	41.3	(37.3)	33.3	(29.6)	26.6
	H				38.1	(39.1)	40.0
H. Purchased local transportation, and personal business	L				6.4	(6.4)	6.4
	M	6.3	6.9	7.1	7.3	(8.4)	9.3
	H				8.2	(10.9)	13.6

Symbols: L — Low   M — Medium   H — High
(   ) — Interpolated; not shown in original source.

Notes on Components of Personal Consumption Expenditures

Although many potential sources were examined, Resources for the Future, Inc. was found to be the only authority having recently published projections giving a detailed breakdown of personal consumption expenditures. The data presented above are from Tables A1-23 and A1-27, in *Resources in America's Future*, Tables A1-23 and A1-27 (see notes to Table 1, Authority "H"). Various types of personal consumption expenditures ("PCE") have been regrouped, by us, into combinations that should be of interest to the architectural profession. Data for 1965 and 1985 were derived by us by interpolation in the percentage distribution of expenditures between 1960-1970 and 1980-1990, respectively, with the resulting percentage distribution being applied to the total PCE for 1965 and 1985.

The method used by RFF to project the PCE components involved judgment extrapolation of past trends in expenditure distributions and in expenditures per capita, giving weight to various assumptions about changing habits and other influences. These influences are discussed at length in Part I of the source volume. The details of the highs and lows do not add to the totals. Each high and low combination is intended to represent reasonable range for each individual type of expenditure, but all expenditures cannot be high or low at the same time. Further explanation may be found in the notes of Appendix to Chapter 1 in the source volume.

TABLE 6. *Disposable Personal Income*
(in 1960 dollars)

Item and authority		1955	1960	1965	1970	1985	2000
Total (billion dollars)							
A. National Planning Association*		309	350	448	(563)	(1126)	x
B. Kahn & Wiener	L	309	350	443	(488)	843	1475
	H				(526)	1124	2458
C. U.S. Forest Service		301	352	(418)	494	(805)	1324
D. Resources for the Future, Inc.	L	301	352	(401)	479	(664)	1134
	M			(418)	499	(864)	1426
	H			(443)	542	(1133)	1998
Per capita (dollars)							
A. National Planning Association*		(1865)	1939	2300	(2720)	(4348)	x
B. Kahn & Wiener	L	1863	1937	2277	(2346)	3267	4638
	H				(2529)	4357	7730
C. U.S. Forest Service		1814	1945	(2155)	2376	(3096)	4075
D. Resources for the Future, Inc.	L	1819	1956	(2100)	2260	(2800)	3500
	M			(2165)	2400	(3260)	4320
	H			(2215)	2510	(3630)	5255

Symbols: * Judged to be the single best projection at this time among those shown.
( ) — Interpolated; not shown in original source.
x — Not given in source, and not considered useful to extrapolate.

Notes on Projections of Disposable Personal Income

GENERAL

"Disposable personal income" is essentially the after-tax income of individuals, or in other words a measure of consumer purchasing power. After deduction of the amounts devoted to consumer "saving" (in the form not only of bank accounts and other investments, but of net increase in mortgage equity and repayment of other debt), the balance is the amount accounted for as "personal consumption expenditures" in Table 6.

Since the growth of gross national product, personal consumption expenditures (PCE), and disposable personal income (DPI) are all closely parallel, the (DPI) measure is chiefly useful in the per-capita form, shown in the second half of the table, which gives a feel for the increasing amount of "discretionary expenditure" which can be engaged in by the average American.

In theory, disposable personal income should be derived out of the income, tax, and income "transfer" flows accompanying given levels and structures of GNP. As a practical matter, however, projections take advantage of the relatively stable (though not necessarily unchanging) relationships mentioned above.

AUTHORITY "A" (NATIONAL PLANNING ASSOCIATION)

The NPA projections, given in the same "NEPS" report cited in Table 2, are built up through a detailed model of national and personal income flows and are based on actual data through 1966. The figures for 1970 have been interpolated by us between the NPA projections, converted by us from 1966 to 1960 dollars, for 1966 and 1972; and the figure for 1985 was extrapolated by us from projections by NPA for 1975 and 1978. The interpolation and extrapolation were done on a per capita basis, and the aggregates obtained by multiplying by the population projections shown in Table 1, herein.

AUTHORITY "B" (KAHN AND WIENER)

The data are given in the source volume in 1965 dollars and have been transposed by us to 1960 dollars. The specific source is Kahn and Wiener, *The Year 2000*, Tables XXIX and XXX, pp. 180-181 (see notes to Table 1, Authority "F"). Kahn and Wiener's projections take off from historical data through 1965 published in the April 1967 issue of *Survey of Current Business*. Their low and high projections are both related to the medium population projection shown in Table 1, herein, and appear to have been derived by extrapolation of the historical relationships of DPI with PCE and/or GNP. The 1970 figure shown in the table has been interpolated by us, based on similar relationships, between projections given in the source for 1965 and 1975.

AUTHORITY "C" (U.S. FOREST SERVICE)

Projections are from the same source cited for Authority "D" in Table 2, and are based on the assumption that, in the future, personal consumption expenditures should amount to about 70 per cent of GNP. The projections take off from historical data presented in the *Economic Report of the President,* January 1962. The source data were presented in 1961 dollars and have been transposed by us to 1960 dollars. 1965 and 1985 were interpolated by us.

AUTHORITY "D" (RESOURCES FOR THE FUTURE, INC.)

The source, *Resources in America's Future,* projects disposable personal income on the basis of assumed relationships to personal consumption expenditures — in other words, assumed percentages of saving — which increase over historical levels in the case of the high, are on the high side of historical averages for the medium, and on the low side for the low. The data for 1965 and 1985 have been interpolated by us, on a per capita basis, between 1960 and 1970 and 1980 and 1990, respectively. Aggregate DPI was then obtained by multiplying by the population projections shown in Table 1. Data are given in the source in 1960 dollars.

TABLE 7. *New Construction Expenditures, by Principal Type*
(billions of 1960 dollars)

Item and authority		1955	1960	1965	1970	1985	2000
Total new construction							
A. Resources for the Future, Inc.	L			(55)	65	(84)	116
	M*	51.8	54.4	(73)	91	(150)	264
	H			(92)	120	(251)	575
B. U.S. Dept. of Commerce		52.9	55.6	70	87	(142)	219
Total private construction							
A. Resources for the Future, Inc.	L			(37)	46	(58)	80
	M*	38.0	38.4	(52)	64	(102)	180
	H			(69)	85	(171)	388
B. U.S. Dept. of Commerce		39.6	39.6	48	61	(98)	147
Private residential (nonfarm)							
A. Resources for the Future, Inc.	L			(19)	26	(35)	51
	M*	21.0	21.1	(31)	38	(60)	118
	H			(45)	53	(103)	243
B. U.S. Dept. of Commerce		23.3	22.5	27	36	(55)	74
Commercial and industrial							
A. Resources for the Future, Inc.	L			(7.3)	7.6	(9.8)	14.0
	M*	6.7	7.0	(8.7)	10.8	(18.5)	23.2
	H			(10.1)	14.6	(32.2)	72.5
B. U.S. Dept. of Commerce		6.7	7.0	8.2	9.8	(17.1)	29.4
Public utilities							
A. Resources for the Future, Inc.	L			(5.2)	5.0	(5.2)	5.9
	M*	5.5	5.3	(6.3)	7.4	(11.5)	18.7
	H			(7.4)	10.3	(21.1)	44.4
B. U.S. Dept. of Commerce		5.4	5.3	6.5	7.9	(13.2)	22.8

TABLE 7. (*Continued*)

Item and authority	1955	1960	1965	1970	1985	2000

Other private construction

A. Resources for the Future, Inc.

L			(5.9)	7.0	(8.5)	9.4
M*	4.4	5.1	(6.1)	7.4	(12.2)	19.4
H			(6.2)	7.5	(14.3)	28.3
B. U.S. Dept. of Commerce	4.2	4.8	5.8	7.2	(12.5)	20.9

Total public construction

A. Resources for the Future, Inc.

L			(17.6)	19.3	(25.3)	35.6
M*	13.8	16.0	(20.7)	27.1	(48.0)	84.1
H			(23.7)	35.4	(80.7)	186.6
B. U.S. Dept. of Commerce	13.4	16.0	21.9	26.7	(44.0)	71.4

Education

A. Resources for the Future, Inc.

L			(3.5)	3.8	(4.4)	5.0
M*	3.3	3.2	(3.6)	4.1	(5.6)	7.4
H			(3.9)	4.8	(7.9)	12.9
B. U.S. Dept. of Commerce	2.9	2.8	4.2	5.0	(6.8)	9.2

Highways

A. Resources for the Future, Inc.

L			(6.3)	7.2	(10.0)	13.8
M*	4.3	5.5	(7.4)	10.1	(19.6)	34.6
H			(8.3)	12.4	(33.3)	86.5
B. U.S. Dept. of Commerce	4.0	5.5	8.0	10.0	(16.8)	27.5

Other public construction

A. Resources for the Future, Inc.

L			(7.8)	8.3	(10.9)	16.8
M*	6.1	7.3	(9.7)	12.9	(22.8)	42.1
H			(11.5)	18.2	(39.5)	87.2
B. U.S. Dept. of Commerce	6.5	7.7	9.7	11.7	(20.4)	34.7

Symbols: *Judged to be the single best projection among those shown.
  L — Low   M — Medium   H — High
  ( ) — Interpolated; not shown in original source.

Notes on Projections of New Construction Expenditures

GENERAL

The statistical specifications of the construction statistics in this table, which are the "construction put in place" figures of the U.S. Department of Commerce, make them slightly different from the figures used in the National Income and Product Accounts and included in gross private domestic investment. The two sets of projections chosen for presentation — those of Resources for the Future, Inc. and of the U.S. Department of Commerce (Business and Defense Services Administration) — are the only ones with some amount of detail by construction types.

AUTHORITY "A" (RESOURCES FOR THE FUTURE, INC.)

Data for all years except 1965 and 1985 come from *Resources in America's Future,* Tables A4-3 and A4-4 (see notes to Table 1, Authority "H"), where they are directly given in 1960 dollars. Projection detail for 1965 and 1985 has been geometrically interpolated by us (between RFF data for 1960-1970 and 1980-1990, respectively), except in the case of residential construction, where a more precise interpolation could be made by utilizing RFF projections on numbers of housing units built together with interpolated unit values. Figures for total private and public construction and for total construction were obtained for the interpolated years by addition.

For the sake of comparability with Authority "B," expenditures on oil and gas drilling (which are shown in the RFF projections detail) have been deducted by us from the aggregates (total new construction, total private construction, and "other" private construction) in which RFF had included these amounts.

The difference in historical level between the "education" figure shown for RFF and that of the Department of Commerce results from RFF's combining "schools and hospitals"; the latter are not shown separately by RFF and we have made no attempt to estimate the separate data for purposes of the table. A compensating difference shows up in "other public construction."

The RFF projections of new residential construction were carried out initially for total new units and then adjusted to add additions and alterations and to distinguish among public, private farm, and private nonfarm. The new-unit aggregates were in turn derived from

128

projected numbers of dwelling units and projected unit values. The numbers of dwelling units were a composite of requirements for net additional households (average annual addition for a ten-year period) and replacement requirements, the latter in turn being projected on the basis of "survival" tables derived from historical data on age of housing stock.

The more important categories of private nonresidential construction were derived by RFF in relation to overall investment levels in the various sectors. Public investment was generally projected in relation to population, although highway construction was related to vehicle-miles traveled. The various reference series were all derived in other parts of the RFF projections system.

AUTHORITY "B" (U.S. DEPARTMENT OF COMMERCE)

Source of the projections, which were prepared by the Business and Defense Services Administration, is the feature article in *Construction Review* for September 1961. Data for all of the desired years, except 1985, are presented in the source in 1960 dollars (details in Appendix B to the article); the 1985 figures have been interpolated by us between those presented for 1975 and 2000.

The BDSA projections depend on stated assumptions as to population, GNP, and the principal components of GNP. The population assumptions are higher than any of those shown in Table 1, except for the high RFF projection. Residential construction expenditures were projected on the basis of assumed housing starts (based in turn on changing numbers of households and assumed rates of replacement of older dwellings), along with projected trends in unit costs. The procedure used for most other components was to project past relationships to GNP. An exception is the projection of expenditures for educational construction, which were related to numbers of school-age children.

PROJECTIONS NOT SHOWN

Projections of the U.S. Forest Service *Timber Trends in the United States* (see notes to Table 1, Authority "G") are specifically given only for total construction, including maintenance and repair; however, the new-construction component is clearly much lower than either of the projections shown herein. National Planning Association projections of total new private residential construction are on a National Income Account basis. If adjusted to a basis comparable to the residential nonfarm figures shown in the table they would run slightly below the Department of Commerce projections.

ACTUAL 1965 DATA

Both authorities made their projections before 1965. Actual 1965 data, converted to 1965 dollars, are as follows:

	(billion dollars)
Total new construction	64.2
Total private	45.0
Residential (nonfarm)	24.1
Commercial and industrial	10.4
Public utilities	4.8
Other private	5.7
Total public	19.2
Education*	4.3
Highways	6.7
Other public	8.3

* Schools and hospitals combined (for comparison with RFF): 4.6.

TABLE 8. *New Private Housing Starts (Farm and Nonfarm)*
(millions of units)

Item and authority	1955	1960	1965	1970	1985	2000
Total units						
A. National Association of Home Builders	1.63	1.25	1.47	1.7	(1.9)	x
B. U.S. Forest Service	1.43	1.26	(1.3)	1.6	(1.9)	2.6
C. Resources for the Future, Inc. L			(1.1)	1.3	(1.5)	1.8
M*	1.58	1.28	(1.6)	2.1	(2.5)	3.7
H			(2.5)	2.6	(3.9)	6.1
Single-family units						
A. National Association of Home Builders	1.50	0.99	0.96	1.1	(1.2)	(1.3)
B. U.S. Forest Service	1.20	0.99	(1.4)	1.1	(1.2)	1.6
C. RFF/Economic Associates M*	(1.4)	1.0	(1.0)	1.6	(2.2)	3.1
Multi-family units						
A. National Association of Home Builders	0.13	0.26	0.51	0.6	(0.7)	(0.8)
B. U.S. Forest Service	0.13	0.27	(0.3)	0.5	(0.7)	1.0
C. RFF/Economic Associates M*	(0.2)	0.3	(0.5)	0.5	(0.3)	0.6

Symbols: * Judged to be the single best projection among those shown.
L — Low   M — Medium   H — High
x — Not given in source, and not considered useful to extrapolate.
( ) — Interpolated; not shown in original source.

Notes on Projections of Private Housing Starts

GENERAL

Total private starts, rather than total starts, or nonfarm starts, was selected as the basis on which it was most easily possible to achieve comparability among the three authorities. Adjustments were required for both the U.S. Forest Service and the Resources for the

Future data, but not for the NAHB data. Minor differences among the series for historical years are caused by revisions in the official estimates, as well as possible errors incurred in the course of adjustment.

AUTHORITY "A" (NATIONAL ASSOCIATION OF HOME BUILDERS)

Projections are given to 1980 in Table 1 of an article entitled *"The Multi-family Market,"* in National Association of Home Builders, *Economic News Notes,* March 1968. Projections for 1985 are our extrapolations. The projections of total units apparently make use of trends in the relationship of dwelling units to household formation. The projected distribution between multi- and single-family housing is based on prospective age distribution of the population, including an expectation of increasing numbers of young adults and retired people, a trend toward 2-home families, and new government housing programs which encourage construction of multi-family housing for low-income families.

AUTHORITY "B" (U.S. FOREST SERVICE)

The data presented are from the source volume — *Timber Trends in the United States,* Table 8, p. 17 (see notes to Table 1, Authority "G"). Adjustments have been made by us to exclude public housing in order to make the data comparable to that presented by Authority "A." The 1955 figures (also so adjusted) are the annual averages for 1950-59. Taking off from Bureau of the Census historical data through 1962, projections of total new units were made by taking account of net new households, vacancy rates (assumed constant), replacement rates (assumed a bit higher than in the 'fifties), and a minimal net availability through conversions. Projections of the distribution between single- and multi-family dwellings are based on assumptions regarding increasing density of population, rising land values, increasing commuting problems in urban areas, and the prospective increases in the number of young families and older age groups. Data for 1965 and 1985 have been interpolated by us between data presented in the source for 1962-70 and 1980-90, respectively.

AUTHORITY "C" (RESOURCES FOR THE FUTURE, INC. AND ECONOMIC ASSOCIATES, INC.)

The data presented under "total units" are derived by us from those on "equivalent residential nonfarm units," as shown in the source volume, *Resources in America's Future,* Table A4-4 (see notes to Table 1, Authority "H") or (for 1965 and 1985) from antecedent data in Table A4-5. Adjustments were necessary, for the sake of comparison, to include farm dwellings and to exclude public housing (or to exclude official-series underestimate and public housing, in the case of the 1965 and 1985 data). The RFF nonfarm series is an illustrative one, designed to express the basic RFF projections in terms of the official housing starts series as revised from 1959; the extension back to 1955 was not governmentally released and is an RFF estimate.

The basic RFF projections, which allowed for mobile homes and government underestimation of permanent units, took into account both net new dwelling unit requirments and replacement requirments. The net new requirements were based on the RFF household projections and allowed for increasing vacancy rates by reason of increasing proportions of second homes. The replacement requirements were derived from assumed attrition/survival patterns for housing units of various vintages; the historical base was the record of apparent attrition as derived from a comparison of the 1956 Housing Inventory and the 1960 Census.

The distribution between single-family and multi-family dwellings is based on an elaboration of RFF data which was made by Economic Associates, Inc. in 1965, in a special study with Mr. William R. Ewald for the General Electric Company. The distribution took into account trends in home ownership by age of household head. Some further adjustments, in the light of more recent historical data, have been made in the figures shown herein.

Although it is possibly a little on the high side, the medium RFF total projection appears to be the single best projection among those shown. It should be borne in mind that housing starts are subject to severe year to year fluctuation and that the projections shown are trend-line averages. Housing starts have been depressed in the last several years by, first, a shortage of mortgage money, and second, high interest rates; but the underlying demand push is apparently already beginning to express itself in increased building permit applications and starts despite the continued high interest costs.

The RFF/Economic Associates projections are also believed to be the most nearly correct of those shown in respect of single-family, multi-family breakdown. Emphasis on the fact that a large proportion of new household formation is accounted for by the quite young and the quite old, who gravitate toward apartments, tends to lead to

133

an over-estimation of new multi-family requirements, by ignoring the second-hand availabilities that occur as maturing families move into single-family dwellings. In addition, attrition rates are probably lower for multi-family structures than they are for single-family, and a considerable proportion of multi-family will be in public housing, not included in the projections in this table. It is of course possible that new styles of construction will evolve (they already have to some extent) which provide the equivalent of single-family living in units which are integral parts of multi-family structures and that such units may come to satisfy a significant part of the single-family demand.

TABLE 9. *Distribution of Civilian Employment by Industry*
(per cent of total)

Item and authority	1955	1960	1965	1970	1985	2000
Agriculture, mining[1]						
A. National Planning Association	10	8	7	(5)	3	2
B. BLS/Economic Associates, Inc.*	(10)	8	(7)	5	(3)	2
Contract construction						
A. National Planning Association	6	5	5	(6)	6	6
B. BLS/Economic Associates, Inc.*	(6)	5	(5)	6	(4)	3
Manufacturing						
A. National Planning Association	27	25	25	(25)	23	21
B. BLS/Economic Associates, Inc.*	(27)	28	(27)	27	(24)	21
Retail and wholesale trade						
A. National Planning Association	20	21	20	(20)	19	17
B. BLS/Economic Associates, Inc.*	(19)	19	(20)	20	(20)	19
Finance, insurance, and real estate						
A. National Planning Association	4	5	5	(5)	5	5
B. BLS/Economic Associates, Inc.*	(3)	4	(5)	6	(8)	9
Transportation, communication, and public utilities						
A. National Planning Association	7	6	6	(5)	4	4
B. BLS/Economic Associates, Inc.*	(7)	7	(6)	6	(4)	3
Services[2]						
A. National Planning Association	15	17	18	(19)	22	25
B. BLS/Economic Associates, Inc.*	(16)	16	(17)	17	(19)	20
Government[3]						
A. National Planning Association	11	13	14	(15)	18	20
B. BLS/Economic Associates, Inc.*	(12)	13	(13)	13	(18)	23

Symbols: * Judged to be the better of the two projections shown.
( ) — Interpolated; not shown in original source.
[1] Includes forestry and fisheries.
[2] All service producing industries not separately identified.
[3] Civilian government only.

Notes on Employment Distribution

GENERAL

Of a number of authorities examined, only the two presented in the table appear to have made long-range projections which both provide reasonably complete coverage of the total labor force (rather than just employees) and extend sufficiently into the future to be useful for our purposes. Even in these two cases, somewhat different coverage concepts are used, but the comparison is still essentially valid. The principal difference is that the NPA series (Authority "A") relates, conceptually, to total number of civilian *jobs* occupied, while the BLS/Ecasso series (Authority "B") relates to total number of civilian *jobholders* — the difference being "second" jobs. This difference may explain the slightly larger historical role ascribed by the NPA series to retail and wholesale trade, as well as part of the future prominence given by them to services.

The two distributions may be seen to be quite close. However, that shown for Authority "B" is considered to be somewhat the more valid. The lesser growth it allows for services can be explained by the heterogeneous mix of this category, some elements of which are relatively slow-growing. The larger role it allows for government stems in part from the assumption that mass consumption will increasingly consist of health, educational, and other services which flow through governmental (including state and local) channels. It will be noted that both authorities project large relative increases in government employment, and the difference is only in degree. (Cf. remarks on Kahn-Wiener projections, at end of these notes.)

AUTHORITY "A" (NATIONAL PLANNING ASSOCIATION)

The NPA projections are from its *National Economic Projections Series,* Report No. 67-N-1. This is the most recent revision of the general projections report in its annual subscription service. Their approximation of total jobs (see above) is arrived at, historically, from data in *The National Income and Product Accounts of the United States, 1929-1965* (Office of Business Economics, U.S. Department of Commerce), Tables 6.3, 6.4, and 6.6, and updating information in the annual National Income issues of the *Survey of Current Business.* The method was to add, to the total of full-time and part-time employees, the difference (self-employed) between full-time equivalent employees and "persons engaged in production" (who are also given by OBE on a full-time equivalent basis). The NPA projections are based on past trends, modified by rough calculations and assumptions about future composition of output. The 1970 projection has been interpolated by us between 1966 and 1977 data as shown in the source volume.

AUTHORITY "B" (U.S. BUREAU OF LABOR STATISTICS/ECONOMIC ASSOCIATES, INC.)

Data are from a special report prepared by Economic Associates for the General Electric Company. Economic Associates, in turn, took its historical data from the U.S. Census of Population. The projections are adaptations to these historical benchmarks of BLS projections shown in *Employment Projections by Industry and Occupation, 1960-75*, Special Labor Force Report No. 28 (March 1963); Economic Associates also made extrapolations to the year 2000. The original table for General Electric presented the data in ten-year intervals from 1950 to 2000; interpolations for 1955, 1965, and 1985 have been made by us now for the present comparison.

The BLS has since worked out revised projections which may be found in the *Manpower Report of the President*, 1967, Tables E-8 and E-9. The changes were slight, however, and should not materially affect the adaptations earlier made for GE.

PROJECTIONS NOT SHOWN

Not presented in the table are projections of the industry distribution of employees in nonagricultural establishments made by Kahn and Wiener in *The Year 2000*. Though these differ from those which are shown by their omission not only of farm workers but of self-employed generally, they may at least roughly be compared in terms of trends in the percentages. Between 1965 and 2000, Kahn and Wiener project, in comparison with the two authorities shown, a greater decrease in the percentage of manufacturing employment, a significant increase in the retail/wholesale trade share, a very large increase in the services share (over 80 per cent), and a steady decline in the government share. Although part of these differences could result from the difference in statistical basis (for example, the squeezing out of small proprietors would cause a series including proprietors to rise less rapidly than one which does not) the Kahn-Wiener projections do represent substantial variations in interpretation of the outlook for future U.S. industrial structure and, most particularly, for the role of government.

TABLE 10. *Rate of Change in Productivity per Manhour
in the Private Economy*
(per cent per annum)

Authority		1955-70	1970-85	1985-2000
A. Water Resources Council*		2.9	3.0	3.0
B. National Planning Association		3.0	3.5	3.9
C. Resources for the Future, Inc.	L	2.6	2.6	2.6
	M	2.6	2.7	2.7
	H	2.8	3.1	3.1

Symbols: * Judged to be the single best projection at this time among those shown.
L — Low   M — Medium   H — High

Notes on Productivity Rate of Change

GENERAL

The data presented reflect hourly productivity in the private economy only. Other authorities have presented such data for the total civilian economy; these are discussed briefly at the end of these notes.

AUTHORITY "A" (WATER RESOURCES COUNCIL)

The data are from "National Projections" (see Table 2, Authority "B"). The source presents private product per manhour in constant (1958) dollars, for historical years and for 1980, 2000, and 2020. For the period, 1965-2020, a 3 per cent growth rate was assumed by them throughout. In 1958 dollars, the source indicates hourly productivity of $3.34 in 1955, $4.42 in 1965, $6.89 in 1980, and $12.44 by the year 2000. The 2.9 per cent rate shown in the table for 1955-70 is implicit and was calculated by us from the WRC data.

The future growth rate of 3 per cent is assumed by the WRC on the basis of workers' being employed with increasing educational endowment, managerial competence, and more and improved capital equipment.

AUTHORITY "B" (NATIONAL PLANNING ASSOCIATION)

In the 1967 National Economic Projections Series, Report No. 67-N-1, NPA projections of output per manhour for the total civilian

139

economy are presented in Table T-12 for 1977, 1985, and 2000, while projections to 1977 for the private sector are in Table 3. The data in the table are our estimates of NPA's implied productivity growth rates for the *private* economy, calculated by applying the long-term historical ratio of such growth rate to that in the *total civilian* economy. That historical ratio of 1.333 was calculated from data in Table 22 of the source volume.

AUTHORITY "C" (RESOURCES FOR THE FUTURE, INC.)

The rates presented above were calculated by us from data in *Resources in America's Future,* Table A1-19 (see notes to Table 1, Authority "H"). Separate projections of hourly productivity were given for the agricultural and private nonagricultural sectors of the economy. The weighted averages of the projections produced hourly productivity of the total private economy, from which the growth rates presented above were calculated (after interpolating productivity data for 1965 and 1985).

PROJECTIONS NOT SHOWN

Kahn and Wiener, in *The Year 2000,* project hourly productivity in the total civilian economy at annual rates of 2.5 per cent for a low and 4 per cent for a high applied to the entire 1965-2000 period. Although these rates are not comparable to those presented above for the private economy, if the historical ratio of 1.333 private productivity growth to that of total civilian productivity were applied (see note on Authority "B" above), some idea of corresponding private economy growth rates may be derived. Such a ratio results in low and high growth rates of 3.3 per cent and 5.3 per cent, respectively.

TABLE 11. *Housing Stock and New Construction, 1950-2000*
(millions of units)

	1950	1960	1970	1980	1990	2000
1. Inventory — Total	46.0	58.3	69	83	97	115
2. Vacant — total	3.2	5.3	7.6	10.0	12.6	16.2
3. Available	.7	2.0	2.4	2.8	3.3	3.9
4. Seasonal or second house	1.8	2.6	4.5	6.5	8.5	11.5
5. Other vacant	.7	.7	.7	.7	.8	.8
6. Occupied — total	42.8	53.0	61	73	84	99

Inventory, by type

	1950	1960	1970	1980	1990	2000
7. Single-family	30.4	43.7	51	61	73	88
8. Multi-family — total	15.3	13.8	15.6	18.0	18.1	20.4
9. Garden or walk-up	13.4	11.3	12.3	13.9	13.8	15.4
10. High-rise	1.9	2.5	3.3	4.1	4.3	5.0
11. Mobile homes or trailers	.3	.8	2.1	4.3	5.8	6.8

New Construction

	1950	1960	1970	1980	1990	2000
12. Total	1.9	1.5	2.4	2.8	3.4	4.3
13. Equiv. official starts	1.6	1.3	2.2	2.3	2.8	3.6
14. Single-family	1.7	1.0	1.6	2.0	2.5	3.1
15. Multi-family	.2	.3	.5	.4	.4	.6
16. Garden or walk-up	.2	.3	.4	.3	.3	.5
17. High-rise	—	—	.1	.1	.1	.1
18. Mobile homes or trailers	—	.1	.3	.4	.5	.6

1. 1950 from *Census of Housing.*

2. 1950 and 1960 from census statistics. Projections from *Resources in America's Future* (hereafter, RFF), Table A4-5.

3. 1950 and 1960 calculated from census statistics (as reported in "Housing Vacancies" report, Series H-111). Projections assume continuation of 1960 proportion of total stock.

4. 1950 and 1960 as in line 3; 1950 partly estimated. Projections are residual, after subtracting other vacancy categories.

5. 1950 and 1960 as in line 4. Projections are judgment extrapolations, taking account of available-vacancy trend. Category includes primarily "awaiting occupancy" and "dilapidated"; these assumed to have counter-balancing trends.

6. Total, less vacant.

7-11. 1950 from census, assuming high-rise to be equivalent of 20-family or over.

12. 1950 and 1960 from RFF, Table A4-4. Projections are averages of ten years centering on years shown. Year 2000 partly extrapolated.

13. Difference is undercount resulting from unreported starts, plus mobile homes and trailers occupied as principal residence. 1950 figure is estimated; comparable official figure not available.

14-15. 1950 and 1960 from Department of Commerce housing start series. Projections as in line 12.

16-17. Projections as in line 12.

18. Projections as in line 12. Data refer only to mobile homes and trailers occupied as principal dwelling unit.

BIBLIOGRAPHY*

THE TITLES included here were selected for the contribution they made as a working base to this particular report. They represent less than one third of those surveyed in this instance. We admit to glaring omissions such as the complete works of Lewis Mumford, Eliel Saarinen, Percival and Paul Goodman, and others to whom we are personally indebted but whose work was not drawn upon directly for this assignment. We do not consider this bibliography either a classic or complete listing. For something of this nature, see the Bibliographic Service on the Future listed here under Ewald.

In our organized search of the literature, we used periodical indexes, newspapers, and the future development library already in place in this office. Periodicals were reviewed as far back as 1965-66. It has been since that time that the greatest supply of useful future-oriented materials has been generated, increasing markedly in 1967 and 1968.

My office was most ably assisted by research librarian Elizabeth Ten Houten.

"American Forecast: Tomorrow's Leaders View the Problems of the Next 25 Years." *Saturday Review* (January 13, 1968).**

American Institute of Architects. *A Study of Education for Environmental Design*. Princeton, N.J.: Princeton University, 1967.

American Society of Mechanical Engineers. *1966 National Transportation Symposium*. New York: American Society of Mechanical Engineers, 1966.

* Those titles marked with asterisks (****, ***, **, *), in that order, are considered the most useful to begin reading into creating a human future environment.

142

Anderson, Stanford, ed. *Planning for Diversity and Choice. Possible Futures and Their Relations to the Man-Controlled Environment.* Cambridge, Mass.: MIT Press, 1968.*

Aron, Raymond; Kennan, George; and Oppenheimer, Robert. *World Technology and Human Destiny.* Ann Arbor: University of Michigan Press, 1963.*

Asher, Norman J.; Wetzler, Elliot; Horowitz, Seymour M.; and Schneider, W. Bartz. *The Demand for Intercity Passenger Transportation by VTOL Aircraft,* Report R-144. Arlington, Virginia: Institute for Defense Analyses Program Analysis Division, 1968.

Barach, Arnold B. *The New Europe and Its Economic Future.* A Twentieth Century Fund Survey. New York: The Macmillan Co., 1964.

——————. *U.S.A. and Its Economic Future.* A Twentieth Century Fund Survey. New York: The Macmillan Co., 1964.

Battelle Memorial Institute. *Final Report on the State of the Art of Prefabrication in the Construction Industry to the Building and Construction Trades Department of AFL-CIO.* Columbus, Ohio: Columbus Laboratories, 1967.*

Beckwith, Burnham Putnam. *The Next 500 Years.* New York: Exposition Press, Inc., 1967.**

Bell, Daniel, ed. *Toward the Year 2000: Work in Progress.* Boston: Houghton Mifflin Co., 1968.***

Boguslaw, Robert. *The New Utopians, A Study of System Design and Social Change.* Englewood Cliffs, N.J.: Prentice-Hall, 1965.

Boulding, Kenneth E. *The Misallocation of Intellectual Resources.* Proceedings of the American Philosophical Society (April 15, 1963).

Boyko, Hugo, ed. *Science and the Future of Mankind.* Bloomington: Indiana University Press, 1965.

Brecher, Ruth and Edward. "Getting to Work and Back." *Consumer Reports* (March 1965).

Brown, Harrison; Bonner, James; and Weir, John. *The Next Hundred Years.* New York: Viking Press, 1957, 1963.****

Butler, William F. and Kavesh, Robert A., eds. *How Business Economists Forecast.* Englewood Cliffs, N.J.: Prentice-Hall, 1966.

Bylinsky, Gene. "U.S. Science Enters a Not-So-Golden Era." *Fortune* (November 1968).***

Calder, Nigel, ed. 2 vol., *The World in 1984.* Baltimore: Penguin Books, 1965.****

Cars for Cities. Reports of the Steering Group and Working Group Appointed

143

by the Minister of Transport. London: Her Majesty's Stationery Office, Waterlow & Sons, Ltd., 1967.*

Chamber of Commerce of the United States. *Rural Poverty and Regional Progress in an Urban Society* (Task Force on Economic Growth and Opportunity), 1966.**

Civilization of the Dialogue, vol. 2, no. 1. Santa Barbara: Fund for the Republic, Inc., 1968.

Clark, Colin. "The Economic Functions of a City in Relation to Its Size." *Econometrica,* 13 (April 1945):2.

Clarke, Arthur C. *Profiles of the Future.* New York: Harper & Row, 1958.*

Clawson, Marion. *New Responsibilities for Government.* (Prepared for Conference 2020, Building the Future Environment — An Atlantic Region Perspective to the Year 2020, January 30-31, 1969.)***

Colm, Gerhard and Gulick, Luther H. *Program Planning for National Goals.* Planning Pamphlet no. 125. Washington, D.C.: National Planning Association, 1968.

Committee On State Planning. *A Strategy for Planning, A Report to the National Governors' Conference,* October 18, 1967.*

Commoner, Barry. "Science and Technology or the Sorcerer's Apprentice." *Population Bulletin,* 23 (December 1967):5.

Cornuelle, Richard C. and Finch, Robert H. *The New Conservative Liberal Manifesto.* San Diego: Viewpoint Books, July 1968.*

Council of State Governments. *State Planning — A Policy Statement.* Chicago: The Council of State Governments, 1962.*

de Jouvenel, Bertrand. *The Art of Conjecture.* New York: Basic Books, 1967.**

Drucker, Peter F. *The Age of Discontinuity: Guidelines to Our Changing Society.* New York: Harper & Row, 1968, 1969.**

Dubos, Rene. *So Human an Animal.* New York: Charles Scribner's Sons, 1968.***

Editors of *Fortune. Markets of the Seventies. The Unwinding U.S. Economy.* New York: Viking Press, 1968.**

——————. *Markets of the Sixties.* New York: Harper & Brothers, 1960.

Eldredge, H. Wentworth, ed. *Taming Megalopolis,* vols. 1 and 2. New York: Frederick A. Praeger, 1967.

Ellul, Jacques. *The Technological Society.* New York: Alfred A. Knopf, 1964.**

Ewald, William R., Jr., *Appalachian Institute Prospectus/Budget/Funding.*

For the Appalachian Regional Commission. Washington, D.C.: Department of Commerce, September 1966.*

——————. *Arkansas National Policy Statement.* (Prepared for Conference 2020, Building the Future Environment — An Atlantic Region Perspective to the Year 2020, January 30-31, 1969.) (And co-signees.)**

——————. *Bibliography of Studies of Future Technology, Change and Philosophies of Life.* (Prepared for American Institute of Planners' Consultation, "The Next Fifty Years/1967-2017, The Future Environment of a Democracy," 1967.)

——————. *Change/Challenge/Response.* A Development Policy for New York State. Albany: Office for Regional Development, 1964. (With State staff and consultants.)*

——————. *Environment and Change, The Next Fifty Years.* Bloomington: Indiana University Press, 1968. (Commissioned and edited.)***

——————. *Environment and Policy, The Next Fifty Years.* Bloomington: Indiana University Press, 1968. (Commissioned and edited.)***

——————. *Environment for Man, The Next Fifty Years.* Bloomington: Indiana University Press, 1967. (Commissioned and edited.)***

——————. *Report of the Appalachian Institute Committee to the Conference of Appalachian Governors and The President's Appalachian Regional Commission.* Area Redevelopment Administration, Technical Assistance Project. Washington, D.C.: Department of Commerce, 1964.*

Faltermayer, Edmund K. "A Way Out of the Welfare Mess." *Fortune* (July 1968).**

——————. "We Can Afford A Better America." *Fortune* (March 1969).**

Fitch, Lyle C. and Associates. *Urban Transportation and Public Policy.* San Francisco: Chandler Publishing Company, 1964.*

"Forecasting the Future." *Science Journal,* 3 (October 1967):10. London: Iliffe Industrial Publications Ltd.****

Foreign Policy Association. *Toward the Year 2018.* New York: Cowles Education Corporation, 1968.

Fuller, R. Buckminster and McHale, John. *World Design Science Decade 1965-1975.* (Documents 1-6.) Carbondale, Illinois: World Resources Inventory (Southern Illinois University), 1967.

Gabor, Dennis. *Inventing the Future.* New York: Alfred Knopf, 1964.

Gans, Herbert J. *People & Plans, Essays On Urban Problems and Solutions.* New York: Basic Books, Inc., 1968.

General Electric Company. *Our Future Business Environment: Developing Trends and Changing Institutions.* New York: April 1968.****

Ginzberg, Eli. *Technology and Social Change.* New York: Columbia University Press, 1964.**

Goldwin, Robert A., ed. *A Nation of Cities: Essays on America's Urban Problems.* Chicago: Rand McNally & Co., 1968.

Gordon, Kermit, ed. *Agenda for the Nation.* Washington, D.C.: The Brookings Institution, 1968.**

Gordon, Theodore J. G. *The Future.* New York: St. Martin's Press, 1965.*

Harvard University Program on Technology and Society. *Second Annual Report.* Cambridge, Mass.: Harvard University Press, 1965-1966.*

—————. *Fourth Annual Report.* Cambridge, Mass.: Harvard University Press, 1967-1968.*

Haydon, Brownlee. *The Year 2000.* Santa Monica: The Rand Corp. P-3571), 1967.

Hearle, Edward F. R. *Are Cities Here to Stay?* Santa Monica: The Rand Corp. (P-2764), 1963.

Heilbroner, Robert L. *The Limits of American Capitalism.* New York: Harper & Row, 1965, 1966.*

Helmer-Hirschberg, Olaf. *Social Technology.* Santa Monica: The Rand Corporation, 1965.***

Hill, Robert L., ed. *America 1980.* Washington, D.C.: Department of Agriculture, The Graduate School, August 1965.

Hodge, Patricia L. and Hauser, Philip M. *The Challenge of America's Metropolitan Population Outlook, 1960 to 1985.* (Prepared for The National Commission on Urban Problems.) New York: Frederick A. Praeger, 1968.

International Communications, Inc. *Science & Technology.* New York: Conover–Mast Publications, April 1968.****

Jantsch, Erich. *Technological Forecasting in Perspective.* Paris: Organization for Economic Cooperation and Development, 1967.**

Johansen, John M. "An Architecture for the Electronic Age." *American Scholar Magazine* (Summer 1966).

Kahn, Herman. *New Roles for Private Enterprise.* (Prepared for Conference 2020, Building the Future Environment — An Atlantic Region Perspective to the Year 2020, January 30-31, 1969.)

Kahn, Herman and Wiener, Anthony J. *The Year 2000. A Framework for*

Speculation on the Next Thirty-Three Years. New York: The Macmillan Co., 1967.***

Kleemeier, Robert W., ed. *Aging and Leisure.* New York: Oxford University Press, 1961.*

Laing, R. D. *The Politics of Experience.* New York: Pantheon Books, 1967.*

Landsberg, Hans H.; Fischman, Leonard L.; and Fisher, Joseph L. *Resources in America's Future.* Baltimore: Johns Hopkins Press, 1963. Bibliographical footnotes.***

Lave, Lester B. *Technological Change: Its Conception and Measurement.* Englewood Cliffs, N.J.: Prentice-Hall, 1966.

Lecht, Leonard A. *Goals, Priorities and Dollars.* New York: The Free Press, 1966.***

Lynd, Staughton. *Nonviolence in America: A Documentary History.* Indianapolis: The Bobbs-Merrill Company, The American Heritage Series, 1966.

Massachusetts Institute of Technology. *The Glideway System. A High-Speed Ground Transportation System in the Northeastern Corridor of the United States* (Report No. 6). Cambridge, Mass.: MIT Press, 1965.

————. *Project Metran: An Integrated, Evolutionary Transportation System for Urban Areas* (Report No. 8). Cambridge, Mass.: MIT Press, 1966.

————. *Survey of Technology for High Speed Ground Transport.* Springfield, Va.: Clearinghouse (PB 168 648), 1965.

Medawar, P. B. *The Future of Man.* New York: Mentor Books, 1961.

Meier, Richard L. *Systems and Principles for Metropolitan Planning.* The Centennial Review of Arts & Science. East Lansing: Michigan State University, 1959.

Meyerson, Martin, ed. *Metropolis in Ferment.* Philadelphia: The Annals of the American Academy of Political and Social Science, 1957.*

Michael, Donald N. *The Next Generation.* New York: Vintage Books, 1965.*

Morphet, Edgar L. and Ryan, Charles O., eds., "Prospective Changes in Society by 1980." *Designing Education for the Future No. 1.* New York: Citation Press, 1967**

National Academy of Sciences. *Communication Systems and Resources in the Behavioral Sciences.* Division of Behavioral Sciences of the National Research Council. Washington, D.C.: Publication 1575, 1967.

National Advisory Commission on Civil Disorders. *Report of the National*

Advisory Commission on Civil Disorders. New York: Bantam Books, 1968.**

National Planning Association, Center for Economic Projections. *Basic Policy Assumptions for Viewing the Future.* Proceedings: Eighth Annual Conference of the Center for Economic Projections. Washington, D.C., July 1967.**

Nelson, R. Ruben. *The Effects of Research, Development on the Economy.* Santa Monica: The Rand Corporation, 1963.

New Communities. Washington, D.C.: American Institute of Planners, 1968.*

Oettinger, Anthony G. and Marks, Sema. *Educational Technology: New Myths and Old Realities.* Cambridge, Mass.: Harvard University Program on Technology and Society Reprint, no. 6. From *Harvard Educational Review,* 38 (Fall 1968):4.*

Outdoor Recreation Resources Review Commission. *Outdoor Recreation for America.* Washington, D.C.: Government Printing Office, January 1962.**

Owen, Wilfred. *The Metropolitan Transportation Problem,* rev. ed. Washington, D.C.: The Brookings Institution, 1956, 1966.

Pickard, Jerome P. *Dimensions of Metropolitanism.* Research Monograph 14. Washington, D.C.: Urban Land Institute, 1967.***

————. *If Present Trends Continue.* (Prepared for Conference 2020, Building the Future Environment — An Atlantic Region Perspective to the Year 2020, January 30-31, 1969.)

Platt, John R. *1982 — Steps to Man.* Washington, D.C.: American Association of University Women Journal, May 1966.***

————. *The Step to Man.* New York: John Wiley & Sons, 1966.***

Polak, F. L. *The Image of the Future,* vols. 1 and 2. New York: Oceana Publications, 1961.*

Prehoda, Robert W. *Designing the Future, The Role of Technological Forecasting.* Philadelphia and New York: Chilton Book Company, 1967.**

————. *Extended Youth.* New York: G. P. Putnam's Sons, 1968.**

Price, Don K. *The Scientific Estate.* Cambridge, Mass.: Harvard University Press (Belnap), 1965.**

Pushkarev, Boris. *The Present Situation — Its Implications.* (Prepared for Conference 2020, Building the Future Environment — An Atlantic Region Perspective to the Year 2020, January 30-31, 1969.)*

Richards, Brian. *New Movement in Cities.* New York: Reinhold Publishing Corp., 1966.*

Rockefeller Panel Reports. *Prospect for America*. Garden City, N.Y.: Doubleday & Co., 1961.**

Schillebeeckx, E., O.P. *God the Future of Man*. New York: Sheed & Ward, 1968.

Schuchter, Arnold. *White Power — Black Freedom*. Boston: Beacon Press, 1968.

"Search for Meaning Amid Change." *New York Times National Economic Review* (January 6, 1969), p. C-141.****

Seidenberg, Roderick. *Anatomy of the Future*. Chapel Hill: University of North Carolina Press, 1961.*

Sheldon, Eleanor Bernert and Moore, Wilbert E., eds. *Indicators of Social Change*. New York: Russell Sage Foundation, 1968.

Shonfield, Andrew. *Modern Capitalism, The Changing Balance of Public & Private Power*. London: Oxford University Press, 1965.

Smith, Bruce L. B. *The Future of the Not for Profits*. Santa Monica: Rand Corporation, 1966.*

Teilhard de Chardin, Pierre. *The Future of Man*. New York: Harper & Row, 1964.

——————. *The Phenomenon of Man*. New York: Harper & Row, 1959.

"Tenth Anniversary Issue: The Image of the Future." *News Front* (Management's News Magazine). Vol. 10 (January 1967), no. 10.

Theobald, Robert, ed. *Social Policies for America in the Seventies: Nine Divergent Views*. Garden City, N.Y.: Doubleday & Co., 1968.*

Tomorrow Is the Question in Electrical Design. Actual Specifying Engineer, E4. Chicago: Medalist Publications, Inc., 1968.

"Toward the Third Millenium." *Progressive Architecture*. New York: Reinhold Publishing Corp., 1966.****

Traffic in Towns. Reports of the Steering Group and Working Group Appointed by the Minister of Transport. London: Her Majesty's Stationery Office, Waterlow & Sons, Ltd., 1963.*

2000+. Architectural Design, London: February 1967.

University of Michigan. *SER 3 — Environmental Analysis*. Ann Arbor: University of Michigan Press, 1965.**

Urban and Rural America: Policies for Future Growth. Advisory Commission on Intergovernmental Relations. Washington, D.C.: Government Printing Office, 1968.**

"The U.S. City." *Life,* 59 (December 24, 1965):26.

U.S. Department of Commerce, Environmental Science Services Administration. *Man's Geophysical Environment — Its Study from Space.* Washington, D.C.: Government Printing Office, 1968.

U.S. Department of Defense, Defense Documentation Center. *COSATI Subject Category List.* Springfield, Va.: Clearinghouse, 1965.*

————. *Long Range Forecasting Methodology.* A Symposium held at Alamogordo, N.M. Springfield, Va.: Clearinghouse, 1967.*

U.S. Department of Health, Education and Welfare. *Toward a Social Report.* Washington, D.C.: Government Printing Office, 1969.

U.S. Department of Housing and Urban Development. *Tomorrow's Transportation, New Systems for the Urban Future.* Washington, D.C.: Government Printing Office, 1968.***

U.S. National Commission on Technology, Automation, and Economic Progress. *Technology and the American Economy,* 7 vols. Washington, D.C.: Government Printing Office, 1966.***

U.S. National Commission on Urban Problems. *Building the American City.* Report of the National Commission on Urban Problems to the Congress and to the President of the U.S. Washington, D.C.: Government Printing Office, 1968.***

U.S. President's Commission on National Goals. *Goals for Americans.* Englewood Cliffs, N.J., Prentice-Hall, 1960.***

U.S. President's Committee on Urban Housing (Kaiser Commission). *A Decent Home.* Report of the President's Committee on Urban Housing. Washington, D.C.: Government Printing Office, 1969.**

U.S. President's National Advisory Commission on Rural Poverty. *The People Left Behind.* Washington, D.C.: Government Printing Office, 1967.**

U.S. Senate. *Developments in Aging.* A Report of the Special Committee on Aging, Report No. 1098. Washington, D.C.: Government Printing Office, 1968.*

Utopia. Journal of the American Academy of Arts and Sciences. Cambridge, Mass.: Daedalus, Spring 1965.*

Wallace, David A. *A Practical Utopia for the Atlantic Region.* (Prepared for Conference 2020, Building the Future Environment — An Atlantic Region Perspective to the Year 2020, January 30-31, 1969.)*

Wattenberg, Ben J. and Scammon, Richard M. *This U.S.A.* Garden City, N.Y.: Doubleday & Co., 1965.

Weismantel, William, ed. *The Postindustrial City.* Albuquerque: University of New Mexico, *New Mexico Quarterly,* Fall 1968.

What About the Year 2000? (Prepared by the Joint Committee on Bases of Sound Land Policy composed of the American Civic Association, American Institute of Park Executives, American Park Society, National Conference on City Planning, National Conference on State Parks.) Harrisburg, Pa.: Mount Pleasant Press, 1929.

Whyte, William H. *The Last Landscape.* Garden City, N.Y.: Doubleday & Co., 1968.

PART TWO

The Building Industry:
Concepts of Change (1920-2000)

MIDWEST RESEARCH INSTITUTE

INTRODUCTION

THIS COMMENTARY on the building industry brings together a mass of data on the way the physical environment is now shaped and attempts to project current trends ahead, in context, to the end of the century. Such an exercise in extrapolation taxes the foundation of technological forecasting. Technological forecasting, at best, helps us cope intellectually with the uncertainties of the near future — the next two years, maybe five, rarely more than fifteen. The fifteen years now before us are special; this is the period referred to by Ewald as the "shock front," a highly pressurized block of time during which the problems of "today" must be partly resolved and realigned, and during which the goals and values established today by individuals, institutions, and societies must undergo a similar process of partial change. Beyond the shock-front years — after 1985 — technological forecasting is inadequate. We distinguish only a few uncertain reference points to suggest what will develop. Part of the inadequacy lies with our consuming societal preoccupation with numbers. What we can't quantify, we tend to minimize — both in forecasting and in overt decision-making.

It is the *qualitative* aspects of the environment which concern architects first, and it is these human factors and human values about which we know least. If, as we sense, changing human values and attitudes will create the greatest share of shock in the "shock front" years, we are indeed working from fragile assumptions.

This report consists of notes composed with varying levels of confidence — combined extrapolations of current trends and isolated events which seem meaningful to us in the larger context of time —

155

to be considered conjecture. By filtering what we have learned about the building industry and its relation to the environment today, we have attempted to sort out here a picture of alternative (and sometimes contradictory) future trends and positions. Many more questions are raised than are answered. Many possibly crucial implications for the architectural profession are buried among these points. Some which have appeared clear to us as issues for the profession to consider are summarized in a final section.

In many ways this report affirms the idea that the future is not inevitable. Man designs his way into it, witting or not, willing or not. The choice is never whether to accept or reject an inevitable future, but how to select among alternative futures. The architect's role in this process may be unique, but it cannot be isolated or even insulated from the others involved. By whatever path society chooses (revolution/reason/response/reaction in Ewald's apt terms), "future building" will involve complex sets of human and professional relationships.

In our view, the leverage of the design professions in the process will depend directly on their ability to explore and expand new working relationships with the countless others involved and affected.

1.

TODAY: BUILDING INDUSTRY ACTORS AND CHARACTERISTICS

HUNDREDS OF THOUSANDS of separate enterprises take part in the process of planning and building the physical environment today, presenting a formidable problem in classification, definition, and interpretation. This grouping might loosely be termed the "construction industry" which is concerned with the total process of preparing, producing, distributing, and servicing the physical environment. But architects more closely identify with that smaller aggregate of organizations which actually produce new or renewed structures and their man-made surroundings and connectors — the "building industry."

This means that any consideration of the future building industry must reflect all of its parts, private and public. These parts are generally viewed as "industries" in their own right — real estate, banking, insurance, building maintenance, title companies, etc., as well as the actual building and design sectors. However, they, along with a host of other specialized actors (lawyers, land surveyors, countless government agencies and functions at all levels), constitute the highly dynamic structure which controls and creates the building process.

This complexity is reduced to a minimal configuration in Figure II-1, setting out approximate numbers of the key groups involved. Even such a simplified portrait eludes the obvious, however: each building project charts its own path through the industry map, bypassing some blocks, incorporating new ones. This is why the few existing building industry studies are difficult to synthesize or com-

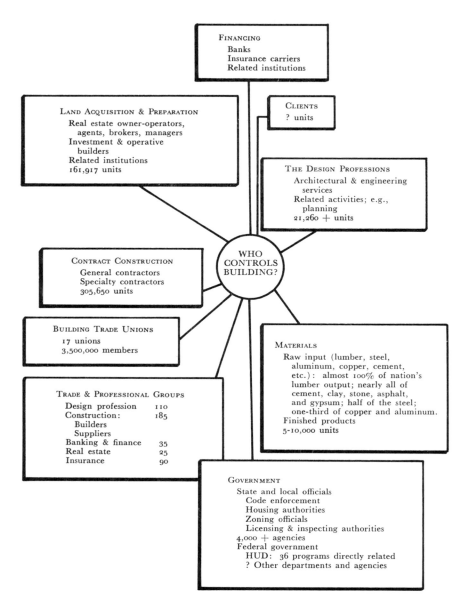

FINANCING
Banks
Insurance carriers
Related institutions

LAND ACQUISITION & PREPARATION
Real estate owner-operators,
agents, brokers, managers
Investment & operative
builders
Related institutions
161,917 units

CLIENTS
? units

THE DESIGN PROFESSIONS
Architectural & engineering
services
Related activities; e.g.,
planning
21,260 + units

WHO CONTROLS BUILDING?

CONTRACT CONSTRUCTION
General contractors
Specialty contractors
305,650 units

BUILDING TRADE UNIONS
17 unions
3,500,000 members

MATERIALS
Raw input (lumber, steel,
aluminum, copper, cement,
etc.): almost 100% of nation's
lumber output; nearly all of
cement, clay, stone, asphalt,
and gypsum; half of the steel;
one-third of copper and aluminum.
Finished products
5-10,000 units

TRADE & PROFESSIONAL GROUPS
Design profession   110
Construction: 185
    Builders
    Suppliers
Banking & finance   35
Real estate   25
Insurance   90

GOVERNMENT
State and local officials
    Code enforcement
    Housing authorities
    Zoning officials
    Licensing & inspecting authorities
4,000 + agencies
Federal government
    HUD: 36 programs directly related
    ? Other departments and agencies

Sources: *County Business Patterns, 1967: U.S. Summary.* Table A-1, U.S. Census Bureau; *1969 Directory of National Trade and Professional Associations,* ed. Craig Colgate, Jr., 3 (Washington: Columbia Books, 1968); Hans H. Landsberg, Leonard L. Fischman and Joseph L. Fisher, "Construction," *Resources in America's Future: Patterns of Requirements and Availabilities. 1960-2000,* Chapter 4 (Baltimore: Johns Hopkins Press, 1963); AFL-CIO Building Trades Department.

FIGURE II-1

pare; they tend to start from the special perspective of a given market segment, actor group, or building function.

In conventional terms, the building industry is not an industry at all in the sense of "textiles" or "chemicals"; rather it is an ad hoc assemblage of skills, resources, and control groups coming together around a defined project. Yet it is a central thesis of this report that this situation has been changing and will shift even more rapidly in the future, so that ultimately a more conventional industry structure will appear.

Looking backward thirty or more years, Donald Schon[1] has concluded that the "industrialization of the building process" (an accumulation of incremental changes in building technology, management procedures, and decision-making) has been forcing the building industry toward more formalization of structure — in effect to become more like a conventional industry. The evidence accumulated in our study indicates that this process will continue at a much faster rate in the thirty years ahead. The process of organizational change has been evolutionary so far; it may well verge on revolution in the next fifteen years.

The building industry has been loosely described as a family business that is tightly held, operating in an environment of nearly cutthroat competition with innovations and financial data well hidden. Although the exceptions are increasing, corporate organization and application of accepted management principles still tend to be antithetical to the industry as a whole. For these reasons, few sound statistical bases exist for analysis and projection. But it is possible to draw inferences from the fragmented studies that have been attempted over recent years:[2]

1. The core of the building industry today includes more than 86,000 general contractors, about 15,000 operative and investment builders, roughly 200,000 subcontractors, and 21,000 design and engineering service firms (see Appendix Table A-1, p. 245).

2. The largest organizations are designated design-construction companies with the top 29 firms in billings (contracts) accounting for $11 billion in 1967. Four firms approached or exceeded the $1 billion level, and the next largest 19 firms had volumes of at least $200 million. Only 18 of the design-construction firms in the top 500 sold less than $100 million in 1967.

3. Design-construction firms range from giant industrial corpora-

tions (the largest is still family-controlled) such as Bechtel with 1967 contracts of $1.4 billion to small, single operators who hire staff and subcontract the work as contracts permit.

4. Home builders, those firms specializing in the most volatile of all construction markets, are producing their own group of giants. In 1967, 22 firms had sales of more than $20 million (average = $38 million).

5. Architectural and engineering firms have also shown vigorous growth; 22 billed at least $10 million in 1967 — up from 12 such firms in 1965. Leading design firms with billings over $1 million jumped from 331 in 1966 to 413 in 1967. Among the 500 largest design, design and construction, and architectural and engineering firms, only 40 billed less than $1 million in 1967 compared with 121 in 1966.

6. Average billings for the top 453 design firms surveyed by *Engineering-News Record* in 1967 were $2.6 million per year, up from the preceding year by 6 per cent. Bechtel led with $1.4 billion (up from $993 million) and the smallest of the top 400 was $14.3 million.

7. Those firms classified as architectural-design companies had the highest percentage gain in 1967, 29 per cent over 1966. Architectural-engineering firms showed a 10 per cent increase, but consulting engineers increased their billings by 18 per cent.

8. Number of employees varies just as much: three architectural engineering firms have more than 1000 professional employees. The largest architectural firm had 300 professionals (not including support staff) and seven of the 68 firms in the top 500 had professional staffs over 100.

9. Firms with top billings are also shifting rapidly. Tishman Reality and Construction moved from twentieth to fifth place in 1967. A new giant has been created by the merger of Chemico, Ebasco Services, and Kidde Constructors into EB&S Systems now occupying third place in the industry. Well-known firms such as Lummus Company and Austin Company have slipped.

10. Profits (measured as percentage of capital investment) were highest for private, nonresidential building contracts with a median profit in 1967 of 18 per cent. Public buildings yielded only 11 per cent and heavy and highway construction had profit medians of 10 per cent.

11. Risk is high but so are potential rewards, attracting many new actors into the industry.

12. A much larger equipment investment required for heavy and highway construction tends to reduce the profit in these markets; also public contracts are often more competitive than private construction.

These, then, are some of the central actor groups in the building industry today. More will be said about the nondesign-construction participants (finance, government, and labor) later in the report. The collective industry might be described in the following way:

> It is a risky, Balkanized industry in which no organization has a dominant position. It is highly competitive, though it engages in ad hoc collaborative efforts; and it is passive in nature, i.e., it responds to external stimuli on a short-term time scale. It has not internalized technology for the purpose of management and it has invested little in research on itself, its products, and its future. The public-private sector relationships of the industry appear inefficient, highly stressed, and negative; thus reflecting the public policies controlling the industry. It therefore seems doubtful that the present productive capacity of the industry is sufficient to handle any major, rapid scale-up in market demand which might result from changing public policy.

2.

TOMORROW: SHIFTS IN STRUCTURE, CHARACTERISTICS, AND MARKETS

TODAY'S BUILDING INDUSTRY lacks market control, tight organization, a solid planning base and an orderly way of dealing with the larger human and environmental dimensions of building. What it produces is done largely ad hoc, combining opportunism, intuition, market experience, and some relatively crude measures of future demand. For many reasons, experimentation is as risky and rare as is longer-term, larger-scale environmental planning. The U.S. building industry has little or no cushion for failure (one "Edsel" and you're out). So, even though the industry operates in a high risk, frequent failure mode, most of the risk and failure is associated with conventional construction in conventional ways for conventional (traditional) end uses.

The Kaiser Committee,[1] The Douglas Commission,[2] and numerous other expert appraisals inside and out of the building industry have generally agreed that the present structure of the industry — given the dominant characteristic of fragmentation — does not offer enough productive capacity to build "Another America" by the end of this century. There is an even stronger consensus that the present industry structure, given both internal and external constraints, cannot produce a radically "different and better America," i.e., an environment much more responsive to human needs and values, unless fairly massive changes occur in structural relationships, operating styles, and the ways in which planning is accomplished.

But what changes? What are the most likely shifts within the building industry, in the larger environmental planning-construction-

162

service industry complex, and in external factors which will enable the production of both more living environment and a better one?

Given the assumption that change will come in response to the quantitatively and qualitatively enlarged demands outlined later in this chapter and by Ewald, we see three strategic and cumulative trends which will speed the rate of change in the structure and output of the building industry. While a host of lesser trends must also be considered (some of them in the "unexpected" or nonforecastable category), most seem likely to be tactical changes subsumed under these overriding forces:

1. Science and technology will have a major and dramatic impact on the internal structure, management, and methods of operation of the building industry over the next fifteen years; thereafter, perhaps, more impact on the "products" of the industry.

2. Public/private sector relations (government/industry) will become more coordinated and positive as accord is reached on many buildings goals, planning policy issues, and on ways to minimize current constraints.

3. These factors, combined with additional pressure from market growth, shifting national priorities, and entry of organizations from outside the traditional building industry, will cause a scale-up in planning and building enterprise to encompass larger projects, longer planning time frames and more attention to human need, stress, and tolerance factors.

These three sets of forces *can* produce a radically different building industry in ten to twenty years. Given a relatively stable world political situation, continued economic growth, and social evolution rather than revolution in the United States, such an outcome seems likely. The central trends are already evident or experimentally underway.

However, the process of public policy formation is likely to set the timetable. Government actions, more than actions taken by the industry itself, will accelerate or decelerate the rate of change. If public decisions on priorities and areas of constraint (codes, zoning, land assembly, union practices, etc.) are not reached early in the 1970's, the industry will find it immeasurably more difficult to scale-up its organization structure to meet the market demands of the 1980's and beyond.

This is one way of stressing the multidimensional and fragmented but pervasive role of government in controlling the shape of the building industry. The various areas of public policy impact are discussed throughout this report and summarized later in this chapter. Rationalization of the many policy questions can occur either systematically, following the master logic of national building and environmental policy, or, more likely, can come about piecemeal, with a slower process of change resulting.

Since we can prejudge neither the order of decision-making which will take place in the political system nor the precise scale, thrust, and direction of the decisions to be reached, we have attempted to set out alternative routes to rationalization of each key issue.

Science and Technology

Science and technology will have a rapidly growing, nearly explosive impact on the industry's structure and methods of operation over the next fifteen or more years. Beyond that, technology may play a larger role in the ways it is conventionally viewed — as a generator of new materials and products, new structural engineering concepts, and new subsystem technologies (energy, waste handling, movement of people and goods, etc.). But the "shock front" impact will be more crucial within the industry — how it organizes, operates, and delivers — than to the character of its products. Technological impact will be most evident in four areas: intra-industry communications, management systems for the industry, interdisciplinary accord and collaboration, and growth of research and development on the industry and building process.

INTRA-INDUSTRY COMMUNICATIONS

The building industry is not immune from the general information explosion which is changing the character of all U.S. industry. A "backroom" problem something like that of the securities industry is developing in architectural and engineering offices as materials suppliers, contractors, clients, and government regulators supply or demand more options at each decision point in the building process. Unlike the brokerage firms, however, those in the building industry have few sophisticated information systems in place to handle the growing volume of communication transactions which must take place. To make matters worse, the building industry does not have a formal structure of information flow, comparable to the securities industry, on which to build new systems.

This appears to be one area where rapid change is predictable with certainty: during the next ten to twelve years, information systems will be created to link both functions and actors within the building industry on a scale approaching a national information utility. Automation of virtually all information intensive activities in the industry will be made possible and profitable by fourth generation computer technology which should cut computing costs by three orders of magnitude in the mid-70's. This development should be well timed to permit rapid implementation on an industrywide scale of systems which are now experimental or limited to single-firm use. Some examples of the trend are:

1. *Specification Production:* A study[3] last year for the Construction Specifications Institute identified 27 partially or fully automated systems already in use by private firms. These range from simple automatic typewriter systems to several tied into larger computer systems which can automatically handle both job modifications and related design decision factors. The same study indicated that perhaps a quarter of all design engineering firms were exploring such systems to cope with specification writing — the major communications message format of the industry. While most present systems are being developed by major firms for their own use, the "information utility" concept is already being tried: Master Systems Corporation in Dallas provides small architectural and engineering firms with on-line terminals tied to a central master specification file.

2. *Master Inventory and Delivery:* The burgeoning growth of new building materials and premanufactured component systems provides another area ripe for automation. As a first step, one New York firm is now offering architects a library maintenance service to guarantee that their supplier catalog collections and technical reference materials will be up to date. Other information service firms are exploring the market for on-line computerized data banks containing systematically arranged materials to supply data. Ideally, such a system would include cost, inventory, and delivery time data and thus provide a complete set of materials and component options for a given requirement, as well as a direct ordering/billing capability. If the system were keyed to performance criteria rather than materials categories, its user value would increase substantially. This futuristic

CREATING THE HUMAN ENVIRONMENT

conception, however, obviously has some important hurdles to cross: Who vouches for manufacturer's claims? Who is responsible for the consequences of delivery estimate errors?

3. *Design Engineering Systems:* Many efforts are under way to cut engineering design costs and enrich productivity of design time by automation of information storage and retrieval, engineering calculation, and design simulation. Most engineering firms already have a battery of such tools available; some are moving toward systems which tie together logic-based calculations and analysis programs with new graphic display and communication devices. The next stage will be closer man-machine collaboration systems probably incorporating public (utility supplied) programs, programs proprietary to the design firm and, finally, a designer's "personal thesaurus" of design shorthand and concepts. Given this possibility, automated design support systems can clearly free the architect somewhat from current time and work limitations and permit increased output volume and/or more exploration of alternatives for each design task.

These are three of the obvious areas for rapid development of automation affecting the design phase of the building process. (Other such developments are outlined in Table II-2 and discussed in Chapter 5 on construction technology.) They point toward an era when design and decision data will be under much better control for the building industry with proprietary concepts and analytic techniques carefully separated from the pool of information which will meet common needs of the industry.

A crucial question then is who will develop, own, and control the pieces of this information utility? So far the development task is being shared by major design and engineering firms — working individually with computer hardware and software companies — by at least one trade association, and by private researchers. If land use, code, and zoning data are to be a part of the information pool, it is likely that government will share in the systems development work as well — probably through HUD, National Bureau of Standards and, perhaps, metropolitan planning agencies as data suppliers.

Yet overall it appears most likely that the utility system (or systems) we are projecting will develop and remain a part of the private sector with service bureau networks leasing equipment and computing time for such functions as is now done for accounting and payroll procedures. A more important question probably is whether "owner-

166

TABLE II-1. *A 1985 Information Utility: Candidate Blue Sky Missions*

· *Land use map service* — computer graphic printouts of area plans providing current and/or projected utility systems, transport systems, socio-economic profiles, building types and zoning, pollution sources and restrictions, and other aspects of land use.

· *National performance standards* — regional variations and local veto/approval for materials usage geared to a national code with on-line inquiry and response to planning and enforcement officials.

· *Financing availability* — cross ties with financial data processing systems to provide a computerized "over-the-counter" market in development capital and debt financing.

· *National multiple-listing service* — a universal listing service for the real estate share of the building industry; land and structures by type, location, cost range, ownership, etc. The National Association of Real Estate Brokers is actively promoting a prototype system now.

· *Design concepts data bank* — an intellectronics library for designers equivalent to those being developed for law (ASPEN system) or medicine (MEDLARS), storing design concepts and solutions as opposed to design engineering methodologies.

· *United engineering information system* — a proposal to merge various existing and planned public and private engineering data retrieval systems under a COMSAT-type management is already being pushed by the Engineers Joint Council and other groups.

---

ship" will rest with neutral service corporations or with giant firms now a part of or entering the construction market themselves. If the latter course is followed, proprietary control of such systems could represent an entrepreneurial asset second only to talent in maneuvering for market position.

MANAGEMENT SYSTEMS FOR THE INDUSTRY

The evolving information utility we have discussed is part of a larger trend in the building industry toward more use of comprehensive and sophisticated management systems to control cost, time, quality, and profitability. Some of the specific techniques relevant here are covered in the technology section later in this report. They range from established control procedures such as PERT and Critical Path Scheduling, which apply to the actual construction phase, to major shifts which appear to be developing in the ways building projects are conceived, planned, and executed from start to finish.

Functions within the building process seem to be shifting both in time order and in who performs them. The project initiation phase for large developments appears to be growing more complex with a greater part of the analysis and decision-making completed before the design team is turned loose. Supporting this trend — or helping to create it — are new analytic tools for determining return on investment, optimum use patterns, and construction phasing as it relates to marketing schedules.

More and more the designer is presented with a predetermined program which limits his role in some respects ("don't concern yourself with alternative site uses"), but liberates him in others ("we know we need this use pattern or end product mix; what is the optimal configuration and design?").

In the next decade, such role shifts may develop much more rapidly, with much of the pressure coming from new actors entering the building industry who bring analytical tools and analysts with them from their home industries. This is probably the most important form of technological change shaping the industry. Outsiders may have as striking an influence on its future shape and control as the arrival of synthetic fibers had on the traditional textile industry — another classic case of invasion by those who possess higher technology.

In its broadest sense, "systems management" is coming to the building industry. Although the term is a fuzzy one even in the defense and aerospace industries where it originated, systems management is probably the best way to sum up the influx of new techniques which are leading to reapportionment and rationalization of building industry functions. For example, should the contractor order materials for a project or should the architect (as is the case in Britain)? Should the architect, general contractor, or subcontractors be responsible for detailing a mechanical subsystem and its ultimate performance? Should the manufacturer of materials component and equipment systems take over the traditional subcontractor role of installation? These and a host of other jurisdictional questions relating to functional responsibilities in the building process are likely to receive closer attention in the next few years. Under a systems management approach, the conclusions reached may well alter traditional roles to a much greater extent than most designers now foresee.

Most of the tools are already familiar in other contexts: capital budgeting, decision analysis, simulation and program budgeting, or PPBS (Program Planning and Budgeting Systems) which constitutes the latest attempt to bring federal agency goals, missions, resources, and policies into clearer perspective. Systems analysis — another loosely used term — is also a methodology which becomes more relevant to the building industry as projects become larger and more complex.

Government's increasing involvement in the building industry may speed up the application of such techniques. For example, the New Communities program (established under Title IV of the 1968 Housing Act) has already attracted proposals from twenty-two private developers and expressions of interest from eighty more. For such large-scale public investments, the control procedures established by HUD will undoubtedly call for elaborate applications of program budgeting, return on investment, and other factors. Ultimately it is clear that the industry will adopt these techniques because they *do* improve management control and profits.

INTERDISCIPLINARY COLLABORATION

New management systems — largely imported from other industries — will have a profound effect on the vertical structuring of the building process. The resultant change will concern roles played by various actor groups in the step-by-step logic of conceive/plan/build.

It appears equally likely that the industry will be just as strongly affected by expanding relationships with other professions. Social and behavioral science based groups, as well as "environmentalists" based in the natural sciences and engineering, are preparing to move in greater numbers into the arena of physical environment design. The cautious growth of such interdisciplinary collaboration has been evident for at least five years. This growth has been motivated by the following:

1. Movement of federal R&D and planning support toward broader discipline involvement in urban and environmental planning.

2. Private sector experiments such as Rouse's use of behavioral planners in programming the Columbia, Maryland, New Town project.

3. Creation of new research and professional services groups offer-

ing "social engineering" as well as traditional economic and physical planning consultation.

4. Growing pressure from federal domestic agencies to factor social and environmental dimensions into larger scale project planning, the most ambitious being the HUD Model Cities Program.

5. Exhortation by Congress, professional groups, and notables from many fields to develop a "total ecology" approach to physical planning.

6. Societal pressures for more citizen participation in the planning process, requiring both a translator/interpreter role by social engineers and new institutional forms to act as clients or advisors.

Certainly, designers and constructors have long sought advice from specialists in other fields on acceptance and marketability factors for their products. But this collaborative process now seems ready to take a more formal, permanent, and important place in building industry decision-making as well as in formation of national planning policies.

The rate at which such collaboration accelerates will depend on both how fast money flows into research and integrated planning programs from government, foundations, suppliers, private developers, and professional associations and the success of current experiments measured against profitability and public acceptance.

RESEARCH AND DEVELOPMENT

No one knows how many dollars or man-years are being invested today in research and development relevant to building industry operations and products. Data on expenditures are hopelessly clouded by poor definitions and scattering of industry segments throughout the various R&D expenditure accounting systems. Yet several points are clear:

1. Much more research is done on materials and products which go into building than on either construction technology or on the other aspects of the total building process (finance, land assembly, management). Probably $300 to $400 million per year is currently devoted to building-related product R&D, virtually all of it by manufacturers and producers of primary building products.

2. The federal government, which will spend about $17 billion on all types of R&D in fiscal year 1970, may devote $30 million of that

(by the most generous definition) to work directly relevant to the building industry.

3. Recent research under both government and private support has begun to clarify where research investment is most needed — the areas of high potential payoff. Most of these are areas of current constraint in the building process (finance, land assembly, codes, etc.) rather than construction technology.

4. Government R&D expenditures in this area, while still small, are rising quickly; at least a tenfold increase in building-related federal R&D to $300 to $400 million before 1980 is probable with $1 to $3 billion being spent in 1985.

5. Building-related private R&D expenditures will also expand rapidly as research-oriented firms prepare to move into building markets from other industry bases.

6. Probably a majority of the building-related research investments before 1985 will be social and behavioral science based (economics and management science, sociology, political science, social psychology). Therefore, the pendulum may swing toward the life and physical sciences and engineering as more emphasis goes toward preservation and restoration of the total environment.

7. A large share of the investment over the next fifteen years is likely to go toward development of management information systems, thus helping to create the information utility system described earlier.

8. There is a current shortage of both institutions and individual researchers equipped to contribute to the build-up of the project R&D volume, thus indicating continued quality and efficiency problems until new organizations and professional groups mature.

Do we conclude from this that the overworked space program analogy holds for the building industry: i.e., "any nation which can send man to the moon in 10 years can certainly rebuild America in 25!" Probably not. The twenty-year taxpayer investment in space is likely to reach $100 billion by 1980 — roughly half of it R&D as opposed to operations. By comparison, a $1 billion investment in building industry related R&D seems a much closer estimate for the next decade with perhaps tens of billions spent between 1985 and 2000.

Government R&D policy is at least as subject to the issue-oriented political process as any other portion of government spending. The fragmented character of the U.S. building industry, which is reflected in an uncoordinated lobbying approach toward the national government, means that most of its problems and constraints are considered only indirectly as parts of more pressing issues confronting Congress and the Executive branch. Hence, global issues such as the "urban crisis" tend to subsume and obscure real issues. Table II-2 attempts to show where related building industry questions may appear in such an issue hierarchy. It is possible that second-order issues such as "low income housing needs" or "congestion" may move to the forefront in years ahead causing a dramatic change in R&D allocation; but questions of codes, zoning, and investment finance tend to have little natural glamour.

It is more likely that the growth of research on the building industry, its problems and opportunities will continue to be supported

TABLE II-2.

NATIONAL ISSUE	POLITICAL ISSUES	RESEARCH TARGETS	ALTERNATE RESOLUTIONS

Urban Development Crisis

- poverty
  - low income housing
    - rent or ownership subsidies
    - more public housing
- pollution
  - breathing space
  - congestion/concentration
  - SST/airport noise
    - new communities
    - new land policies
    - new transport concepts
    - national airport plan
- participation
  - new institutions
  - ownership/management
    - urban development corporations
    - local housing partnerships

Rural Development

- population dispersal
  - slowdown megalopolis growth
    - income maintenance policies
- suburban sprawl
  - land costs integration
    - new communities
- rural decline
  - services/amenities
  - growth center plans
    - new TVA concepts
    - adjusted tax scales

through fragmented channels for most of the 1970's with strong coordination or "systems management" applied only after 1980. This means that the performance of R&D is also likely to remain fragmented, shared among great numbers of private, independent and public sector institutions (universities, research institutes, builder-developer consortia, etc.).

In the definitional terms of this report, the spectrum of research involved is extremely broad. Some work, such as that done by the Building Systems group at National Bureau of Standards, has impact on the building industry directly. Other research, however, is much less clearly relevant in an immediate sense.

For example, those convinced that stronger market control will ultimately be necessary if industrialized building systems are to flourish in this country, as they have in Europe, are carefully watching the progress of three large-scale demonstration projects (described in Table II-3). Other such plans are waiting in line for public support if these programs succeed. They hope that a pattern will be established for (1) government support of demonstrations, (2) subsequent policy revision (codes, zoning, etc.) followed by (3) commercialization through private sector channels.

Perhaps more important, but less obviously related, is the growing research on such issues as income maintenance. If some form of guaranteed annual income should be implemented over the next few years, the requirement for low income housing might change drastically. Similarly, a new and massive home ownership program could also cause radical shifts in current housing-demand projections.

Table II-4 identifies some of the major areas of research focus expected in the years ahead. Each has links to the building industry, to its markets and products which are extremely complex. The list does offer, however, some framework for considering both the type of research community which will evolve and the possible relationship of new and old participants in the building industry to the "contract research market" as a possibly attractive form of diversification.

Public Policy

A major contention of this report is that relations between government and industry will become more positive as accord is reached on many building goals, on planning policy issues, and on ways to minimize current constraints.

173

TABLE II-3. *The Demonstration Approach:*
Three Market Assembly Experiments

Three examples show the range of market assembly techniques which can lead to government guarantees of "underwriting" of new construction systems and the types of organization relationships involved:

1. *School Construction Systems Development* — The now classic "SCSD project" led by architect Ezra Ehrenkrantz at Stanford since the early sixties, has (1) created a market block of 30 school districts pooling their future building requirements, (2) developed performance standards for basic construction systems, (3) led five manufacturers to design component systems for construction, investing their own R&D funds, and (4) begun building schools using the chosen systems at cost savings of approximately one-third. Architects, educational planners and psychologists were the central collaborators, but market innovation has been the central theme. Initial support came from the Ford Foundation.

2. *HUD In-City Low Income Housing Demonstration* — Kaiser Engineers won a competitive contract in 1968 to study, develop, design, construct and test "several thousand" low-income housing units in up to 20 model-city neighborhoods. This project, which involves market guarantee aspects by government, may well be a forerunner of more direct federal involvement in shaping the markets needed for valid tests of industrialized housing systems. In addition to its own interdisciplinary project staff, Kaiser has important subcontracts with social engineering firms to review neighborhood dynamics, client desires and priorities.

3. *Military Housing Systems Construction* — A Defense Department program, closely assisted by the National Bureau of Standards, to use a controlled market — the requirement for 6000 units per year of military base housing — to test building systems concepts on a national scale. General Electric, architect Carl Koch, and a third consortium studied the market opportunity and submitted competing solutions. DOD hopes to start building soon with a system which combines the best ideas of all three systems, but is heavily tied to the GE concept of near-site factory production of components.

The building industry is not a "regulated industry" in the formal sense of the airlines, railroads, drug industry, or the securities business. The building industry has no Securities and Exchange Commission, Food and Drug Administration, or Interstate Commerce Commission equivalent of its own. Instead, it must attend to the rules, regulations, and policies of 20 to 30 federal departments, agencies, and commis-

TABLE II-4. *Possible Areas for Heavy Public R&D Investment Relevant to Building*

1970 to 1985	*1985 to 2000*
Organization of technical information	Behavioral design research
Management information systems	National land use planning
	Ecology
Buildup of relevant professional skills	Social values
	Retirement and leisure
Large building market control demonstrations	Lifetime education renewal
	Open space development
New communities	Climate control
Citizen participation	Life support for alien environments (undersea, arctic, space)
Ownership/financing mechanisms	
Zoning rationalization	Human intelligence augmentation
National performance codes	
Conversion to metric system	
Environmental pollution	
Intergovernmental relations	

sions as well as 5000 to 10,000 state, local, and regional government agencies which share "control" of the industry and its market.

The best recent count of federal grant-in-aid programs, totalling about 1150 separately administered assistance programs, includes more than 150 which provide funds or technical assistance relating in some way to physical planning and construction. Many more are of indirect concern to the building industry because they help regulate labor and money supply or other factors crucial to construction. Thus, some diversified builders today must be nearly as expert in "grantsmanship" as a mayor or city manager.

If Congress or the President cuts construction funds for education by $175 million (as proposed for fiscal year 1970), the impact on the school building market is substantial. If Washington succeeds in opening craft unions to larger minority participation, backed up by new job training programs and subsidies, the impact on labor availability for construction may be even more important. If the governors succeed in winning a larger role for state government in urban development, the building industry again may be strongly affected by changing policies and decision channels.

The fact is that government is a part of the building industry today, involved in the building process as client, "designer," land owner, financier, and regulator in uncountable direct and indirect ways. Assuming government is here to stay — to the end of the century and beyond, how will its multidimensional relationships with the building process change? Will shifting public policy bring more government control or less? More rational, coordinated control, or further fragmentation? Will the building industry ever have its own SEC?

Specific trends, much less specific answers, are very difficult to define. Yet many isolated factors seem to point to a gradual improvement in the overall climate of relations between government and the building industry, based on better coordinated policy and planning on both sides. The following is evidence of this:

1. Management science is affecting government and inter-governmental relations as it is the building industry. In the next decade this should bring about rationalization and simplification of grants-in-aid programs and their associated decision-making apparatus (Why should eighteen separate clearance points be required for a building innovation in New York City?); some consolidation of geographic jurisdictional lines for various programs, policies, and authorities; and better tools for predicting and controlling the money markets which underlie construction.

2. Government policy studies are becoming more sophisticated, longer range in outlook, and broader in coverage. Both internal study groups and special Presidential commissions (where policy breakthroughs are often pioneered) are better staffed and funded than a few years ago and appear to build on each other with more continuity. This process is likely to continue with shortening lag times on White House and Congressional implementation.

3. The political issues tied most closely to building (urban decay, low income housing, population dispersal) are all "growth issues." Short of global disaster, they will continue to breed pressure for shifts in national priorities favoring more construction.

4. Information systems technology (and much lower cost computing power) may well make it possible to decentralize and reapportion more government decision-making to regional levels. The growing strength of Councils of Government, which are now established in 144 metropolitan areas, makes them obvious targets for newly consolidated governing functions before 1985.

5. Government policy decisions on conglomerate mergers can have a profound effect on the organizational change in the building industry and on the fate of the giants now entering it. Since scale-up of operations seems crucial to meet increased building demand, it seems likely that some "optimum compromise" or friendly solution on building-oriented conglomerates will be worked out.

6. If present government experiments in building market assembly succeed (e.g., military base housing, Model Cities housing, "Project Breakthrough"), this form of "control" is likely to be used on a far larger scale in the 1975-1985 period.

7. Similarly, the success of the National Housing Partnership concept as a new form of government/industry collaboration can lead to its expansion into other areas of public building.

8. It is also apparent that definitions of "public buildings" are gradually broadening to include more and varied types of service-cultural-amenities structures (e.g., Neighborhood Facilities centers) and "private buildings" which serve public functions (private hospitals; nursing homes, colleges, research centers) which are receiving both direct and indirect federal subsidies for construction. We expect this trend to continue.

9. Finally, our forecast of greatly increased federal investment in R&D on the building industry and its processes and products should lead to better understanding and closer acquaintanceship on both sides. As government invests in development of building-related technology and information systems, awareness of issues and problems should grow much sharper.

These trends all point toward increased ties between government and the building industry. But they also portend better organized and coordinated relationships. On the industry side, this should include a more forceful and directed lobbying effort in Washington where about 200 union, professional, and trade associations now present a disorganized, fragmented and weak forum for discussion. In our view, it

TABLE II-5.

ISSUE: *Building Codes*. The Douglas Commission found that of 4067 units of local government with population over 5000 surveyed, 80% had a building code. About half (53%) "substantially incorporated" a national or regional model code; 15% were "based" on such a code. Eighteen per cent were based on a state model code; 12% were not related to any code, and in the remaining cases (3%) any relationship to a model code was unclear or not reported. (In addition, many of the jurisdictions reported separate plumbing and electrical codes.)

Key Federal Agencies Concerned: HUD, especially FHA; National Bureau of Standards, Building Research Division; National Academy of Sciences, Building Research Advisory Board (BRAB).

Other Key Groups Concerned: Entire construction industry, especially the generators of the four major model codes — the Basic Building Code (Building Official's Conference of America), the Uniform Building Code (International Conference of Building Officials), the Southern Standard Building Code, and the National Building Code (American Insurance Association). These groups will probably be the leading edge of the industry's pressure for more rationalized procedures.

Alternate Solutions in Current Thinking:
Shift to performance rather than materials code.
Shift to national code, again based on performance rather than materials.
Shift to regional codes, perhaps overseen by Regional Councils of Government, with overriding jurisdiction in area covered.
Imposition of federal building codes on all federally-assisted construction.
State regulation of factory-built components and systems at factory rather than on-site with just an occupancy permit required locally.

ISSUE: *Zoning* (see pp. 204-210). Nearly 10,000 governmental units now have regulatory powers over land-use including some 5000 jurisdictions within metropolitan areas. These ordinances usually cover at least the following:

(Continued)

seems likely that centralization of building policies and programs in fewer government agencies (with perhaps nearly all consolidated under HUD or a succcessor agency by 1985) will be matched by emergence of one or more new supersized "associations of associations" along the lines of the National Security Industrial Association (NSIA) which plays this role in relation to defense industries.

Indeed one of the more intriguing and far-reaching recommendations of the Kaiser Commission calls for HUD to fund creation of a national "Association for Urban Technology." The concept is that

178

TABLE II-5. (*Continued*)

---

activities or uses (i.e., dwellings, business, or industry); population density; building bulk; off-street parking. The conventional pattern of zoning regulations has been local self-executing, and negative, although allowing for change through appeals, variances, special exceptions, and amendments. Zoning has often been used to keep out people (blacks, poor) as well as activities which are thought to depress property values.

Key Federal Agencies Concerned: HUD, Department of Commerce, Civil Rights Commission, Small Business Administration, Advisory Commission on Intergovernmental Relations.

Other Key Groups Concerned: Planners, developers, real estate operators, businessmen, builders, local and regional public bodies, and private special interest groups.

Alternate Solutions in Current Thinking:

Performance standard; e.g., odor limits, rather than a ban on all paint plants.

Planned unit development; i.e., instead of lot-by-lot requirements, apply specifications to entire or area development.

Conditional rezoning to make certain that applicants carry through their stated intentions for the property.

Zoning ordinances controlled by Regional Councils of Government or state agencies with overriding jurisdiction in area covered.

ISSUE: *Urban Renewal* (see pp. 204-210). The innercity is overcrowded, dilapidated, and losing its tax base as established businesses and middle-income families move out, leaving only new businesses in the ghettoes and the poor. Supermarkets, department stores, light industries are concentrating on establishing outlets and factories in suburbs rather than in the ghetto. Urban renewal has historically meant "Negro removal." Residents displaced by meager attempts at renewal cannot afford to move into replacement or rehabilitated

---

(Continued)

urban development, centering on building industry technology, needs to build a communication and information transfer system comparable to the elaborate professional journal system, professional society structure and network of data systems which physical scientists now enjoy.

The policy-making processes and general trends discussed above are some of the parameters which help filter the prospects for change on particular issues of concern to the building industry.

Table II-5 sets out some of these direct issues in context — the

TABLE II-5. (*Continued*)

housing without some kind of subsidy. Ghettoes are first areas to be disturbed by freeways, recreational parks, etc.

Key Federal Agencies Concerned: HUD

Alternate Solutions in Current Thinking:

Fuller's "floating city" concept where residents could be relocated while their dilapidated housing was renewed.

Temporary housing, perhaps made of paper, or quickly assembled factory produced mobile units for same purpose.

Income support programs (e.g., "guaranteed annual income"; reverse income-tax concepts).

Rental or home ownership support programs reaching lower-income groups than present FHA or VA standards.

Federal acquisition of land for federally assisted or wholly supported housing in the central cities (e.g., through Model Cities or Project Breakthrough).

Economic development to create jobs and satisfy consumer needs for those remaining in central cities, coupled with aggressive efforts to encourage migration for some to "New Towns" and existing suburbs.

Formation of neighborhood development corporations with some powers pertaining to zoning, condemnation, inspection of neighborhood properties.

Advocacy planning.

Short-cutting or abolishing the craft union apprenticeship system so that central city residents could derive income from rebuilding of the central cities.

ISSUE: *Relocation/Integration.* The cost of housing in both established suburbs and "New Towns" eliminates low- and moderate-income families. (Average price of a new home at Reston is currently $34,000. Rouse has yet

(Continued)

current situation, principal groups and policy-makers concerned and some possible routes to resolution. We have not attempted to set specific dates or priorities; all in our view are relatively short-term, immediate problems which need some degree of resolution now. However, we can safely predict that if no substantial progress is made on these issues in the early or mid-70's, then the timetable for the scale-up of building industry operations and output discussed in the final part of this chapter will be badly set back.

If politics and policy-making were not "process," but a simpler

TABLE II-5. (*Continued*)

to construct any low-cost housing at Columbia.) "New Towns" seem especially attractive as a solution to relocation of some ghetto residents, but the basic problem is the same as in the suburbs — housing is too expensive, even though self-contained communities would provide jobs for some residents. Some aggressive attempts are being made to encourage middle-income blacks to move into the suburbs. There are numerous private fair housing groups operating in these areas. The Ford Foundation has just given $200,000 to a Washington, D.C., group to help their efforts to move blacks who can afford it into existing suburban communities.

Key Federal Agencies Concerned: HUD, Veterans Administration, DOT.

Alternate Solutions in Current Thinking:

Federal dollars involved in New Towns can be made contingent on commitment to build housing for low- and moderate-income families. (Some see a danger that this could lead again to subsidizing segregated housing, as occurred in the extension of FHA and VA guarantees to consumers and loans to builders of Levitt-like subdivisions which were allowed to discriminate — and did.)

Aggressive public/private cooperative efforts to convince blacks who can now presently afford it, to try the suburbs and New Towns, especially when they already have jobs in these areas. Suitable candidates for this consortia would be the Equal Opportunities Division of HUD, AIA, AIP, NAREB, the life insurance industry, etc. as well as volunteer groups.

ISSUE: *Tight Money* (see pp. 195-203). Several major capital sources have relatively low participation rates in providing funds to the construction industry, notably time deposits of commercial banks, life insurance, and pension funds. Many investments more attractive; construction most sensitive to inflation.

(*Continued*)

kind of yes/no binary system, then the building industry could simply push a "yes" or "no" button after each of the 300 or so policy recommendations set forth by the Kaiser and Douglas Commissions. These considered recommendations cover most of the short-range alternatives which can lead to longer range strategies for rebuilding both America and the building industry.

But public policy is "process." There is no such button. And there is no clear building industry consensus on the "how's" and "why's" of resolving most of these issues.

TABLE II-5. (*Continued*)

Key Federal Agencies Concerned: HUD, Federal Reserve Board, Federal Home Loan Board and related apparatus, Farmers Home Administration, Veterans Administration, Council of Economic Advisors, Department of Commerce.

Other Key Groups Concerned: Entire building industry and the public.

Alternative Solutions in Current Thinking:

Eliminate tax exemptions on real estate owned by nonprofit groups.

Control inflation by fiscal and monetary policy manipulation.

Guarantee market through federal subsidy directly to builders.

Guarantee mortgages unequivocally.

Federal guarantees extended aggressively to short-term construction loans.

ISSUE: *Land Cost* (see pp. 204-210). Increasing scarcity of vacant land in urban areas adds growing cost of raw land and land development. In residential sector, land component as percentage of combined building and land costs equals 28% in 1968; 45% projected to the year 2000.

Key Federal Groups Concerned: HUD, USDA, Department of Interior, Department of Commerce.

Other Key Groups Concerned: All segments of the construction industry, especially those engaged in the land acquisition and development phase, conservation groups, the public, state and local departments of finance and taxation.

Alternative Solutions in Current Thinking:

Tax land on real value, not present use.

Remove tax-exempt status of real estate held by various nonprofit groups (e.g., 34% of midtown New York property has this tax-exempt status).

Accelerate sale of federally owned land in urban areas. (Perhaps a better idea would be for the federal government to lease this land to local,

---

(*Continued*)

Scale-up and the "Mega-Builders"

The third theme which emerges from a broad review of building industry trends is one of growing pressures on operational scale. There appears to be a nearly compulsive desire by many actors, new and old, to break through an invisible barrier standing firmly in the way of scale-up — to larger projects, more complex ones and longer time frames.

The innovators rush the wall and are repelled. What is the barrier? It is not simply a change resistant marketplace. Nor is it simply

TABLE II-5. (*Continued*)

---

regional or state public or quasi-public development bodies, thus retaining right to impose federal standards on codes, use, occupancy, etc.)

Greater use of "air rights."

Develop open spaces and new communities.

Increase construction of high-rise residential units, currently accounting for about one-fifth of multi-unit housing starts. (N.B. Although high-rise construction decreases land cost per unit, increased building cost quickly takes up the slack.)

Accelerate reclamation and conservation of urban fringe land to be used for recreation and parking, to free up valuable in-town sites for more pressing uses.

ISSUE: *Construction Manpower Cost/Availability/Efficiency* — In the MRI survey of the literature, manpower problems were cited most often as a principal constraint to a breakthrough in either methods, costs, or time of construction. Some surveys say construction worker productivity is low and decreasing (E.g., *The Economic Report of the President and the Council of Economic Advisers for 1968* showed a 0.3% decline in construction labor productivity from 1959 to 1966. A study done for the Association of General Contractors has a preliminary estimate of a 6% decrease in productivity over the past six years). Others, however, disagree; a study by Christopher Sims for the Kaiser Committee shows an annual average rate of *increase* of 2.3% since 1947. There is strong feeling and some evidence that construction manpower, through its unions, does have practices and policies which restrict the number of new entries into its force and which hamper innovations in methods, materials, and processes which might speed up projects or lead to off-site fabrication. The Kaiser Committee seems to feel that some outcries against labor are too strong; often new techniques/materials have not been used for fear that the unions will react without ever directly approaching them. Recent Supreme Court decisions seem to leave the way open for unions to continue to

---

(*Continued*)

John Hersey's "Wall" of indifference and fear transplanted to America. It is a wall at the face of the shock front which consists of all the issues and constraints discussed earlier (and displayed in Table II-5). These specific issues now receiving attention tend to be symptomatic. The basic issues go much deeper.

No one can chart the precise underpinnings of our current national dilemma, although the Ewald report sets out many of the warning signals and attitudinal trends. Perhaps the wonderful Mobius Strip best expresses the through-the-looking-glass and circular nature of the

TABLE II-5. (*Concluded*)

guard against use of prefabricated parts, etc., in violation of union contracts. Seasonality of projects and thus employment lead to the paradox of high hourly wages but low annual income. The Kaiser Committee found that of workmen who report earnings in construction, only slightly more than half received the major portion of their income from that industry. The fact that the building trade unions are organized along craft rather than industrial lines means that contractors have to deal with as many as two dozen unions on any one job.

Key Federal Agencies Concerned: HUD; Department of Labor, Office of Federal Contract Compliance, Manpower Development and Training Administration, OEO, Civil Rights Commission, Equal Employment Opportunity Commission.

Other Key Groups Concerned: Civil rights and civil liberties groups, builders, contractors, building trades unions.

Alternative Solutions in Current Thinking:

Switch from on-site construction to factory production of components and buildings.

Encouragement, through lead of federal government, which accounts for about one-third of construction, to year-round letting of construction contracts with special incentives for winter building.

Abolition or modification of apprentice systems.

Portable pension and fringe benefit packages to get workers to move where there is work.

Improvement of construction process management through techniques such as PERT and CPM to eliminate piecemeal instructions which now lead to "stand-around time."

Compensation on annual contract basis, rather than hourly, seasonal wages.

Organization of manpower on industrial, rather than craft, basis.

---

wall. When the dominant values of the two cultures are intertwined, as in Figure II-2, the "tactical" issues we discuss in this report come into some strategic focus.

But a review of the current problems, trends, and potential of these issues leads to our central conclusion: The building industry is moving toward a classic industry configuration. Fragmentation will be gradually replaced by coherence and cohesiveness.

Why?

The dominant pressures today are threefold: (1) general eco-

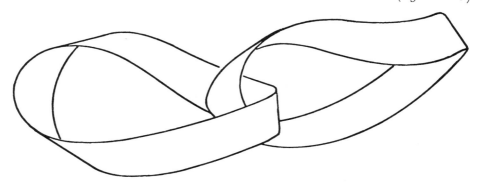

AFFLUENCE   EDUCATION
INFLATION   EMPLOYMENT
ALIENATION   INCOME MAINTENANCE
INNER CITY DECAY   HOUSING
SUBURBAN SPRAWL   HEALTH

FIGURE II-2. *Two Cultures: A Mobius View*

nomic/efficiency measures, (2) housing requirements for the whole population, and (3) the new or renewed physical environment demanded by a people with rising affluence and rising expectations.

The process of scale-up to larger and longer term building projects seems to us likely to be well developed by the end of the 1970's and should encompass an increasing share of the total building market through the following decade.

The trends supporting this conclusion are discussed throughout the report. Perhaps the simplest one is sheer growth of market demand for new structures which is summarized in the building forecast section at the end of this chapter. Another, subtler force is the realignment of industry structure and practices being caused by new management and building technology.

Two other trends need to be summarized here: (1) the new large-scale builders and (2) the new large-scale clients. Both appear to be needed if substantial scale-up is to occur. Both appear likely.

The large-scale building combines of the future — "macro-" or "mega-builders" in the terminology of this report — represent the major organizational manifestation of innovation by invasion. Virtually all include one or more corporate entities with a traditional base outside the building industry, and most have and will continue to have major nonconstruction components.

From a MRI survey of approximately 100 new actors (individual companies, conglomerates, joint ventures) now planning or engaged in building projects, a representative selection is listed in Appendix Table A-2 (p. 247). They are divided into four groupings which set out the principal motives and avenues for exploration of building markets by "outsiders."

1. *Conglomerates.* There are two basic varieties. The first is classic conglomerates such as ITT and Gulf and Western who are moving into the industry through direct acquisition of builders or through creation of building/developer subsidiaries. The second group is principally ad hoc partnerships combining firms with major resources in land, finance, materials, design, and construction. The recently announced joint venture activity of Aetna Life, Kaiser Industries, and Kaiser Aluminum and Chemical suggests the total project leverage or capability which such a giant combine might exercise.

2. *Vertical Integrators.* Most of the conglomerate giants are oriented toward horizontal integration of building functions. A second group are more directed toward vertical integration of the building process from raw materials to finished structure, and are currently less involved with the land, planning, and financial aspects of building. Boise-Cascade, not long ago primarily a lumber producer, now shows 40 per cent of its multi-hundred million annual sales as "shelter." Raw materials, products, product systems, mobile homes, and total housing projects are part of this housing-oriented approach by a rapidly growing giant.

3. *Asset Convertors.* Rails, insurance, and petroleum companies have vital assets in the form of land and money which are leading them to building growth markets as a major area for potential diversification. While such activity is not entirely new, it appears to be occurring on a stepped up scale. At least some of the asset converters are likely to team up with other major joint venture groups to form ad hoc conglomerates. Howard Hughes' acquisition of major underdeveloped land holdings in Nevada represents another classic form of asset conversion on a new scale.

4. *Product/Service Market Expanders.* Another group which sometimes overlaps with those above consists of manufacturers and service firms exploring ways to expand their leverage and hence in-

crease product sales to the building market. General Electric's three year study of new community building, now scaled back, was in part an attempt to analyze town building as an "appliance systems" market. How much of a total structure can be manufactured, sold, financed, and maintained as home appliances and automobiles now are? Many other manufacturers are exploring similar concepts, working from their particular product base. A number are experimenting in the low and moderate income housing market where such treatment is encouraged by government subsidy.

Along these four major avenues, or by combination routes, we expect to see a group of permanent mega-builders emerge over the next decade. The questions of "how soon" and "how many" are intimately linked to the other central issues in this report — particularly government policy on housing, finance and new community, or open space development.

Clearly, the advantages of mega-builder scale increase as project scale goes up. Figure II-3 suggests the dramatic S-curve relationship which ties together the wall of current constraints with building location. If public policy decisions favor the building of new cities and open space development ("What will Howard Hughes *do* with Nevada when he owns it?") in the time frame our chart suggests, then we can envision a handful of mega-builders (5 to 15 conglomerates) controlling a majority of the development.

But given continuation of current trends toward more megalopolitan concentration and prime governmental emphasis on inner-city redevelopment, it will be more difficult for the new giants to flex their real muscle.

"Project Breakthrough," the new mass housing development program of HUD, presents a middle ground prospect. The central emphasis is on large-scale market assembly; governors have been asked to identify scattered sites for thousands of housing units in their states. It is expected that innovative building systems will thus finally be given a large enough trial to measure economic effects accurately. But will the government choose one, two, three, or twenty development and building combines to produce the needed housing?
A very few such decisions will cause major shifts in the mega-builder timetable and strongly influence the total shape of the industry.

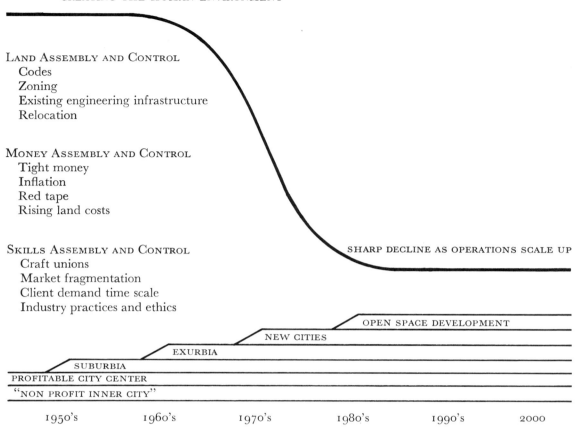

LAND ASSEMBLY AND CONTROL
   Codes
   Zoning
   Existing engineering infrastructure
   Relocation

MONEY ASSEMBLY AND CONTROL
   Tight money
   Inflation
   Red tape
   Rising land costs

SKILLS ASSEMBLY AND CONTROL   SHARP DECLINE AS OPERATIONS SCALE UP
   Craft unions
   Market fragmentation
   Client demand time scale
   Industry practices and ethics

OPEN SPACE DEVELOPMENT

NEW CITIES

EXURBIA

SUBURBIA

PROFITABLE CITY CENTER

"NON PROFIT INNER CITY"

1950's   1960's   1970's   1980's   1990's   2000

FIGURE II-3. *Constraints to Building Scale-up*

Clients for the Mega-Builders

Tradition has it that the landowner decides what is built and by whom on his acreage. That tradition is somewhat scarred and fading today. While the individual or corporate landholder is likely to remain the dominant client in absolute numbers through the rest of the century, other types of clients will play an ever larger part and may be of special consequence to the mega-builder. These will be both "interim" and permanent clients; some will be private but many are likely to be public or quasi-public in nature and commitment. Attempting to pinpoint actual private landholders who will be operating on a scale large enough to attract mega-builders attention would call for a de-

188

tailed review of real estate holdings and trends. There are few "Irvine Ranches" left intact.

Some of the major property holdings rest with, or are being assembled by, people already in the development business. (The Rouse Company assembled 1500 separate holdings over four years to develop Columbia, Maryland.) Some huge tracts are held by major industrial firms such as Ford and Chrysler who have yet to decide what role they may want to play in direct development. Others may only be assembled by government intervention and condemnation, even where private development will ensue.

It is again government action and public policy which is likely to set the basic patterns and determine the role of the mega-builders in development. Aside from the "Project Breakthrough" concept of market assembly which has already been mentioned, many other models for possible new forms of public or quasi-public clients exist. Some are:

1. *Local Housing Partnerships.* Both nonprofit and for profit development corporations are being established under the National Housing Partnership section of the 1968 Housing Act. Most will concentrate on low and moderate income housing (turnkey and conventional), but some will probably develop light industrial and service facilities as part of concentrated site programming.

2. *Urban Development Corporations.* On a larger scale, this type of institution may take over much of the actual public development and building process control function in existing cities with various profit-sharing and incentive fee arrangements being used. The New Jersey model is the most advanced with a statewide Urban Development Corporation now in operation which has strong management links to subsidiary Local Development Corporations in various cities. A similar, though more monolithic, development control agency is being established by Edward Logue in New York State.

3. *Advocate Planning Agencies.* The U.S. Office of Economic Opportunity favors a different approach in which planners and designers work with neighborhood residents to develop an acceptable plan. Some consideration is being given to allowing these groups to act as interim clients, controlling the building process for housing and other types of construction.

4. *The Regional COMSAT.* A logical future step may well create super-sized nonprofit or limited profit "public" corporations to plan

and control development and building for a major geographic region. The territory covered could be limited to a metropolitan area, or could encompass a multi-state region along the lines of the Tennessee Valley Authority. (Presently, the six Regional Commissions created under the Economic Development Act of 1965 view themselves as candidates for such a broad mission. So do a number of the stronger regional Councils of Government now established in 144 urban areas across the country.)

The only clear forecast to be made about such organizations today is that many new forms are likely to be tried before strong, tested patterns emerge. Such an era of experimentation in institutional change is likely to last through most of the 1970's.

Considering only those possibilities mentioned, however, it is clear that such new "client institutions" could encompass a multitude of functions relating to building. The TVA example, drawn from another era, suggests that the whole series of functions we term the building process might be involved — land assembly, planning, research, codes, zoning, finance, relocation and construction can all be affected or controlled to varying degrees by the institution chosen.

The Outlook for New Construction: 1970-2000

While the ultimate client forms and distribution are unclear, as are the market shares to be held by the Goliathan mega-builders versus the traditional David-sized independent builders, there is much building to be done.

The remainder of this chapter sets out our forecasts for building and construction markets on a segment-by-segment basis over the next thirty years.

Total expenditures for new construction, measured in terms of constant 1960 dollars, are expected to rise from their 1968 level of $65.6 billion to about $190 billion by the year 2000. This represents nearly a threefold gain, equivalent to an average compound growth rate of some 3.4 per cent annually.

Table II-6 shows the total expenditures by various construction categories for selected years over the 1955-2000 period. Again, all figures are in constant 1960 dollars.

Anticipated growth varies widely among the different classes of construction. In general, engineered construction (i.e., the "nonbuilding" categories listed in the table) is expected to grow at a slightly

TABLE II-6. *Total Expenditures for New Construction*
(billions of 1960 dollars)

	1955	*1960*	*1965*	*1968*	*1970*	*1985*	*2000*
Residential buildings							
Single-family dwellings	17.9	13.3	12.0	10.4	11.4	14.3	14.3
Multi-family dwellings	4.2	3.8	6.7	7.5	7.8	15.4	24.7
Additions & alterations	3.9	4.4	3.9	3.9	5.2	7.7	11.9
Nonhousekeeping units	0.4	0.9	1.3	1.1	1.5	2.6	4.6
Total	26.4	22.4	23.9	22.9	25.9	40.0	55.5
Private nonresidential buildings							
Industrial	2.8	2.9	4.6	4.4	5.6	10.2	10.8
Commercial	3.8	4.2	6.0	6.5	6.9	12.6	21.8
Religious	0.8	1.0	1.1	0.8	0.8	1.1	1.2
Educational	0.5	0.6	0.7	0.8	0.8	1.3	1.7
Hospital & institutional	0.5	0.6	1.2	1.2	1.3	2.4	3.6
Misc. buildings	0.6	0.9	1.2	1.0	1.5	3.3	6.3
Total	9.0	10.2	14.8	14.7	16.9	30.9	45.4
Private nonbuilding construction							
Public utilities	5.6	4.6	4.6	5.7	5.9	10.5	16.7
Other	2.2	1.6	1.4	1.4	1.5	2.2	4.3
Total	7.8	6.2	6.0	7.1	7.4	12.7	21.0
Public nonresidential buildings							
Educational	2.8	2.8	3.8	4.8	4.2	8.0	10.1
Hospital & institutional	0.4	0.4	0.5	0.6	0.5	0.7	0.8
Misc. buildings	1.8	1.6	2.2	2.3	2.9	5.1	7.0
Total	5.0	4.8	6.5	7.7	7.6	13.8	17.9
Public nonbuilding construction							
Highways & streets	5.1	5.4	6.4	8.5	8.6	16.6	25.3
Water & sewer	1.4	1.5	2.1	2.3	2.9	6.2	10.7
Other	2.9	3.5	3.5	2.4	5.2	9.4	13.8
Total	9.4	10.4	12.0	13.2	16.7	32.2	49.8
Total construction	57.6	54.0	63.2	65.6	74.5	129.6	189.6
Buildings	40.4	37.4	45.2	45.3	50.4	84.7	118.8
All other	17.2	16.6	18.0	20.3	24.1	44.9	70.8

higher rate than building construction, especially in the public sector encompassing highways, streets and roads, water supply and treatment plants, and wastewater and sewage treatment facilities. Annual growth rates for the major construction categories estimated for the 1970-1985 and 1985-2000 periods are summarized in Table II-7.

TABLE II-7. *Projected Average Annual Increase in New Construction*

(based on 1960 dollars)

Type of construction	Time period		
	1955-1970	*1970-1985*	*1985-2000*
Residential buildings	— 0.1	2.9	2.2
Private nonresidential buildings	4.3	4.1	2.6
Private nonbuilding construction	— 0.3	3.7	3.4
Public nonresidential buildings	2.8	4.1	1.8
Public nonbuilding construction	3.9	4.5	3.0
Total new construction	1.7	3.8	2.6
All buildings	1.5	3.5	2.3
All nonbuilding construction	2.3	4.2	3.1

Source: Projections by MRI

An average of about a million new households have been formed annually in the United States over the past twenty years. During the same period, an average of 1.6 million new housing units have been constructed each year (see Table II-8).

TABLE II-8. *Construction of New Housing Units* (1950-2000)

Year	New housing units (thousands)		
	Single-family	*Multi-family*	*Total*
1950	1600	352	1952
1955	1332	314	1646
1960	1009	287	1296
1965	965	545	1510
1968	898	645	1543
1970	955	655	1610
1985	1080	1170	2250
2000	1060	1840	2900

Source: Projections by MRI

During the 1970-1985 period, there will be about 18 million new households formed, resulting in a demand for about 30 million new housing units. Between 1985 and 2000, 26 million new households will be formed, accompanied by the construction of about 38 million new housing units of all types.

Based on these projections of new household formations, an estimated 1.6 million new housing units will be built in 1970; 2.3 million in 1985; and 2.9 million in 2000.

In terms of constant dollars, the cost per new housing unit built will increase by only about 16 per cent between 1968 and 2000. The major question is what *type* of housing will be built, not how many units will be built or how much will be spent per unit. Consequently, there are wide differences of opinion regarding the split between single-family and multi-family dwellings.

In 1950, 82 per cent of the new housing units were single-family; in 1968, the single-family dwellings comprised 58 per cent of the new housing units constructed; and in 2000, just 37 per cent of the new housing units will be intended for single-family occupancy. The manner in which federally funded construction for housing and redevelopment projects will be allocated will, of course, have a strong influence on the single-family versus multi-family proportions.

Additions and alterations will account for a slightly higher percentage of total residential construction dollars in 2000 than in 1968, climbing from the current 17 per cent to just over 21 per cent. Non-housekeeping units, while increasing at a more rapid rate than the other residential categories, will still amount to only 8 per cent of the total residential construction expenditures in 2000.

Privately owned nonresidential building construction is expected to increase at a rate of about 4.1 per cent annually through 1985, then slow down to a 2.6 per cent rate for the remainder of the century. Commercial buildings will show a rate of increase of 3.9 per cent annually, moving up to nearly half the 2000 expenditures for this category of construction. The hospital and institutional field will also show above average growth; but industrial buildings, with an annual growth rate of just 2.2 per cent, will drop from their present one-third to less than a one-fourth share of total expenditures for private nonresidential building construction.

Total growth in the public nonresidential building sector will be from $7.6 billion in 1970 to $17.9 billion in 2000, an overall rate of increase of 2.9 per cent annually over the 30-year period. Growth will be most rapid over the first half, showing a 4.1 per cent annual increase between 1970 and 1985, and only 1.8 per cent annually thereafter. Educational buildings will continue to dominate this category, growing at about the same rate as the total and continuing to account for 55 to 60 per cent of the public nonresidential building construction expenditures.

Expenditures for construction of privately owned utility plants and other nonbuilding projects, while showing little or no growth since 1955, should increase at a respectable 3.7 per cent annual rate through 1985, then continue at only a slightly decreased 3.4 per cent level until 2000.

Public works programs have perhaps the brightest future of any of the major construction categories. They should increase from a current level of $13.2 billion to nearly $50 billion by 2000 — a compound growth rate of 4.2 per cent annually. The most rapid growth will be between 1970 and 1985 (at a 4.5 per cent annual rate), as public funds are expended to improve transportation facilities and to combat water pollution.

3.

FINANCING CONSTRUCTION

MONEY IS IMPORTANT to the building industry. Our concern here is not to dress out such a truism for the hundredth time, but rather to signal certain changes in the financial sector which appear destined to have lasting impact upon the organization and operations of the building industry.

These changes have to do with the forces which assemble and control construction funds; and these financial entities are so thoroughly interwoven with federal policy that it would be accurate to state that financial and governmental matters are warp and woof of the same fabric which binds construction activity.

If it goes without saying that finance is important to construction, we should note that the reverse is also true. Projections of *Finance* magazine's January 1967 figures[1] show that the current total national wealth of the United States is very near $3 trillion, and more than half of it is represented by structures. Half of the structures' value is residential, and one-fourth each is business and public. The structures' value, interestingly enough, is more than three times as large as the nation's aggregate land value.

These figures show rather dramatically that construction is by far the greatest single creator of lasting wealth in the country, even though it accounts for only a tenth of the nation's total output of goods and services (GNP) each year. This is precisely where the rub comes. Because of construction's value permanence, it involves the long-term commitment of its money and requirements. Dollars invested in a building remain in the building for many years as a residual form of wealth. The building is not "consumed" as rapidly as a meal, a suit, or even an automobile; and so the money invested in it cannot "turn over" as often as most other forms of investment. In other words, the construction dollar does not have as many chances to "work" — to make a *number* of profits — as the nonconstruction dollar.

In an energetic, optimistic, escalating economy such as we have seen in this country almost continuously since World War II, ambition tends to outrun capacity. The collective demand for money soars beyond the supply, and the pursuit of funds becomes highly competitive. Naturally, the price of money rises and inflation results. Inflation reduces the attractiveness of long-term lending because it sharply reduces the return compared with rapid-turnover loans which carry higher interest rates. The lender finds his money tied up for twenty years at 5 per cent interest, while his competitors are relending their money each year at interest rates which have been rising to 6 per cent, 7 per cent, 8 per cent, and more.

Fortunately for the construction industry, lenders' decisions about money allocations to various demand segments are not always discretionary. Federal laws, particularly in the form of charter obligations, severely limit institutional latitude in several important instances — most notably savings and loan associations. The S & L's are virtually forbidden to put their money anywhere except in mortgage loans. Mutual savings banks are similarly (but not so tightly) limited. Without the direct statutory commitment of these agencies' assets as a stable resource for long-term funds, the residential construction industry would surely have foundered during the tight money crisis of 1966.

The possibilities of further increasing the funds available for residential construction through statutory allocation are impressive, and we believe they should be examined in detail. A glance at Table II-9 shows that commercial banks, life insurance companies, and pension funds are providing relatively minor assistance to this most neglected sector of the economy.

The very low participation of the pension funds is particularly noticeable. Pension funds are now reported to be the largest buyer of common stocks in the country, accounting for one-tenth of all transactions of the stock market, according to the July 1967 *Pension and Welfare News*. More than any other entity, the pension funds have exerted an inflationary force in stock prices and resultant deflationary force in long-term bond prices which undergird much of the mortgage market. The funds' recent ventures into land investment are also

TABLE II-9. *Allocation of Capital to Residential Mortgages, 1967*

Capital	Savings and loan associations	Mutual savings banks	Commercial banks' time	Life insurance companies	Pension funds
Total capital ($ billion)	125	66	181	177	115
Capital in residential mortgages ($ billion)	113	45	37	41	7
Portion of total capital (%)	90	68	21	23	6

Source: Report of the President's Committee on Urban Housing, December 11, 1968.

exactly antithetic to the construction capital market because they bid up the prices of land and thereby directly increase the amounts of mortgage money needed.

Vigorous competition for funds always hurts the building industry, and the impact is inevitably most severe in new residential construction — especially in low-cost housing where higher interest rates simply cannot be afforded. The shallow pool of low-interest money literally dries up. Government financed or guaranteed housing programs based upon limited interest rates have usually collapsed in such situations because of their statutory inability to respond flexibly to changes in market interest levels.

This is precisely what happened following the Revenue Act of 1964 — the act which established the 7 per cent tax credit for business investment. It took a while for the law to go into effect and for the business community to plan and execute responses to it. But by the beginning of 1966 the business borrowing spree was in full swing and the demand for money surged beyond the available supply. Total new plant and equipment expenditures climbed nearly 40 per cent[2] in the two years following May 1964, about $12 billion above its normal trend line. To make matters worse, business inventories *also* expanded about $12 billion more than normal in this same period.

Interest rates were bid upward, well beyond the reach of low-cost housing. Construction loans in this sector stopped instantly when it became obvious that the supply of low-interest mortgage money was disappearing, and the projects were shut down forthwith. On a seasonally adjusted basis, nonfarm residential starts declined by nearly *one-half* in the ten months following December 1965.[3]

A little recognized factor made itself felt for the first time during the 1965-1966 crisis in construction capital. It was just one of the many straws that broke the camel's back in that situation, but it will loom large in the future. This is the cost of sending the "postwar baby crop" to college. As the first of this expanding population wave arrived on campus in 1965 and 1966, expenditures for higher education surged by $3 billion, an increase of one-third over 1964.[4] It is important to observe that higher education and residential construction compete for exactly the same kinds of long-term, low interest-rate funds; and the government views them both as worthwhile investments in the nation's future. Moreover, the family savings — either as time deposits or as loans against life insurance — which are used to buy more and more advanced education are withdrawn *directly* from the bloodstream of residential construction capital, the savings of loan association and savings bank depositories, and the insurance companies. This kind of direct competition for funds between housing and higher education continues apace, and one cannot help wishing that housing could choose a more vulnerable direct adversary.

The soaring capital requirements of higher education are but the first vestige of the construction industry's collision course with the money needs of the nation's postwar generation. Considering that the 45- to 65-year-old age group traditionally accumulates the capital which the 20- to 45-year-old age group borrows to build homes and rear and educate its children, it is something of a shock to examine the age distribution patterns of existing population as they relate generally to capital supply/demand imbalances. Figure II-4 shows this relationship graphically.

Figure II-4 deals with established fact, assuming only time will continue to pass. The people who make up these projected age groups are already living, so it requires little imagination to see that the tendency to imbalance between capital suppliers (savers) and borrowers will mount rapidly during the 1970's and 1980's. Increasing pressure on future capital supplies is inevitable even *without* the generally expected increase in the nation's standard of living.

As Hayes and Harlan[5] have pointed out so well, the financial community has been slow to recognize and appreciate the investment possibilities of the building and real estate industries as they have been shaped by modern tax laws. This was believed to have been due

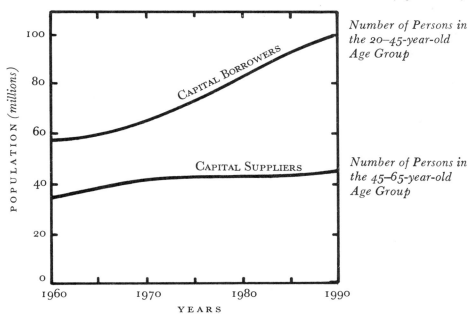

FIGURE II-4. *The Growing Imbalance Between Age Groups Which Supply and Demand Capital*

to the uncomfortable strangeness and complexity of the real estate industry's bookkeeping concepts which generate profits by accumulating losses. Wall Street has tended to view such manipulation with great suspicion, and this alienation has hurt the building industry's access to capital in the past.

There is now a general awareness in the investment community, however, of the tremendous profit possibilities of multi-industry corporate operations which are structured to exploit differences in the tax laws applying to various industries. There are exceedingly complicated realtionships involved here, but they all fit neatly into modern computer programs.

The computer thus becomes the key to modern investment programs, and big capital corporations with vast information systems and well-developed computer capabilities are beginning to replace the individual developer whose savvy is no longer exclusive, or even adequate, and whose access to capital was nearly always somewhat tenuous at best.

Using computer-based techniques, big capital manufacturing

199

corporations can enter the building, real estate and life insurance industries and develop programs to control cash flows, depreciation rates, tax write-offs, and other bookkeeping elements in each industry operation, to maximize total corporate profits by reducing taxes in perfectly legal ways. Well-designed simulation models enable them to determine almost instantly the effects of changes in interest rates, government monetary or construction policies, tax laws, economic activity, or whatever. The speed of these determinations gives them the opportunity to make immediate response to the changes, and thereby increase their competitive advantages over less modern corporations.

The Future

Of all the conjectural statements we might make about finance and the future building industry, it seems most safe to say that the pressures of demand for money will continue to outrun available supplies in anything approaching a free market; the role of government as a sensitive and responsive agent of economic monitoring and control will become increasingly dominant; the big capital manufacturing corporations will become increasingly interested in the building and real estate industries — and increasingly articulate and influential as their spokesmen in government policy-making circles.

If we project these three basic premises forward through the last thirty years of the twentieth century, we set the stage for some interesting logical conjecture.

INFLATION LOCKED IN

Inflation and high interest rates are here to stay. The basic demand for capital supplies will be too great — particularly during the 1970's — for traditional relationships to return in matters of short- and long-term investment. The important thing to observe here is that everyone has inflation programmed into his future plans; so if a lender has a certain level of return on investment in mind, he automatically adds 1 or 2 per cent per year to it. This kind of advance programming has a way of locking inflation into the system because the element of recurrent bargaining is preempted — i.e., bargaining for lower interest rate and lower prices is not seriously undertaken.

Under these circumstances it will become absolutely impossible to obtain funds for low-cost housing except by government subsidy, either in the form of public housing or (more likely) interest or rent supplement programs.

THE ROLE OF GOVERNMENT

The government can ill afford to lose substantial revenues by failing to anticipate the means by which private industry earns money by avoiding payment of taxes. We may presume that the government will marshal its immense information systems, and that it will purchase and program computers as necessary to keep abreast or ahead of the science of legal tax dodging.

There has been an unmistakable trend in recent years, however, for the Executive Department to know more than it can get Congress to do something about, e.g., the unpopular oil depletion tax policies. We see no reason to expect that senatorial conscience will be reborn in these matters during the next thirty years. So it seems likely that government legislation will continue to overlook the complexities of tax reform (which industry understands) and concentrate instead upon housing acts and subsidies (which the voters understand).

Both existing laws favoring multi-industry operations as tax-saving devices and government subsidy programs for such appealing public causes as housing and education may thus be seen as lasting political realities.

Hopefully, the government will make increasingly sophisticated use of computer capabilities in making new laws and monetary policies. Simulation can be of tremendous assistance in structuring changes in such control measures, and it would be lamentable indeed if industry consistently outmaneuvered new controls to a point endangering their effectiveness.

There will undoubtedly be a strong increase in the government's use of tax laws to motivate (and thereby control) investment patterns.

THE MEGA-BUILDERS AND MONEY

The huge, well-capitalized, tax-savings-oriented, computer-minded, multi-industry corporation — usually based in manufacturing, but with significant operations in building, real estate, and life insurance — looms as the central figure on the construction scene over the next thirty years.

He will be both buyer and seller — a client in his own right and also a servant to the government and to commerce and industry.

By the standards of anyone who has ever been involved in the building industry before, this macro-operator will be incredibly well informed about all major sectors of the economy. He will know the full case for and against proposed new legislation while it is still in committee, and he will be an articulate and uncommonly influential spokesman for the building industry's position in the concerns of government at all levels.

The features which distinguish him from previous giants who have attempted to amalgamate variegated construction interests in the past are nimbleness, breadth of knowledge, and financial solidarity. His predecessor was usually limited by money and by personal knowledge within a practices sphere of operation. By the time new peripheral opportunity information reached him and he had assembled the money to exploit it, smaller operators had already responded to it. In contrast, tomorrow's giant will be the first to know, the first to evaluate, the first to respond — and his response will be a whole pattern of simultaneous moves, solidly financed, and each one programmed to augment and strengthen the others.

The potential power of tomorrow's macro-operator is astounding. Consider first the financial leverage he wields from a sound manufacturing base which generates extra profits from tax losses in his building/real estate operations. This higher return attracts new investment capital, of course; and as a growth company, he will not be expected to dissipate his capital in dividend payments. Second, his information, opinions, counsel, and guidance will be actively sought by policy-makers in the investment community, professional and trade associations, press, and especially government. This last is a tremendously influential position to have! (A glance at the membership list of the President's Committee on Urban Housing makes this point.) In addition, of course, he has the advantages of reciprocity sales, fall-out benefits, bargaining leverage — and the all-important capabilities of keeping meaningful track of widely diverse events and programming cool-headed, nimble responses to them . . . in advance.

In the future, the building industry will become increasingly polarized between government on the one hand and the macro-operator on the other. They will tend to be mutually influential. The lines of force in between them will be money and information. The industry's smaller participants will find themselves increasingly oriented to one source or the other or both.

This bipolarity should make the building industry more stable and prosperous, particularly in the larger projects, but this increased security will be purchased at the sacrifice of considerable independence on the part of those who elect to serve the poles.

4.

LAND AND LAND USE

IF THE NATION'S 200 MILLION PEOPLE were spread out evenly over its total land area of 3 million square miles (excluding Alaska and Hawaii), there would be 67 people on each square mile. That amounts to 10 acres apiece for every man, woman, and child — hardly a critical shortage.

A number of recent studies have used this kind of reasoning to show that there is an abundance of land. The Kaiser report[1] showed that the entire population could be comfortably housed on less than 2 per cent of the land — an area the size of the state of Iowa. That would be roughly 3,600 persons per square mile, approximately the density of Kansas City which is one of the most sparsely populated major cities in the country. (Manhattan's density is 75,000 persons per square mile.) The Douglas Commission Report[2] shows that one-eighth of the land within large cities (over 250,000 population) actually remains undeveloped altogether. The problem with such calculations is that they do not recognize that the nation's land abundance is either located long distances from places where most people are economically obliged to be, or else it is priced above what anyone will pay for it to build upon — up until now, at least.

Our particular focus here must be upon the land which people want badly enough to purchase for occupancy of one sort or another. This is where tomorrow's building activity will take place. And the kind of structures to be built upon this land will depend largely upon what the land buyers think will be most urgently needed and most profitable in any given area. Many factors will influence this kind of judgment, but most important among them will probably be land

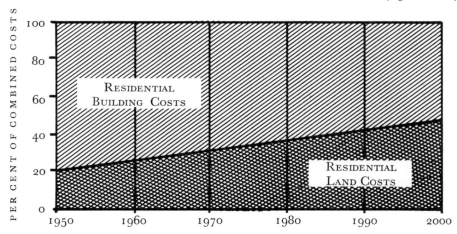

FIGURE II-5. *The Trend of Relative Land and Residential Building Costs, 1950 to 2000*

(land + building costs = 100 per cent)

cost, appreciation potential of the property, and taxes. Federal, state, and local government will no doubt have a good deal of influence on all three.

Since land is a fixed-quantity, essential resource continuously at auction in a prospering economy, it is axiomatic that land costs will rise. Figure II-5 shows that 1950-1968 residential land costs have risen sharply as a percentage of total project costs; and all of our evidence indicates that the trend will continue at a brisk pace projected over the next thirty years, despite the expectation of healthy increases in building costs.

The disproportionate rise in land costs exerts increasing pressure for intensification of land use, both in the inner city and in suburbia. Inevitably this must result in increased verticality or smaller lot sizes or both. The verticality route seems more likely because it is a pure economic dictate in commercial investment: multi-story revenue is absolutely essential to service mortgages inflated by exorbitant cost of land acquisition. Smaller lot sizes for residences will come more slowly because there is more room in family budgets for discretion about the matter — most people would rather have a larger lot and add five years to their mortgage.

A third inevitable result of disproportionate land cost increases is

205

the default of private initiative to government-financed downtown construction programs — redevelopment, highways, and public buildings. There are few organizations today which have both the money and the free inclination to assemble large enough parcels of downtown land to contain the sizes and kinds of projects which would arrest the decay cycle and restore investment confidence. The massive public housing projects of the 1950's replaced many slums with pleasant and attractive low-income apartment buildings, but they failed to restore the confidence required for large scale projects on private initiative. Experience up to this point indicates that the best — and perhaps the only effective — way of accomplishing the revitalization of high-cost downtown land areas is by direct government subsidy to private investment.

The true value of land has historically been determined by the number of economically viable alternative uses it has. A large corner lot in a commercial zone can be used for scores of profitable purposes; and the stubborn seller can usually cover his taxes by renting it out virtually undeveloped as a lot for used cars or parking, and simply wait until some buyer comes along and pays his asking price. (The influences of zoning and tax policies are thus clearly seen as paramount factors in determining land prices, and they will be discussed later.)

In the past, central locations have offered potential business occupants a maximum variety of choice among employees, services, ancillary facilities, and customers. Central residential locations offered employees maximum choice among easily accessible jobs, goods for purchase, public facilities, and entertainment.

These historical determinants of land value are now being disturbed by certain socio-economic, techno-economic, and political-economic developments. Central cities are becoming less attractive as business locations because of social and racial unrest, the decline in the number of employees to choose from (usually caused by a combination of white exodus and deteriorating public transportation), the withdrawal of customers to the suburbs, the high tax rates required to support expanding welfare and educational programs on shrinking tax bases, property insurance problems, and — perhaps most important of all — a pervasive feeling of hopelessness or doubt, at least, about the appreciation potential of downtown property in the near term compared with other investment opportunities.

Downtown vs. Suburban Land Uses

In most inner-city areas, the sidewalk traffic has declined to levels incapable of supporting the great miscellany of specialty shops, restaurants, and activity centers which so characterized the charm of downtown twenty years ago. An immense number of people never go downtown anymore because traffic, parking problems, and even the threat of physical violence discourage it. The deterioration is depressing; and the suburbs are now, in many cases, virtually self-sufficient.

America's vast middle class has all but abandoned downtown to the municipal functions, visitor facilities, entertainment, and business enterprises which are importantly involved with central affairs. Downtown residential populations are still moving toward the economic extremes — the luxury apartment dwellers and the ghetto poor.

The former heart of downtown operations — the physical distribution of goods — has followed its customers to the suburbs. Information handling and control functions — office work — which formerly required physical presence in a community of buyers and sellers, are now fully effective at remote locations.

Downtown still controls; but for most people it is just a phone number. Suburbia is where the economic bounce is.

The nature of differences between downtown and suburbia as building sites is profound, and no public policy shifts will alter this basic fact. They are two different worlds, and they will remain so. Suburbia has cut the Gordian knot, and it looks ever outward. When the radical extension becomes untenable, it forms independent satellite cities of its own. It will clearly require enormous changes in the mix of inner-city functions and services to cause parents to view downtown as a great place to raise a family. Left to the free market and "natural choice," the parent, the employee, the employer, the professional man, and hence most potential new-building investors will continue to choose suburbia.

Suburbia will remain the site of fresh, natural, strong self-renewing economic growth and building activity — involving projects of all sizes and descriptions. And downtown will either become an island of local government buildings in a sea of slums, or else an island of local government buildings in an ocean of government-stimulated rebuilding investment. Without such new stimulus, downtown cannot be restored to middle-class economic viability of any kind remotely approaching a natural order. Its residential populations will be wealthy (especially in apartments as second homes), childless, or poor; and its business populations will be limited to the servicing of a constantly narrowing arc of commercial activity.

Restoration of the inner city either by subsidized mass rehabilitation or replacement, or by subsidized piecemeal rehabilitation or replacement will be an incredibly expensive matter; but it must be done if the nation is to avoid progressive self-destruction.

Hopefully, earlier attention will be brought to the intermediate rings of cities before it is too late to salvage any spirit of self-regeneration there also. It is in these intermediate-ring areas that private capital can still develop its own momentum if large enough projects are undertaken.

Urban Revitalization

Government, at one level or another, holds the key to the problems of uneconomic use of land. The key is control, or more specifically, the instruments of control and the willingness to use them courageously in the public interest.

The instruments of government control include zoning regulations, taxes, and various kinds of building and housing codes at the state and local levels; and income tax allowances, investment subsidies, and rent supplements at the federal level.

Exorbitant hold-out land pricing could be discouraged by progressive property or license taxation rates on undeveloped or poorly maintained real estate. It makes no sense for the nation to pay downtown land barons increasing rewards for holding land out of economic use or paying blackmail prices to rid the cities of their unsightly treasures.

On the positive side, more use of tax holidays should be used to stimulate private investment in new building and rehabilitation of highly desirable nature, particularly in the intermediate-ring areas of central cities where hope of revitalizing private investment still remains alive. This kind of incentive tax policy has been effective in stimulating construction in the South for a number of years, especially in South Carolina where, in addition, all investment in beautification and employee comfort is permanently tax exempt.

Zoning regulations and building codes are generally fairly administered and written in the public interest; but at worst they are tools of political favor, and in any case they require constant attention by the local press to assure a well-informed and watchful citizenry. The Douglas Commission,[3] forecasting that 18 million acres of new urban land will come into use during the next thirty years (about half again what is now in use), went to the raw nerve of the matter in proposing:

1. Action to assure that local governments exercising regulatory authority are responsive to the needs of broad segments of the population and are competent to exercise land use controls in a fair and effective manner, coupled with state and federal action to recognize and strengthen local decision-making wherever it does not clearly conflict with broader regional, state, or national goals.

2. Establishment of state or regional machinery to reconcile conflicts among local governments and special-purpose agencies, and to plan and act on matters demanding a broader-than-local perspective.

3. Establishment of policies and measures aimed at providing persons of all income levels with a wide choice of places to live and providing employees an opportunity to live near their work.

4. Formulation of clear, statewide rules allocating costs in new subdivisions between the public and the developer, and thus, in effect, between taxpayers and home buyers.

5. Actions and procedures to assure the protection of built-up areas which provide an acceptable environment, and to eliminate blighting influences and encourage rebuilding in presently unsatisfactory neighborhoods.

6. Action to encourage and assist developments which are large enough to create their own environments and thereby to eliminate the need for some detailed controls that inhibit imaginative development, promote racial and economic segregation, and contribute to inefficient land-use patterns and strains on the control machinery.

7. Greater reliance on direct public action to prevent undesirable private development, provide public initiative for desired development which the private market cannot or will not supply, recapture land value increases for public use, and assure the realization of other public objectives.

The Commission specifically recommended state legislation granting public assistance for land assembly in the public interest, state authorization for land banking, and federal creation of a National Institute of Building Sciences to develop a suitable national building code, conformance to which would be a condition of eligibility for federal assistance programs.

In urging federal legislation in the critical field of housing codes to meet the challenges of urban redevelopment, the Commission noted that the 1949 Housing Act called for a "decent home and suitable living environment" for all Americans; but there is not yet even a uniform workable definition of standards of decency. For example, the 1960 Census of Housing showed that 20 per cent of Washington, D.C.'s 263,000 houses were substandard — but another survey in 1965-1966 showed that 48 per cent were substandard by the Commission's own definition.

The Commission put its finger squarely on the slum-exploiting absentee landlords who buy dilapidated property from each other for its "depreciation" value as an income tax shelter, and do little or nothing to maintain the property. It was observed that most cities already have laws requiring minimum housing conditions to be maintained, but that the city governments look the other way when it comes to enforcement. This is usually accomplished very neatly by failing to provide an adequate inspection budget.

Under circumstances where there is suburban preoccupation by the general public, apathy or even collusion with slum property exploiters by local governments, and federal tax laws which nurture and reward such exploitation, it is not surprising that the problem of urban degradation has grown to such staggering proportions.

5.

CONSTRUCTION TECHNOLOGY:

CHANGE AND IMPLICATIONS

PROMISES, PROMISES — the oft foretold revolution in the construction industry is still around the corner. The myriad of factors discussed elsewhere generates solid conviction that new technical developments will soon alter the nature of building. Any realistic appraisal of technological change in construction — and the possible impacts on the professional designer — demands new perspective on the process of technical change.

The construction of buildings in 1968 aggregated $59 billion, generating 7 per cent of our GNP. Even discounting inflationary trends, the value of all building construction requiring the services of the professional designer will double by 1985 (see Table II-6). Building construction volume is growing at a faster pace than the supply of architects and building design engineers.

As discussed before, the building industry is made up of tens of thousands of building contractors; 21,000 architectural and engineering firms; countless materials suppliers; federal, state, and local governments each with multiple controlling groups; building workers and their unions; brokers, realtors, and entrepreneurs of building enterprises and their financial backers. No one group has controlled a dominant share of the building dollar. The structure of the industry is changing, however. Large-scale builders continue to enter the residential market. Business is tending to concentrate in fewer firms, and the large firms are tending to integrate functions, as in the case of realtor-engineering-designer builders.

This tremendous size and universal distribution of construction activity have created sufficient mass and momentum that monumental changes are required to accelerate or deflect the steady progress of historical trends. Specifically, even the most important technical or engineering developments have relatively minor effects upon the movement of such a juggernaut.

It is clear that among the major determinants of change for the construction industry, three classes of influence can be identified:

1. *Regulating factors* have direct, fast response linkage to the *extent* of building activity. Major factors include the performance of the overall economy, the state of the money market, the effect of government construction programs, and labor union practices.

2. *Underlying determinants* exert subtle but powerful control over the *kind* of structures to be built. These determinants include the changing requirements for buildings, the structure of the construction industry, with new entities, mergers, giant firms and package vendors, and the prevailing government policy regarding construction.

3. *Long term influences* are indirect, and relatively slow acting, but lead to basic changes in the *nature* of building. Major influences include evolving building codes, the changing roles of the professional environmental designer, and technological change — in both the "hard" technology of the building process and the management techniques by which this process is controlled.

Attempts to peer thirty years or so into the future have been beset by two kinds of error. First, the timing or rate of acceptance of technical change has been overestimated; i.e., expected too soon. Second, the extent of the impact on those affected is almost always understated.

The potential impact of advanced construction technology is most often assessed in terms of ability to reduce construction costs. Focusing exclusively upon the criterion of reduced cost badly neglects important "multiplier effects" of technological change. The impact of new technology is multiplied via increased building value, through more effective use of resources in achieving building goals, and in terms of increased human values derived from an improved environment.

Technological advances in the construction process are important at the present time for a number of reasons. Approximately 30 to 35 per cent of the total design effort is spent developing solutions to basically technical problems — heat load, efficient structure, lighting, air conditioning and environmental control, parking accommodations, moving people inside the building, traffic flow, etc. The amount of effort which must be devoted to technical considerations has been increasing rapidly in recent years, and this trend is expected to continue through 1985. Although this trend may possibly affect other groups in the building industry more than architects, it denotes a major change in the process in which all are involved.

About 40 per cent of total construction cost for major building projects goes for technical and engineering equipment. Increasing attention to problems of acoustical treatment, pollution abatement, waste disposal, changing transportation modes, solar control, seismic codes, etc., is steadily increasing the cost of providing these technical aspects of the building process.

Perhaps most important, innovation in construction technology multiplies the range of choices available to the user (the owner) and the environmental designer. The ultimate judgment of the impact of technological change in construction rests with the coming generation. The early evidence suggests, however, that this judgment will be weighed far more heavily on our ability to meet construction goals for the future in terms of human values than in terms of cost reduction.

Technological Innovation in Building

During the last thirty years — as we have noted — the U.S. building industry has undergone a radical change of character. Project and corporate size has increased greatly. Equipment, materials, design, planning, and management practices are different in many ways from those employed before World War II. Nevertheless, while the industry as a whole has undergone major change, this change has proceeded piecemeal, in the small segments of the industry. There has been no radical change of great technical and economic significance; no single invention or family of inventions. In the building industry, change has been evolutionary — and much of the most important change is usually not described as technical at all. The most significant changes have had to do, rather, with methods of managing and organizing the building process. These innovations mark the emergence of industrialized buildings.

Entrepreneurs in postwar construction patterned their activities after large-scale manufacturing processes in industry. They stimulated adoption of a variety of managerial and production techniques —

cost analysis, job analysis, time and motion study, prefabrication, on-site mass production, etc. — which resulted in treating building as a manufacturing process. The mass-production house was one of the more striking outcomes of this effort, and served to focus attention on prefabrication techniques of all kinds. This new approach to the building process increased efficiency in use of labor and material. Costs were lowered, speed of construction was greatly increased, and product quality became subject to the same sorts of criticism leveled at other mass-produced products — "Ticky-Tacky."

Along with these changes in management and methods evolved a series of building techniques, components, and materials adapted to the concept of building as a manufacturing process — to the idea of the building as a product. These included the movement of segments of the building operation into the factory: premanufactured houses, premanufactured components, and off-site preparation of materials. New materials and components were invented or adapted to fit these trends toward premanufacture: plywood, prestressed concrete, new thin-walled lightweight structures with new insulating and structural materials. Much of the building operation was moved off-site into the factory itself; on-site activity was made as much like factory work as possible. New power tools and equipment were adopted, both on-site and in-factory, to replace previous craft operations. One common aspect of many new components (gypsum wallboard or resilient floor coverings) was the extent to which they reduced craft-based labor.

Time lags are associated with the adoption and exploitation of new concepts. Four key stages can be identified in tracing the acceptance of innovations:

1. *Invention* — discovery or first description of the concept or idea involved — often a patent application or seminal publication.

TIME LAG

2. *Innovation* — the first commercial-scale trial of the new idea.

TIME LAG

3. *Adoption and diffusion* — the point in time after which information about the innovation spreads rapidly and modifications or new applications are developed. Typically the period during which the innovation is most "newsworthy."

TIME LAG

4. *Acceptance as standard* — use of the innovation continues to

214

grow, but more slowly. The new idea has now become one of the standard options; it is considered part of the state-of-the-art.

The construction industry has responded to changing market requirements, and to shifting economic pressures, by adopting a wide variety of technical and institutional innovations.

The time period required between the initial demonstration of a construction idea on a commercial scale and the acceptance of the innovation as standard practice has been traced for a selection of relatively significant innovations. The "incubation period" of eighteen innovations is shown in Table II-10. Several important conclusions can be drawn from even this small sampling.

TABLE II-10. *Acceptance of Construction Innovations*

Innovation	*Years required for "acceptance"**
Nonresidential construction	
(1) Shell roof construction	36
(2) Climbing tower crane	8
(3) CPM scheduling for major projects	11
(4) Folded plate construction	19
(5) Curtain wall construction	13
(6) Total energy installations	17
(7) Prestressed concrete building components	17
(8) Weathering steel for exposed structure	24
(9) Strategic decision theory for competitive bidding	> 16

Average nonresidential 17.8 years

Residential Construction	
(1) Guaranteed amortized mortgage	15
(2) Mobile home units	22
(3) Asphalt impregnated fiber sheathing	16
(4) Radial arm saw on site	12
(5) FHA minimum standard codes	13
(6) Combination forced air heat with air conditioning	28
(7) Preassembled window units	18
(8) Tilt-up frame wall assembly	13
(9) Prefabricated homes	16

Average residential 17.0 years

Average period for acceptance 17.4 years

* Years between first commercial scale use and general acceptance as a standard, state-of-the-art option or practice.

First, contrary to some opinions, the evidence does not suggest that the construction industry is slower to innovate or to adopt technical change than other segments of American industry. Neither does it appear that either the weight of tradition or the concern for preserving property values has rendered residential construction less progressive or more reluctant to implement changes than the nonresidential building community. Most important for this study, the average period for acceptance — the interval of most rapid growth and major impact — spans fifteen years. While there are reasons to expect somewhat more rapid diffusion of innovation in the future, the length of this period of active growth and influence will not be drastically reduced.

We may confidently expect that technical change in construction through 1985 will be wrought mainly by the adoption and growing use of innovations which have already been tested on a commercial scale. Methods, materials, and management techniques pioneered within the next few years are likely to have their major impact in the post-1985 period.

Certain kinds of innovations, of course, have been adopted fairly swiftly. But major developments now brewing do not have the characteristics which have marked rapid acceptance in the past. What are the factors which favor rapid acceptance? Innovations are quickly adopted where:

1. Direct substitution is involved; an improved material or a better process for accomplishing a well-defined objective.

2. Only one element in the building program — design, engineering, construction, or program management — is directly affected. (Example: pumped concrete affects only construction practice.)

3. Minimum new resource commitment is required. (More often innovation lags for want of specially skilled people than for lack of funds.)

In contrast, innovations which affect several aspects of construction, require retraining of personnel, or accomplish some basically new function — rather than displacing a standard technique — have taken longest to reach acceptance. These are precisely the characteristics of some of the most significant innovations now under development.

Technical Change in Construction

The construction business will be subjected to both structural changes and procedural or process changes as a direct consequence of adapting to a steady stream of innovations. Some new technology will develop totally within the construction field as the result of experimental construction work — research and development. However, construction-industry R&D spending over recent years has been so low that few innovations are anticipated. "Innovation by Invasion" has been the traditional source — and for the next ten years will remain virtually the sole source — of new construction technology. New technology altering the construction field will continue to be infused from a host of industrial and public sectors — chemicals, electronics, basic materials, machinery, military, aerospace, foreign builders, and the service industries.

The form in which new technology enters the construction industry is more important than the exact origins of the innovation outside the building field. Major vectors of construction change enter the industry in different forms at four major points: technological advances relating to materials, construction techniques, design management, and program management.

For each of these areas, highlights of the principal trends and changes anticipated to 1985 are discussed in the following sections. Projected consideration of the construction scene for the period 1985 to 2000 follows.

MATERIALS AND BUILDING PRODUCTS

Shifting patterns of materials use and building products will continue to influence four industry functions — *design, engineering, construction,* and *management.* Relatively few surprises are anticipated. The materials expected to have the greatest influence on construction activity in the next fifteen years have comfortably familiar names — concrete, plastic, steel, and plywood. But the prefixes and adjectives needed to characterize these products virtually foretell the future when strung together: cast-high-strength, maintenance-free, composite-preassembled system.

A sampling of the principal materials which will change construction activity has been assessed to determine which construction functions would be affected, the significance or degree of influence exerted, and the time period during which the influence would be greatest. These evaluations are summarized in Table II-11.

TABLE II-11. *Construction Materials, Products, and Subsystems*

	Functions affected*	Significance	Period of maximum effect
Chemically prestressed concrete	D-E-C	8	1971-1983
High strength structural steels (A572, A441, A514, A517, etc.)	D-E-C	7	1972-1985
Weathering steels for exposed structure	D-E-C	6	1967-1980
High performance sealants	C	6	1965-1974
Sandwich panels	D-C	6	1965-1982
Total energy systems	D-E-M	7	1968-1978
High strength–light weight concrete	D-E-C	6	1977-1990
Ultra high strength, notch-tough reinforcing bar	D-E-C	6	1976-1984
Cast, prestressed concrete, load-bearing exterior wall panels	D-E-C-M	8	1972-1989
Phenolic and epoxy extrusion foams	D-C-M	4	1976-1988
Polymeric concrete	D-E-C	4	1977-1990
Foamed in place plastics	D-E-C	5	1974-1988
Soil stabilizing chemical treatments	E-C	5	1964-1989
Plastic pressure piping	E-C	6	1973-1981
Durable, long-life protective coatings	C	6	1972-1987
Acoustic control materials	D-E-C	7	1966-1977
Packaged sewage treatment unit	D-E	6	1965-1989
Complete waste disposal systems	D-E	4	1974-1994
Precast concrete building components	D-E-C	9	1965-1988
High strength mortar	C	3	1974-1989
Prefinished metal siding	C	4	1967-1979
Exposed aggregate panels and components	D-C	6	1966-1977
Prefabricated residential walls	E-C	7	1970-1979
Maintenance-free surfaces	D-C	7	1968-1990
Plastic-coated hardboard	C	5	1971-1987
Prefinished wood siding	C	3	1974-1985
Soil-binder blocks	D	1	1976-1989
Chemically treated, rot-resistant lumber	D-E	2	1972-1990
Predecorated dry wall	C	6	1975-1992

TABLE II-11. *(Continued)*

	Functions affected*	Significance	Period of maximum effect
Flake and particle board	D-C	6	1963-1988
Composite (faced) exterior plywood	D-C	6	1966-1982
Liquid poured resilient floor covering	D-C	4	1970-1983
Metal roofing	D-C	5	1967-1985
Plastic flashing	C	6	1972-1988
Plastic door and window frames	D-C	6	1973-1989
Laminated timber beams	D-E-C	4	1962-1979
Prefinished wooden windows	C	2	1972-1984
Extensive & special outdoor lighting	D-E-C	1	1973-1988
Solid state electric controls	D-E-C	4	1975-1990
Variable transmission glass (photochromic, Varad, etc.)	D-E-C	2	1976-1992
Preshingled roofing sections	D-C	5	1978-1992
Prefabricated plumbing vent systems	D-E-C	7	1974-1990
Single-ply membrane roofing	D-E-C	6	1974-1986
Jet-Set concrete (20 min. set)	E-C-M	6	1977-1991
24" composite ceramic-urethane flooring	C	5	1976-1988
"Total Comfort" control systems	E-C-M	4	1973-1988
District heating & cooling utilities	D-E-C-M	4	1975-1990
Prefabricated utility core	D-E-C	8	1973-1989
Surface applied electrical "trim" system	E-C	3	1977-1994
Double-tee concrete roof slab & beam	D-E-C	2	1978-1990
Stone aggregate surfaced plywood	D-C	3	1974-1986
Electric heating panels	E-M	6	1976-1998
Foamed or cellular concrete	E-M	5	1977-1989
Integral-rib steel panels	E	7	1978-1996
Radiation cured polymers	D-E-C	4	1978-1990
Hydrothermal silicate synthesis	E-C	6	1982-2000
Structural thermoplastics	E-C	7	1983-1995

*KEY: D = design
       E = engineering
       C = construction
       P = project management

The greatest change in construction activities can be expected from the imaginative use of a handful of the versatile, workhorse materials. New technology involving these materials is expected to have the maximum effect on building design, construction techniques, and structural engineering.

Another type of change for the construction field will stem from the continuing trend to convert building materials into building components. Fabrication, preassembly, and integration into packaged building subsystems will play an increasingly important role in construction. These trends alter the distribution of effort between design and engineering. More important, increasing use of subsystems alters the project management process — affecting programming, specifications, purchasing, scheduling, installation, site inspection, acceptance, warranties, and liability.

For the 1970-1980 period, concrete materials and components will show the strongest growth. Beyond 1980, steel is expected to replace many of the vertical wall panels and functional modules formerly cast in concrete. By 1984, more manufactured products will be made of plastic than of any other material, but structural plastics are not expected to have major impact until the post-1985 period.

Changes in building materials are slated to have greatest influence on the construction process itself. Design and engineering will be affected less, and impact on design will precede that on engineering by about three to four years. Materials will have little influence on project management.

CONSTRUCTION METHODS

Technical changes in methods used for building fabrication and erection in the decade 1970-1980 may be so spectacular as to obscure the longer term changes in design, materials, and management practice. Even two or three years ago, any description of radical building methods read like a foreign travelog. Most techniques which represent a sharp break with construction practice are so new in America that significant impact is not expected until the mid-1970's.

As in any new technology, the nomenclature is confusing. Well over sixty industrialized building methods have been described — and each month sees further proliferation. Only the major trends and different approaches to building production and delivery can be considered here.

Industrialized building. In timorous forms, industrialized or factory building production has been on the scene for many years. Industry leaders expect smooth and gradual transition, with progress most likely occurring in two phases. The years 1970-1975 will be a period of consolidation and aggregation. The manufactured building will bring together prefabricators and makers of sectional buildings, mobile homes, and preassembled utility cores, to form a major segment (perhaps temporary?) of industrialized building. For the next few years, most of these groups will be loose associations of consortia brought together by joint ventures and front money. Clear evidence of this trend can be seen in organizations such as Builders Resources Corporation, and Laird Incorporated, or in such joint efforts as Kaufman and Broad with U.S. Steel and the Campbell Engineering group.

By 1975, mergers and acquisitions will have wrought lasting structural change in industrialized building. Most of the successful fabricators will be aligned with package builders, developers, or one of the systems builders. Harbingers of the emergence of "total construction firms" can be seen in the corporate acquisition of American Standard, Jim Walter, Continental Consolidated, Boise-Cascade, IT&T, and Chrysler Corporation. On a smaller scale, the synergy of combining financial resources, land, and modern construction capabilities is generating turmoil among the more successful builders and developers. Redman Industries (mobile homes) first acquired Kansas Quality Construction (apartments) and Albritton Engineering (aluminum windows) before merging into the Titan Group. Nearly fifty organizations currently face a knotty decision — merge, be acquired, or go public.

Even where Big Business has not forced a shotgun wedding, systems builders promote "keeping steady company." The Mitchell system presently depends heavily upon use of a plastic bathroom utility module; and the U.S. Gypsum Structi-core, with Lockheed's Lock-Panel system, has brought together Commodore Corporation (mobile homes) and a manufacturer of prefabricated kitchen-bathroom modules. The cost-effectiveness criterion of system building inevitably restricts the choice of compatible elements.

Clearly, the target for most industrialized building in the next ten years will be housing units — primarily low-rise apartments and town houses, under section 221(d)(3) — together with low-cost block housing for the inner city. The mobile homes group may be able to

respond most rapidly. The new and experimental lure of FHA mortgages for mobile units represents both stimulus and stabilizing influence. The speed and efficiency of industrialized building for mobile
homes far exceeds that of any other rationalized building approach.
A two-bedroom housing unit complete with furnishings and utilities
can be completely assembled in thirty minutes and sold at $4500. At
present, this is the only approach to come close to the FHA's goal of
a single-family housing unit plus land for $5000. Experimental hous-
ing authorization, and temporary code suspension where needed,
should provide the proponents of the factory-assembly approach opportunity to develop the full potential for multi-family housing units.

A different market orientation is represented by the producers of
structural modules, utility-core modules and subsystems. These fac-
tory-produced units are directed toward high-rise construction, both
apartments and commercial buildings. As building products and engineering subsystems, preassembled "plug-in" units will see increasing
use in all types of construction. Present producers of structural shells
of concrete, plywood, steel, and eventually plastic are candidates for
merger with organizations committed to proprietary building systems.

Systems building.[1] The most sophisticated approach at present is
the components or systems-building concept which brings to bear both
the production capabilities and the flexibility of American industry.
The various experimental projects involving the systems approach
should hold even greater import for the environmental designer than
for the engineer. Presently at issue is the question of trade-offs between achieving an "efficient" building versus a "humanized" building. Defining the building in terms of its systems interfacing and
functional performance requirements invites maximum ingenuity in
realizing the design. However, the volume required to defray development costs suggests that for the next ten years, systems building is
most suitable for institutional and government controlled building
programs.

Proprietary building methods. The common factor in most proprietary building techniques is the emphasis on erection methods at
the job site. The objectives are speed and cost reduction. They are
more "process"-oriented than concerned with the building as a
"product." For the next few years at least, the operative words will
be: precast concrete, hoist to stack, and foreign license. Many proponents are confident that U.S. industrial ingenuity by 1975 may

leave the Europeans far behind. There is urgent need for contributions from the professional planner and designer. The preponderant emphasis on process efficiency has endowed many of the current projects with all the aesthetic charm of a Warsaw worker's flat.

Perhaps six or seven proprietary systems are now in serious contention for a slice of the building construction market. In method of assembly, they can be classified as skeleton hung panel-wall systems, load-bearing walls and slabs, stacked-box systems, and modular vaults and spans.

Regardless of which approach gains the most momentum in the next five years, a definite trend can be seen toward load-bearing masonry walls for low-rise construction. After seventy years of structural steel skeletons, the contrast between the Monadnock Building and the Palacio del Rio provides one way of assessing the importance of technological change in the construction field.

On-site fabrication. At the same time that the process of on-site building is being moved back to the factory, factory equipment and methods are being moved to the job. The extent of job-site fabrication will increase, and the nature of production will tend toward factory techniques. Use of specialized equipment for flexible manufacture of building components will grow at least 12 per cent annually and represent a substantial market by 1978. Use of such equipment will shift construction toward a capital intensive base.

Between 1970 and 1980, much job-site production will be directed toward casting; prestressing; and curing of concrete slabs, modules, and components. After 1975, however, some of the emphasis on concrete will diminish, yielding to metal and composite assemblies as CO_2 welders, NC punches, presses, and plastic foaming equipment come into greater use. Exterior panels of prefinished steel and of textured, anodized aluminum will offer advantages in weight and post-construction movability. Steel roof panels formed on the job can be made in any length and will provide superior fit.

Most of these developments in on-site production represent comparatively straightforward transfer from factory practice. New construction techniques can be anticipated from R&D programs sponsored by the U.S. Army Corps of Engineers, Bureau of Standards, and HUD. Typical of such experiments is the General Electric-Gibbs and Gibbs approach of a mobile factory to be housed in an air-supported structure at the construction site.

The task of assembling fairly large numbers of modular building sections will increasingly be handled by computer control. Savings due to better quality control and faster mating of parts for high-rise construction may be even more attractive than savings in direct labor. An early example of this trend is the punched-tape controlled, wall-building machine used by Kellner and Sons to manufacture interior and exterior frame walls at the rate of 20 feet per minute. Quick changeover to alter window placement, holes for wiring runs, and selection of panelling or siding can be as simple as switching loops of tape.

Because these construction methods require substantial capital investments and will affect numerous aspects of the building process, little impact is expected until 1976-1980. For large scale multiple unit projects, however, the effects will be important: reducing cost of construction by 12 to 15 per cent, halving construction schedules, and increasing productivity per man-hour by 20 to 25 per cent.[2]

Advances in "conventional construction." By no means will all future change in construction involve radical departures from rationalized building. Through 1980, substantial change will be effected by wider use of methods now in use but not fully exploited. Areas of major impact, relative significance of technical advances, and the time period for maximum effect for the principal shifts expected are summarized in Table II-12.

Changes in construction methods will significantly influence the management of building projects: new sources of supply and new services will be brought in; scheduling will be speeded up; and different job supervision, acceptance, and warranty provisions will be demanded. The magnitude of this impact will be at least triple that of changes in building materials. New construction methods will have the most dramatic impact between 1973 and 1979. The influence of new technology in building procedures will have long lasting effects — especially on design — persisting well past 1985.

Subtle but immensely powerful changes in the nature and appearance of buildings within the past few years must be attributed to shifting methods by which building projects are conceived and produced.

The role of the professional designer over the next twenty years will surely be shaped by further changes in management — as much or more than by changes in the product or in the process of construction. The AIA has recognized the importance of expanding management functions in building — for example by the establishment of the "Package Deal" committee.

Significant technical improvements in management of both the conceptual planning phase and the construction project phase are now close to realization. But whether new management technology will play an important part in environmental design depends upon resolution of nontechnical issues: Will the architect's role and freedom of choice in the planning of building gradually deteriorate? Will buildings be designed backward from an analysis of investment yield or forward from basic requirements?

The crucial management decision to be made before 1985 relates not to computer aids or information processing but to pre-emption of the designer's contribution and decision-making role.

Buckminster Fuller, in characteristic style, recently exaggerated these trends for purposes of emphasis:

> The present decade's crop of buildings are designed primarily by the computerized "Landlords Optimum Occupancy-and-Earnings Analysis" for a given spot in a given city. The engineering departments of the elevator manufacturers design the main stacks to get the mortgaging bank's computer-specified number of occupants and their customers aloft on that much real estate. To serve that many people on that many vertically superimposed decks, the air conditioners surround the elevator shafts with their ducting and cap the giant skeleton structures with their large cooling towers crowded alongside the elevators' roof-top motor housing.
>
> Next, the electrical and hydraulic engineers design the enormous networks and manifolds of power, light, and telephone wires, organic plumbing, and fireproof sprinkler systems which rise from the city's mains and return the wastes to the city's sewers. Next, the engineers of the steel-producing companies design the structural skeleton that will support and accommodate the weight and configuration of those main vertical transport stacks and organic systems. In the next-to-last design phase the exterior decorators play with the few permitted esthetic variables in the choice of materials and in the mechanical and structural componentation of the building's exterior. Among them are windows, embracing prefabricated modules, lobby lighting fixtures, and elevator-car decor. Lastly come the interior decorators employed by the individual tenants.
>
> The client who retains the architect tells him that he has already determined to produce a mortgage-bank prelogisticated building for a specific purpose on a specific site for a specific sum of money. The architect has

TABLE II-12. *Construction Changes Due to Advanced Building Methods*

	Functions affected	Significance	Period of major influence
Industrialized building			
Prefabrication	D-C-M	7	1959-1988
Mobile homes	C-M	8	1966-1984
Stacked mobile homes	D-E-C-M	6	1973-1982
Sectional buildings	E-C-M	5	1966-1982
Shell homes	C-M	2	1963-1976
Utility core modules	D-E-M	6	1967-1980
Steel framed modules	D-E-C-M	5	1974-1988
Structural modules	D-E-C-M	8	1972-1989
Systems building for:			
Public buildings	D-E-C-M	9	1970-1986
Private institutional	D-E-C-M	8	1971-1987
High rise commercial and housing	D-E-C-M	6	1974-1989
Low cost housing	D-E-C-M	3	1979-1990
Proprietary building methods			
Panels on structural skeleton	D-E-C	6	1973-1980
Load bearing wall and slab	D-E-C	8	1972-1984
Stacked box modules			
Checkerboard stacking	D-E-C-M	7	1973-1984
Cantilevered stacking	D-E-C-M	8	1976-1988
Zip together vaults and spans	E-C	5	1974-1986
On-site manufacturing			
Portable batch plants	C-M	4	1965-1974
Precast concrete	D-E-C	8	1975-1990
Steel and aluminum fabrication	E-C	7	1978-1995
Plumbing and utility units	D-E-C-M	5	1974-1992
Framed housing modules	D-E-C-M	7	1972-1986
Mobile factory	C-M	8	1976-1991

226

TABLE II-12. (*Continued*)

	Functions affected	Significance	Period of major influence
Advances in "conventional" methods			
Load bearing thin masonry walls	D-E-C	8	1974-1990
Cranes (crawler, gantry, cradle, and tower)	E-C-M	9	1963-1995
Helicopter airlift	C-M	4	1974-1985
Sonic pile drivers	E-C	4	1966-1986
Filament wound structures	D-E-C	2	1979-1991
Tilt up slab	E-C	6	1964-1986
Slipforming	D-E-C	7	1973-1988
Pumped concrete for high rise	C	6	1974-1986
Suspended ceilings	D-E-C	3	1968-1988
Textured and decorative formwork	C	4	1972-1980
SCR masonry process	E-C	3	1972-1982
Metal stud partition	E-C	4	1977-1990
Prefabricated commercial metal buildings	D-E-C-M	7	1964-1988
Airless paint spray	C	2	1974-1986
Gunite concreting	E-C	3	1959-1984
Post and beam construction	D-E-C	4	1971-1980
Spray on roofing process	C	3	1973-1981
Suspended membrane roofs	D-E-C	3	1976-1990
Buckling shell roof techniques	D-E-C	2	1977-1992
Unitized utility cores	E-C	6	1973-1990
Lift slab construction	D-E-C	4	1960-1980
Foamed in place concrete	E-C	5	1979-1999
Conveyorized systems	C-M	4	1973-1980
Acoustical plaster application	C	5	1962-1983
Built-in wire ways and ducting	D-E-C	3	1977-1989
Finger-jointing	D-E-C	2	1978-1991
Automatic welding units	E-C	8	1977-1995

no original design initiative, for he must design the kind of building the client already has in mind. Usually he must please not only the client, but the client's wife, business partners, lawyers, bankers, real estate agents, and their respective committees of "experts."

By and large the architect has to work with what is available in the industry's architectural and engineering building-components catalogues. Furthermore, he must design within the already preconceived building codes, the zoning laws, and the restrictions set up by various labor unions. The architect also is greatly controlled by what the organized contractors can do, the kinds of tools they have and the price that they bid to do the work. The architect is, finally, just an aesthetical, good-taste purchasing agent and ways-and-means detailer — who is practiced in finding and organizing the usable space amongst the columns, pipes, and elevator stacks.[3]

Powerful technical aids to more efficient and imaginative design and production may provide viable ways to reverse trends which subordinate the role of the professional planner and architect. Developments in management technology will be considered as they relate first to the design process and second to the building project itself.

TECHNOLOGY FOR DECISION AND DESIGN

Technological advances currently available, or under development, to strengthen the design function are generally computer related. Perhaps inordinate attention has been given to computer graphics. Many observers agree that the greatest potential of the computer lies in strengthening the designer's contributions at the earliest stages of planning and programming. Maximizing the architect's contributions before too many options have been foreclosed should be a major goal for the future. Although less advanced at present, technical aids for decision-making and for conceptual and schematic design may have far greater influence than the myriad programs aimed at more efficient handling of technical details.

Before 1975, the use of computer aids in the conceptual phase of building design could become vital — because of increased complexity of building projects, the quickened pace of competition, the ready availability of computers, and the existence of new and powerful software. Designers agree that the increasing complexity of programming makes proper handling of all details difficult — some factors are neglected. Recognizing the iterative nature of design, one goal

228

is to increase the number of factors that can be juggled in the preliminary decision phases. Just as computerized cost-accounting systems often pick up 15 to 20 per cent of time charges formally unaccounted for, the emerging design and decision networks permit additional requirements to be weighed in the schematic phase, offering both greater rigor and increased options of choice.

Two different approaches to automation of design are currently under development. These have been characterized as the "glass box" approach versus the "black box" approach. Proponents of the glass box approach believe that enough can be learned about the decision-making process to establish priorities, values, and criteria and that previously identified patterns of logic can be applied, either to guide the range of choices made by the designer or to indicate the optimum decision set. Indications are that glass box decision-making may be applicable to financial programming, scheduling, site evaluation, and the analysis of building function trade-offs. At least until after 1985, there is no indication that prestructured logic will deal adequately with the larger questions of design — the generation and manipulation of structural form.

For the near term, the black box approach offers greater promise. The fundamental tenet allows the designer to make all of the choices, while the computer displays the full range of alternatives, consequences, and costs. Development of this approach over a ten-year period may be anticipated in four stages:

1. The first stage is the evolution of computer routines for factor analysis, efficiency, cost, functionality, and design "checklists."

2. The second is the flowering of CRT computer graphics suitable for the generation and manipulation of building form, perhaps with a few optimizing routines built in.

3. The third is the marriage of the analytical routines (in alphanumeric form) and graphic display capabilities; at the designers option, control can be transferred back and forth between computer-optimizing routines and the designer's overriding choices.

4. Finally, by 1985, emergence of an interactive system incorporating a personalized designer's thesaurus of forms, subsets, relationships, and values.

The role of simulation and gaming in design is expected to develop concurrently. Design functions will probably tend more toward a gaming approach where "competing" allocations can be evaluated in compressed time; whereas, engineering and technical considerations are generally more amenable to modeling and simulation. Urban planning, landscape design, and regional or neighborhood dynamics are receiving attention in the form of design games. Simulation is progressing in terms of structural dynamic simulation (especially moment-yielding designs for the California seismic codes). Within a few years techniques should be generally available to permit full analysis of structural response to dynamic inputs, based upon simple static-test data. Other programs are being developed for simulating the building environment — observing the performance of building controls over a wide range of environmental conditions.

Whether computerized or not, information retrieval techniques will play an important part in modifying design procedures in the next ten years. Interim systems utilizing microfiche for both handbook and catalogue data are well developed. Units permitting selective call up and display of facade modules and decorative treatments superimposed on the preliminary design represent a foretaste of more elaborate systems to come. The emergence of various commercial information utilities appears a certainty before 1980. Information-handling techniques after 1980 may take several forms:

1. High density optical storage systems; best suited for storing graphic information.

2. Time-sharing information processing and retrieval; best suited for specifications, building codes, and engineering and cost data.

3. Real-time information systems; best suited for handling management data and project programming, rather than design related data.

Prior to 1972, most attention will be devoted to streamlining the handling of detail design and engineering considerations rather than the conceptual phase.

Programs for the generation of specifications should be developed to a generally useful stage before 1975. The generation and manipulation of architectural renderings, perspective views and some working drawings is developing rapidly. Most observers expect this function to evolve as a service under contract to architectural and engineering firms. Adaptation of aerospace techniques for configuration change control are anticipated prior to 1980. As system building becomes better established, computerization of changes in specifications and drawings must be used to insure error-free interfacing of all components and subsystems.

The development use of real-time inventory systems for materials and building components is not expected before the early 1980's. This type of logistic information will not be essential until both building methods and industry structure have undergone substantial change.

Computerized routines for optimizing specific technical elements of detail design are becoming more readily available. Both smaller architectural firms and consulting engineering groups will be major users of design-optimizing programs by 1975. Today these programs are typically table-look-up or simple computational routines for optimizing space and volume allocation, traffic flows, cuts and fills, heat gain calculations, plastic structural design, lighting arrangements, etc. The evolution of both program-sharing agreements and time-sharing computer terminals appears certain to increase the importance of these routines. These are basically techniques for preproving proposed solutions before finalizing the design.

Summarizing changes in design technology to 1985, the forecast is for much greater emphasis on the conceptual phases of design, development of new techniques uniquely suited to the visualization of architectural form and space, delegation of technical optimization to the appropriate specialist groups, with the designer's major contributions to be made in early decision-making, programming, and aesthetics. Phillip Daniel has commented on the aesthetic aspect: "Surprisingly enough, the architectural designers feel a tremendous release and relief when they realize they don't have to worry about remembering to consider hundreds of details, or remember that they've already considered this point or that point, and that it was or was not important. They hated the computer at first but now — gosh, do they concentrate on aesthetics!"[4]

PROJECT MANAGEMENT TECHNIQUES

While the use of management technology to streamline the administrative activities of the firm and to control costs, schedule, and performance on the building project may lack the glamour of technical aids to design, improved automation of management functions can be expected to contribute importantly to profitability.

Over 60 per cent of design-engineering firms now use computer programs for accounting and for cost estimating. Unlike heavy construction, where CPM methods of scheduling are routinely used, new techniques of project management have not been widely accepted in commercial, institutional, and residential building. Large-scale builders believe that optimal routing, PERT calculations, and the PPBS approach to programming will spread into general use by 1980. Industrialized building requires industrial control; and systems building requires systems analysis.

In the fifteen years to 1985, the environmental designer must develop the capability to provide his clients — quickly and economically — with the following additional services:

1. Computerized feasibility studies.

2. Predetermination of building costs, owning costs, and operation costs — as a function of building quality.

3. Analysis of the relationship of cost to revenue-producing capacity of a project, i.e., economic soundness.

4. Analysis of insurance and tax structures as they apply to the design of the project.

5. Strict management and documentation of quality control regarding materials, equipment, contractor performance, and liability protection.

6. Determination of competitive bidding factors and analysis of contractors bids.

The task of providing these services to the client suggests that the sharpened pencil may give way to the time-shared computer terminal.

Almost certainly, business services and cost analyses will be performed via time-sharing. In 1968, over $100 million was spent for computer time-sharing in the United States. In 1965, the amount was practically nothing. This is quite a growth in a very short period of time. And, obviously, the end is not in sight.

Beyond programming, the supervisory functions of the professional designer will be aided by on-site inspection techniques such as time lapse photography, video tape recording, and on-site data loggers. Performance certification for engineering subsystems can be performed more rapidly using preprogrammed acceptance tests. Test data also provide a fully documented base line for supervising warranty and maintenance agreements. Such inspection, documentation, and reporting techniques are expected to dovetail with emerging trends toward computerized building control systems. The International Monetary Fund building in Washington, D.C., is the first commercial office structure to employ a high degree of computerized automation in its operation and maintenance. A dedicated 12,000 word core computer controls and operates the refrigeration system, electrical system, heating, ventilation, lighting, and plumbing systems, as well as providing an analysis of the operational efficiency of major equipment.

New technology expected to influence management and control functions in the design and construction of buildings is summarized in Table II-13. Unlike technological change expected in building materials and construction methods, technical advances in the management area are expected to have maximum impact after 1980. Improved programming of the building process will have the earliest

TABLE II-13. *Management Technology for Design and Control*

	Functions affected	Degree of significance	Period of maximum effect
Design related techniques			
Requirements analysis	D-E	6	1973-1980
Project economic feasibility	D-E-M	7	1971-1984
Preliminary programming	D-M	8	1970-1982
Design, zoning, and code checklists	D-C-M	5	1976-1985
Environmental planning games	D-M	4	1975-1983
File review IR	D-E	5	1971-1980
Catalog IR	D-E	5	1970-1980
Handbooks IR	D-E	5	1974-1982
Programmed decision networks ("glass-box")	D-M	6	1978-1990
"Black-box" decision techniques	D-M	7	1974-1986
CRT "sketchpad" techniques	D	6	1975-1984
Generation and manipulation of form	D	8	1977-1988
Iterative design techniques	D-E	6	1980-1990
Microfiche data banks	D-E	4	1970-1978
High density optical storage	D-E	6	1978-1990
Video file of form manipulations	D	7	1980-1992
Perspective views	D	4	1968-1979
Architectural renderings	D	5	1971-1980

(Continued)

233

TABLE II-13. (*Continued*)

	Functions affected	Degree of significance	Period of maximum effect
Engineering and detail design development			
Shared program agreements	D-E-M	6	1974-1981
Time shared terminals	D-E-M	9	1970-1984
Commercial information utility	D-E	7	1978-1990
Structural analysis			
Plastic design	D-E	4	1972-1980
Ultimate strength design	D-E	4	1973-1982
Moment yielding calculations	D-E	5	1974-1984
Seismic code compliance	E-M	5	1972-1986
Space frames	D-E-C	4	1971-1986
Space trusses	D-E	4	1972-1980
Suspension structures	D-E	3	1975-1986
Staggered truss designs	E-C	3	1974-1986
Hyperbolic structures	D-E-C	3	1976-1988
Cost analysis	D-M	7	1971-1986
Specification generation	E-M	8	1973-1988
Specification update	E-M	4	1978-1990
Heat gain calculations	E	3	1970-1980
Cuts and fills	E	3	1972-1982
Lighting design	D-E	3	1975-1984
Floor space and volume allocation	D-E-M	8	1972-1986
Elevator design	E-M	6	1974-1982
Traffic flow	D-E	4	1973-1980
Piping design	E	4	1968-1977
Design revision routines	D	6	1980-1995
Working construction drawings	D-E-M	7	1978-1989
Building simulation	E-M	5	1977-1984
Construction project simulation	M	6	1976-1990
Computerized building control	E-M	5	1976-1995
Administrative management and control techniques			
Project programming	D-M	9	1976-1995
Financial and tax structure analysis	M	6	1972-1982

TABLE II-13. (*Concluded*)

	Functions affected	Degree of significance	Period of maximum effect
Administrative management and control techniques (Concluded)			
Operating and maintenance costs	E-M	4	1974-1984
Efficiency analyses	E-M	3	1972-1986
Project scheduling			
PPBS	C-M	7	1973-1985
CPM	C-M	7	1966-1975
PERT	C-M	5	1968-1975
PERT-COST	C-M	5	1971-1980
Materials and components inventory	D-C-M	6	1980-1990
Real-time logistics	C-M	7	1985-2000
On-site supervision aids	C-M	5	1972-1985
Project management information centers	C-M	6	1971-1988
Documentation aids	M	7	1973-1980
Performance and inspection routines	E-M	5	1972-1984
Maintenance scheduling	E-M	4	1970-1979
Periodic projects reporting	M	5	1972-1984
Client visual communication aids	M	4	1972-1980

effect. Fundamental changes in the approach to environmental design are expected to have consequences which will persist for the balance of this century.

Innovations and technological advances which will influence building materials, construction methodology, engineering, architectural design, and management of the production phases of building have been considered in this chapter. Rather than suggesting how the architectural profession will respond to these changes, the foreseeable trends and opportunities may be summarized by considering the present distribution of professional time. Technological factors may then be assessed in terms of potential shifts among the efforts and time allocations of the professional designer.

For building projects of moderate complexity, the distribution of professional time and costs are shown in Table II-14. Linkage with

TABLE II-14. *Technology and Traditional Architectural Practice*

Functions of the Architect-Engineer	Current allocation of cost and effort*	Future trend
Architectural services		
Conceptual, schematic design		
Principal architect's time	5-10%	Increase
Detail design development		
Construction documents		
Specifications		
Construction drawings	15-18%	Decrease
Blueprinting and reproduction		
Engineering services		
Inside staff	5%	Increase
Outside consulting	25-40%	
Structural		
Mechanical		
Electrical	30-45%	
Other		
Client communications		
Meetings, reviews,		
Contracts, renderings,	2-5%	Increase
Models, specifications		
Construction supervision	7-10%	Decrease
General activities		
Office administration		
Nonproject activities	15-30%	Decrease
Overhead		

* Current distribution of architectural efforts modified from AIA "Economics of Architectural Practice," based on billings for 485 buildings; Categories I and II (modified by Committee judgments).

1970 to 1985	*1985 to 2000*
	Commercial information utility "Sketchpad"
File and catalog Microfiche	Planning "games"
Computer design aids ("Black Box")	Personalized interactive computer design techniques
Time-sharing terminals for programming	
Cost analysis and estimating	Iterative "Glass Box" decision networks
CRT landscaping	"Omnibuildings"
3-D form generation and manipulation	

Specification generation methods	Configuration change control techniques
CRT display — computer graphics —	Computer directed preparation of construction drawings
Massive scale projects	
Automatic revision and update of plans and specifications	
Automatic code and zoning checkout	High density optical information storage

Time-sharing optimizing routines	Real-time inventory and logistics
New materials High rise stacked modules	Structural plastics
Performance specifications	Building project simulation
Newer structural design theories	
Seismic codes Simulation of building environment	
Propietary construction systems	
Load bearing concrete walls	Computerized building controls
Componentation "Open" building systems	

Client programming Automatic rendering and models	
Project management information center "War Room" briefing	
Visual communication aids	

Industrialized modular building	On-site data logging
Mobile factory	
On-site factory methods	Automatic test and acceptance
Supervision and documentation aids	Baysian state-space control methods

PPBS application	
Shared program agreements	Organic change in "Environmental Design Community"
Computer cost accounting	
Bidding strategy	Financial simulation of the design firm

relevant technical trends and innovations indicates ways in which the allocation of the designers' efforts in the future may be affected.

In 1967, Robert Hastings predicted directions for the future.[5] Creative use of new technology can play an important role. "The architect of the future will devote more time to value judgments, proper use of space and total design concept. He will spend less time on technical and mechanical details. These will become the responsibility of the building component manufacturers, who will become specialist experts in building systems, and subsystems. The manufacturer will develop, test, fabricate, install and guarantee the system."

SUMMARY: CHANGE, ISSUES, AND UNCERTAINTIES FOR THE ARCHITECT

THE FUTURE examined in this report calls for a new role for the architectural profession, and for a redefinition of professionalism.

The role of the architect — or rather, the design team with the architect as catalyst and coordinator — will be necessarily more comprehensive if the profession is to retain or build a major degree of influence on the shaping of the environment. Specifically, this means that the architect's role may be less one of design activity itself than of managing the design-implementation process in which there will have to be more active collaboration with the client on all aspects of the problem, and with a large number of other skill resources. Architecture will have to earn the right to play this coordinative role; it is not likely to be conferred automatically.

In this context, professionalism takes on new meaning. To a great extent, the artist-patron model still seems to apply to architect-client relations — at least from the point of view of the architect. This work style both reinforces and is reinforced by fees and billing practices, common methods of office organization, and the tendency to "farm out" aspects of the design problem which are viewed (incorrectly) as wholly technical or peripheral to the central design task. The limited data available on the nature of design assignments undertaken by many members of the profession tend to reinforce this picture: large segments of the profession appear to spend most of the time in types of client assignments which will have a static or declining future; few seem to have gained much experience in the increasingly comprehensive design tasks (of socio-physical-political systems) which will become more common.

This suggests that each element in current architectural practice (in terms of actual activities — not intentions or academic principles) be examined to determine the extent to which these features of current activity in the profession are preventing architects from coping with both threats and opportunities.

We believe that a number of frequently heard assertions about the environment and role of architectural practice should be challenged. Even beliefs strongly supported today by current conditions need re-examination, since these conditions are changing rapidly. Yet, as is well known, beliefs are slower to change than conditions which cause them. Below are a number of lay assertions about the situation of the architect, and what we regard as plausible alternatives to these views.

Assertion: New technology will encourage wider practice of professional design.

Alternative: Both the invention and application of new technologies in all fields — especially building but also in information processing, communications, management, environmental control, transportation, etc. — will be guided primarily by political considerations, secondly by engineering/economic considerations. Criteria such as aesthetic elegance, "customized" approaches, flexibility (to allow for multiple use as well as changes in use over time), derivation of design criteria from socio-psychological requirements determined through research will probably be in third place.

Assertion: Wider application of good design is blocked by union-controlled work practices, obsolete or "protectionist" building codes, and zoning regulations.

Alternative: The environmental crisis — housing shortages, urban disorganization, low income through lack of employment opportunity or low education, and the other evidence of social malaise — is creating powerful forces for change in all these previously restrictive forces. The profession needs to gear its practice and education preparation to an environment in which removal or modification of these practices will be increasingly the norm.

Assertion: Most people don't care about design.

Alternative: People are intensely aware of and affected by bad design or a lack of attention to design. However, there is no vocabulary

240

in which these concerns can be expressed, particularly in advance of design and construction. There is also little or no opportunity for direct communication between the "users" of designed space and the designers of that space.

Assertion: The current social reaction to an increased rate of change will harden, resulting in a possibly violent repression and rejection of new technology.

Alternative: There is little prospect of an "anti-technology" reaction in terms of a retreat from present increasing commitment to cybernetics, computer-centered processing of mass data for both analysis and decision-making, and increasing automation of production (e.g., in all aspects of building materials and components). Responsible, sophisticated, pragmatic practice of design becomes more important than ever in this context, since the trend will be away from one-of-a-kind design solutions toward mass application. But this more effective practice will have to be carried on in the context of, therefore attuned to, increasingly "technologized" environments, production techniques and managerial or decision-making process.

Just as it is possible to conceive of two "environments" for the profession in the next thirty years — one in which there is ad hoc uncoordinated action with respect to the environment and another in which there is national policy coordination for urban ecology, population distribution, housing, etc. — so it is possible to conceive of two "strategies" for the profession. One would evidence little change from present practices in design activity, project management, client relations, etc., and the other would reflect a movement toward "design management" — a better articulation, assembly, and control of professional skills in the service of improved planning and structuring of the environment. Thus, four possibilities exist:

1. *Professional practice and environment policy essentially as today.*

Under these conditions, we can expect to find ourselves in a national social crisis of which present urban illnesses are the leading edge. With emergency conditions in effect, the independent practice of architecture would be seen as irrelevant or beyond the ability of the society to support in terms of time and money. Professional skills still needed would be "co-opted" by public agencies and other mechanisms for "top down," short-term solutions.

2. Practice remains the same, but national environmental policy is developed.

Here, too, architecture would be pushed to the periphery. Environmental design and planning decisions would be made largely by other professions — lawyers, economists, engineers, planners, perhaps social scientists. Criteria of utility would tend to take precedence over aesthetic values and customized solutions. The practice of architecture would become bureaucratized and the "planner/architect" would emerge as a technical specialist in a combination of planning and design.

3. Architectural practice moves toward "design management" but without corresponding evolution of national environmental policy.

This possibility is the least likely of the four, since the scope and depth of the current environmental crisis has already produced environmental control strategies at the local and regional level in such areas as pollution and noise abatement. These trends may be expected to continue. Also, national environmental policy would tend to encourage a more comprehensive approach to the design task. (Whether or not the architect would be at the center of a thrust toward design management is another question.)

4. "Design Management" emerges in the context of comprehensive policies of environmental planning and control.

This is the most likely and, in our view, hopeful alternative. Trends in public policy and in the profession already emerging would be mutually reinforcing. For the architect to be at the center of this comprehensive approach, massive renewal and augmentation of professional skills will be necessary, both in the professional schools and among practitioners. Much of the new experience and skills needed would be developed on the job as a result of multidisciplinary teams working in the context of organizations larger and more diverse than the bulk of today's architectural firms. "Clinical," problem-centered experience, with wider dissemination of "successful" design solutions and techniques, will be the norm.

To prevent professional obsolescence and to prepare for the more comprehensive practice of design which would seem inevitable if architecture is to survive as a distinct profession and one seen as salient by society, a renewal process via continuing education both on and off the job seems essential. This must start with practicing professionals;

the urgency of the design challenge will not permit a primary reliance on change in professional school curricula. New curricula for professional education should be derived heavily from challenges being encountered in practice and innovations developed there. Elements in mid-career renewal of the architect might include:

1. applied cybernetics

2. applied behavioral sciences: problem-solving and consultation based on diagnosis of social systems ranging from small groups through organizations to communities or regions

3. management techniques: particularly the prediction and implementation of change

4. design implications of other new technologies

5. design implications of new concepts in education, government, industrial management, community services, communications, and other institutional spheres

6. demographic attitudinal and value trends, particularly at the community and regional level

It would be useful and responsible for the profession to play possible scenarios of the future for the society as a whole against possible scenarios of the profession in terms of types of practice, professional education, relations to other design professions and to the environment — client groups and other significant publics such as government. The analysis presented in this report can be viewed as one kind of prototype for this sort of forecasting.

AIA might consider a continuing "Forum on the Future" to be presented through such media as the *Journal;* annual national, regional, and local meetings; the mass media (in concert with other design professions); and specialized information services such as subscriber supported data banks, briefings, etc. All these media might have as content such subjects as:

1. encounters with "significant others" (representatives of key present or potential client groups, public policy-makers, academics outside the design professions, etc.) to present their views of the profession as a basis for dialogue

2. wider reporting of "successful" solutions to design problems, including description of the design process and problem-solving, differences between expectations and results, client-professional relationships, views of "third parties" affected by the project though not involved in its implementation

3. AIA might aggressively develop information collection and screening programs to do a more effective knowledge-transfer job in these areas through tie-ins with the new Urban Information Clearinghouse now being planned by HUD and the National Institute of Mental Health's information system

4. study of the design team in relationship to various types of design problems — how to create the team, appropriate modes of collaboration between the architect and other team members (e.g., systems specialists, engineers, social scientists, planners, economists), typical problems of interdisciplinary collaboration and ways of alleviating these, etc.

5. current and potential relationships between professional students and practitioners

6. the discovery and use of social criteria for design and design implementation.

TABLE A-1. *Employment, Payroll, and Number of Reporting Units By Phase of Construction*[a]
(United States, March 1967)

Construction phase	SIC code	Employment	Payroll ($M)	No. of reporting units[b]
Land acquisition and preparation		625,534	650,119	161,917
Real estate owner-operators	651	280,934	340,974	114,127
Real estate agents, brokers, managers	653	93,688	115,865	21,274
Title abstract companies	654	14,941	18,212	2,364
Investment builders	655	60,741	75,795	8,374
Operative builders	656	41,856	56,930	6,942
Combination real estate, mortgage loans, insurance and law offices	66	33,374	42,343	8,836
Financing		1,883,365	2,824,646	54,351
Commercial and stock savings banks	602	776,983	1,067,225	14,955
Mutual savings banks	603	26,059	38,873	413
Rediscounting & financing institutions (for credit other than banks)	611	1,335	2,143	112
Savings & loan associations	612	91,805	132,848	5,680

(Continued)

245

TABLE A-1. *(Continued)*

Construction phase	SIC code	Employment	Payroll ($M)	No. of reporting units[b]
Financing (Continued)				
Bond & mortgage companies	6,152	44,953	69,019	3,883
Loan correspondents & brokers	616	5,071	8,112	718
Insurance carriers	63	937,159	1,506,426	28,590
Designing		250,465	520,960	21,260
Architectural & engineering services	891	250,465	520,960	21,260
Contract construction		2,962,733	4,928,126	305,650
Building construction by general contractors	15	889,069	1,419,260	86,221
Non-building construction by general contractors	16	554,239	964,009	28,560
Construction by special trade contractors	17	1,490,437	2,477,793	190,229
(Administrative & auxiliary personnel)		28,988	67,064	640
Total (all phases of construction cited above)		5,722,097	8,923,851	543,178

[a] Data understated in two ways: First, mid-March is the middle of the slow construction season; second, some groups, such as planners and title lawyers, could not be isolated from their larger SIC listing and included here.

[b] Number of Reporting Units means number of establishments in each state; therefore a multi-state operation would be included in this count more than once.

Source: *County Business Patterns: U.S. Summary, 1967*. U.S. Department of Commerce, U.S. Bureau of the Census.

TABLE A-2. *Major New Actors in the Industry*

Actors by type	New roles and activities
CONGLOMERATES (Existing Organizations and ad hoc partnerships):	
Aetna Life & Casualty, Kaiser Industries, and Kaiser Aluminum & Chemical	Land — Acquisition and Development: Plan to pool $175 MM in cash on properties to move strongly into all types of real estate. Design — Structural and Environmental: Kaiser Industries — prime contractor for HUD's "in-city" R&D program. Construction: Kaiser Aluminum & Chemical purchased a California producer of relocatable structures.
Southern California Edison; Bechtel Corp.	Construction: 10-year, $250 MM project to build showcase all-electric residential community for 15,000 people.
ITT	Construction: Acquisition of Levitt & Sons, nation's largest private home builder.
Gulf & Western Industries	Land — Acquisition and Development: Set up a real estate subsidiary to put to work excess land acquired as part of its expansion activities.
Holiday Inns of America; U.S. Gypsum; John Hancock Mutual Life Insurance Company	Money — Debt and Equity Financing: John Hancock and U.S. Gypsum providing $2 MM financing to Allied Mortgage Development Company organized and directed by Holiday Inns. Design — Structural and Environmental; Construction: Holiday Inns is the organizer and director of Allied Mortgage Development Company, an independent corporation set up to develop and use various systems approaches to construction of low-cost housing.
Connecticut General Life Insurance, Teachers Insurance Annuity Assoc., Chase Manhattan Bank	Money — Debt and Equity Financing: Equity position in land acquisition and development of Columbia.

(Continued)

TABLE A-2. (*Continued*)

Actors by type	New roles and activities
CONSTRUCTION INDUSTRY VERTICAL INTEGRATORS:	
Boise-Cascade	Construction: Long-range plan — nationwide residential construction — from base of lumber and other building materials supplier through land development, manufacture of mobile homes and permanent structures and components, both on-site and at factory. Current projects: prime consulting contractor for renewal of downtown Boise, rent supplement projects in Boston, Indianapolis, and Pittsburgh, commercial, industrial-residential complex in Long Beach, California, middle-income development in Boston.
Tishman Realty & Construction Co.	Other — A one-industry conglomerate: locates land; designs building; arranges interim and permanent financing; builds; leases and manages; and tests new production materials for the industry.
U.S. Plywood-Champion Papers	Land — Acquisition and Development: Runs 35 resident developments in 8 states.
ASSET CONVERTORS:	
Penn-Central RR	Land — Acquisition and Development: One of nation's largest realty owners. Owns and operates two recreational parks in Texas and Georgia; building a third in California. Investment return in railroad is 3%; return on realty 15-20%.
Norfolk & Western Rwy.	Land — Acquisition and Development: Within 12 years hopes to develop all of its off-track acreage (13,000) and buy some more. Three current projects: in joint venture with Chicago's Railway Properties, $18 MM residential-commercial-industrial complex in Ham-

TABLE A-2. (*Continued*)

Actors by type	New roles and activities
ASSET CONVERTORS: (*Continued*)	
Norfolk & Western Rwy. (*Continued*)	mond, Indiana; $10 MM industrial park near Cincinnati; $100 MM residential-commercial complex near Kansas City.
Humble Oil Company	Land — Acquisition and Development: Turning 25,000 acres originally acquired for oil and gas prospecting into a "new town" on the outskirts of Houston. Also planning a residential-commercial-industrial complex on 50,000 acres near Houston airport.
Standard Oil of California	Land — Acquisition and Development: Formed real estate subsidiary to find uses for 250,000 acres of company-owned surplus land.
PRODUCT/SERVICE MARKET EXPANDERS	
American Standard Corp.	Land — Acquisition and Development: Has $17.5 MM investment in real estate. Money — Debt and Equity Financing: Also with Celanese has formed a corporation to finance low-income, federally assisted housing. First project: a $1 MM apartment in East Harlem to be designed and built by blacks.
General Electric Corp.	Other: Has disbanded a special division created four years ago to study the applications of its products and services to "new towns" creation. One successful product of the new disbanded division was the housing systems proposal for DOD which was considered the most valuable of three competing concepts.
Campbell Engineering	Design — Structural and Environmental; Construction: Engaged in experimental housing project in Detroit to test use of standardized components and computerized planning in reducing cost and time of construction.

(*Continued*)

TABLE A-2. (*Concluded*)

Actors by type	New roles and activities
PRODUCT/SERVICE MARKET EXPANDERS (*Continued*)	
Westinghouse Electric Corp.	Land — Acquisition and Development: Acquired a Florida real estate company which is developing a planned community near Ft. Lauderdale. Plans to use it as an urban lab to test its production systems. Other: In mid-1968 formed urban systems development subsidiary to develop, build, and rehab low-income federally assisted housing.

TABLE A-3. *Total Cost Index*

Year	Land cost	Bldg. cost	Land component	Bldg. component	L & B	Total resid. cost index 1960 = 1000	% In	
							Land	Bldg.
1950	585	770	585	2310	2895	724	20.2	79.8
1955	765	885	765	2655	3420	855	22.4	77.6
1960	1000	1000	1000	3000	4000	1000	25.0	75.0
1965	1250	1105	1250	3315	4565	1141	27.3	72.7
1968	1530	1310	1530	3930	5460	1365	28.0	72.0
1970	1640	1350	1640	4050	5690	1422	28.8	71.2
1985	3450	1950	3450	5850	9300	2325	37.1	62.9
2000	7250	2950	7250	8850	16100	4025	45.0	55.0

Bldg. cost: Based on Boeckh Residential Building Cost Index, 1950-1968.
Land cost: Based on USDA Farm Real Estate Values, 1950-1968.

PART THREE

Future of the Profession

GERALD M. McCUE

CHAIRMAN OF THE
AMERICAN INSTITUTE OF ARCHITECTS COMMITTEE
FOR THE STUDY OF THE FUTURE OF THE PROFESSION

INTRODUCTION

THE FUTURE of the design professions and the building industry is an integral part of the future of our society. In order to assess the future of the profession of architecture, the AIA Committee has reviewed the range of possible futures, identified those factors of change which might be most critical, and projected their probable consequences upon the profession. The identification of future trendings has proven to be a simpler task than projecting their impact upon architects, for the existing profession is not subject to direct causal relationships from external forces. Even if future developments outside the profession were certain, it is questionable as to whether one could predict their consequences on even the majority of the persons and organizations which make up the field of architecture. It is possible, however, to make several important conclusions from the studies completed.

The Committee concludes that a precise description of the future of the profession is neither possible nor desirable. To make such a definition would suggest a homogeneous profession, and it appears safe to conclude that it will be even less monolithic in the future than it is today. Most important, a precise description would imply that the future was preordained and that by adding all the factors, one could arrive at a specific answer. As the studies progressed, it became increasingly clear that this was not the case. The Committee does believe, however, that a range of future roles can be identified and that the architect's position within this range is still open to some degree of choice. This section is intended to identify those areas of choice and to provide a background for the commitments which the Committee believes that the profession must make in the near future.

The objectives set for the first view of the future of the profession were three:

1. to identify those factors which in the future would have the greatest impact upon the physical environment and upon the processes and persons who would shape that environment.

2. to study the principal factors in depth and to identify the problems which the changes from these influences would present to the architectural profession.

3. to project the probable range of futures which are available for the profession and to identify the areas of decision and suggest actions which should be taken now in order to keep open the range of future choices.

It was concluded that "original" research for investigation of each of these areas should be considered as a long-range and ongoing task. Thus, the decision was made to limit this review to a reconnaissance and analysis of available projections for the future, in what are believed to be the most critical areas, and to bring this work to a conclusion in order to provide a context for immediate action.

In order to reach its conclusions, a conceptual model for the profession was sought which would afford a method for relating the vast number of seemingly unrelated trends and projections which might influence its future. The model is discussed in detail later, but in essence it views architecture and the other design professions as an interface between society and society's demands from the environment at one side, and on the other side the verified knowledge and available resources for meeting those problems. In this construct, the profession is a delivery system, applying its values and utilizing its skills to bring the resources and knowledge to bear on society's environmental problems.

This report, which includes two studies of the forces deemed most critical, does not take into account all of the external factors which will influence the design professions in the future. For example, the review was limited to an analysis of probable future influences in the United States, although the Committee is strongly aware of the critical importance of international developments, both social and technological. Similarly, no detailed studies were made of industries other than those closely related to the present construction process, and some sources believe that innovation may be most apt to come from outside the present industry. As the studies progressed, other areas of critical importance began to be identified; and although the William R. Ewald, Jr. study projects the general social environment, there is a great need for further study of the public's demand from the micro-physical environment.

Given our conceptual model of the profession, it is also clear that before more complete predictions can be made as to the nature of the architectural profession, it will be necessary to study the character and strength of the existing profession and its institutions. In particular, these studies should concentrate on the capabilities, personality traits, and ambitions of young architects and students.

Equally as important as additional knowledge about our own profession is the need for further study of the related design professions with which we will share our future responsibilities. The two preceding studies give an overview of the external context in which architects and the other design profession will act their roles, but neither contains an adequate data base to compare their capabilities or to predict the choices each will make as to its own future. Most important, the lack of any study of the existing field of architecture — and in particular its schools — prevents an adequate review of the capability of architects for assuming the roles to which they aspire. One cannot assess their probable success as compared to others outside the profession, many of whom will have strong capabilities and the same hopes for the future. The Committee strongly urges that the American Institute of Architects not stop at this point, but rather continue its studies of the most relevant factors pertaining to the future of the field of architecture.

1.

HIGHLIGHTS OF THE STUDIES

THE COMMITTEE and the consultants agreed on one critical point; the character of the future is not forclosed. There are trends and directions that may be projected, but real options remain open to both society as a whole and architects as individuals.

In a very real sense, no single, clearly defined role emerges for the architect. In the period of rapid and profound change which is likely to continue for some considerable number of years, no man may be wholly the master of his fate. Nonetheless, for the architect and for others in the environmental design professions, the choices to be made have significance.

The factors likely to shape the future American society and the construction industry are complex. There is no need to summarize them; but the following highlights, selected by study coordinator Henry Bruck, are critical and are fundamental to the Committee's own conclusions.

Societal Trends (from report by William R. Ewald, Jr.)

1. The present and foreseeable future, 15 to 30 years, is a shock front of change similar in its depth and consequences to the agricultural and industrial revolutions. Potentially, the years before us can be one of the great epics of mankind.

2. At the present time, the United States is a low morale society. In order to take advantage of the opportunities that are open, the United States must become a high morale society.

3. The greatest need is for social inventions to control the use of technology and to direct it to human ends.

4. More effective two-way communication to assure a sense of genuine participation is a key factor, especially between professionals and laymen.

5. Nonprofit institutions offer a unique basis for dialogue and participation in creating a human future.

6. The present crisis is a national, not just an urban one. The driving forces of change are population growth, migration patterns and technology.

7. U.S. society cannot afford everything it wants, but it can afford anything it wants.

8. Four paths to the future seem possible — revolution, reason, response, and reaction. The fixing of priorities will depend on the path followed.

9. A number of "system breaks," that is, discontinuities of past trends, may affect the future environment. Among these are a low birth rate and longer life expectancy, a national settlement policy, expanded civilian R & D, and novel telecommunication technology.

The Building Industry (from report by Midwest Research Institute)

1. At present, the building industry is an ad hoc assembly of skills, resources, and control groups. It is not a high technology industry.

2. The industry does not now have the capacity to build "another America."

3. Firms from other industries have recently begun to explore the total building market.

4. The building industry could change rapidly and dramatically during the next fifteen years.

5. The major forces for change are:
  • science and technology, especially in communications and management.
  • public policy leading to greater accord between the public private sectors.
  • market growth.

6. The direction of change is likely to be toward a more conventional, large-scale industry structure integrating now separate functions.

7. Pressure of demand for money will continue to outrun the available supply.

8. Government policy will be the critical factor in the provision of stable financing for the industry.

9. Land costs will continue to increase sharply as a percentage of total project costs with resulting pressure for intensification of land use.

10. The pattern of rapid and vital suburban growth will continue.

11. Revitalization of urban centers may be achieved only by government action.

12. Building construction volume is growing faster than the supply of architects and building design engineers.

13. Because of a conventional lag pattern, innovations in technology of construction will have their greatest impact after 1985.

14. Existing constraints on innovation can be expected to give way under pressure of necessity in the next ten years.

2.

THE PHYSICAL ENVIRONMENT

WE ARE ENTERING AN ERA of extreme social stress created by the need and demand for greater economic parity by low income groups, for equality of opportunity and choice by minorities, and for greater participation in decision making by all groups in society. These issues will form the context for a search for new social values and will be the most critical factors in determining both the extent and nature of the development of the environment. Persons and organizations which emerge as effective instruments to deal with these issues will have a major influence on the form of the physical environment, affecting both the public and private sectors. Even those aspects of the private sector which appear unrelated will be highly influenced by public policies and methods for effectuation created to deal with the central social issues.

The critical questions relating to society's objectives for the environment have been identified by Ewald. Can images of the environment be put forth which will be sufficiently strong and worthy of achievement that the public will support their fulfillment? Will the public be sufficiently concerned about the quality of the environment to allocate a significant portion of the growing GNP to develop, improve, and maintain it? Will sufficiently high goals be set, such that new development represents a step forward in achieving the highest level of amenity which an advanced technological society can provide? Will the same high standard be set for the nation's low income groups? Will the public recognize a priority for greater overall improvement as compared to a higher level of luxury for a privileged few? The answers to these questions will develop from the individual and collective ideologies of our citizens and from those groups who come forward to lead in establishing these goals.

The need for setting coordinated objectives and for developing theoretical constructs of idealized environments cannot be overestimated. The extent of new development in the next few generations will be unmatched by any time in history; but whether it will develop a higher standard of living, a more rewarding physical environment, or will result in a slow deterioration of human values will depend upon the objectives and skills of the individuals who are concerned, the ideals which they visualize, and the degree to which they convince the public that their visions are worth achieving.

The Large-Scale Environment

The form and quality of the large-scale physical environment will be social and political and will be most affected by the following factors:

Public Objective. The nature of the life styles and environments to which the public aspires and is willing to support; the extent to which the public makes its concern for the physical environment a high priority; the extent to which citizens groups become actively involved in the planning process; all will be critical factors.

GNP/Population. The ratio of the growth of the GNP to the growth of the population will result in a mean per capita income which will establish the degree of individual affluence. The higher the mean, the more willing the public will be to put greater expenditure into preservation and improvement of the physical environment.

Governmental Fiscal and Taxation Policies. At local, regional, and national levels, policies related to the exploitation and conservation of the physical environment will be formed to reflect the public's objectives at the macro-scale. Equally as important, policies designed to stimulate or retard improvement of various sectors of the economy or segments of society or geographic areas will be formulated at the national level, and these policies will have more influence on the physical environment than any other single factor.

Taxation policies will be formulated and revised and will have a major influence on the development of the physical environment. The extent to which real property, as opposed to income, is taxed for support of government, education, and public environmental improvements will be a significant factor in determining public support.

262

Demographic Patterns. The urban migration will continue by an even more mobile population, and it will create new demographic settlement patterns related to climate, employment opportunities, and opportunities for sought-after life styles and recreation, rather than the earlier historic ties to natural transportation routes or raw-product centers.

Transportation. Long distance transportation is sufficiently advanced to predict a high degree of world mobility for an increasingly more affluent population. The character of public and private transportation for short distances is more difficult to predict, however, and the actual commuting time between home, place of work, and recreation will strongly influence the residential pattern and ratio of center city to suburban development. No significant new technological advances are projected in the near future, and the effectiveness of local transportation will be determined primarily through priorities established between existing systems.

Income Support. The creation of an income floor, negative income tax, rent supplement or similar subsidy program (this does not include public housing) would constitute a system break which would permit free choice of location and type of accommodation and would effectuate a more natural settlement pattern. If no program of support is generated to permit natural settlement pattern, then the center city and suburb will become increasingly more polarized with black government and population in the cities, white government and population in the suburbs. The tensions, conflicts, and war for resources which would result would be highly destructive to the social environment and would mitigate against a high quality physical environment.

Supply and Demand. The demand factor will affect most severely the cost of land near metropolitan areas, in beneficial climatic zones, and near natural recreational resources. This will, in turn, result in higher residential and commercial densities. The demand for construction will outpace the ability of the construction industry to produce, thus maintaining relatively high costs and permitting the industry to lag in efficiency in comparison to other segments of the nation's production. The continued high cost for both land and construction and an even greater increase in the complexity of the development process will jointly contribute to a greater trend for purchase or rental of property already developed by others as opposed to individuals initiating construction for their own needs.

The form and character of the large-scale physical environment are clearly more related to the life-style ambitions of each segment of society than to any other consideration. The factors are primarily sociological in that they will be dependent upon the social conditions which will influence individual decisions. The degree and amount of government imposed economic control for assisting and for encouraging change in each of the areas described above will be the most significant additional determinant. It will be the public, led by those professional and social institutions that project images and assist in formulating policies regarding these issues, which will make the ultimate choices through government, at both local and national levels.

THE SMALL-SCALE ENVIRONMENT

The conditions which will affect the form of the small-scale environment are both sociological and technological and largely depend upon whether there is a relatively free market or tightly controlled development and upon the extent of technological advance in the building industry. The major factors are as follows:

Life Style. Increased affluence will permit an even higher percentage (ideally all) of the population to select places of habitation which will implement the life style they seek. The form of the small-scale physical environment will still reflect the balance between the life pattern sought after and its relative cost. The primary difference between living in an apartment and a single-family house will be the relation to private or public use of adjacent land and the relation to other available facilities rather than the physical configuration of the living space itself. The most significant changes in the future will be not in the physical form of the facilities which house activities but in social patterns and family groupings, in the kinds of activities which are made available, and in new groupings and relationships among activities.

Government Involvement. Direct purchase, construction, or implementation by governmental agencies will greatly affect particular kinds of development, particularly in the urban core; but it is less apt to influence new growth in undeveloped areas. Outside of the

264

urban core, government-inducement programs which produce financial investment incentives will be the most critical factor.

Government Control of Criteria. The degree to which planning laws, ordinances, codes, and financing criteria will apply will strongly affect the extent of innovation in new construction technologies.

Public Control of Criteria. The extent to which the local populace, through local commissions and public hearings, has a voice in the decisions regarding development programs will be a major factor in the level of social amenity which will be achieved.

Motivations of Project Initiators. Most critical are the objectives of the project initiator, whether public or private. The underlying motive for providing either exceptional quality for a competitive market or minimum amenity for a closed market is most fundamental. Similarly, whether the project is for the initiator's own use and long term retention or for quick resale, or whether the development is a response to a known need rather than merely an investment vehicle, are all significant factors in determining the quality of the improvement.

Means of Implementation. By establishing the balance of decision-making, the means of development critically affect the finished product. When decision-making is linear and fragmented, each group in turn sets its own criteria and the next must work within them. In contrast, when development can be an interaction between all of the interested parties — developers, occupants, supervisory authorities, finance, designers, and contractors — the net result can optimize the contributions of each and permit true innovation. The critical determinant will be the degree to which quantifiable criteria such as the highest investment return per cubage, the maximum cubage permitted by zoning, minimum spaces permitted, etc., are weighed against subjective values which reflect psychological needs such as light, space, convenience, privacy, and activity and status fulfillment. The means of project implementation affects the methods by which these criteria are fixed, the extent to which they are negotiable, and the relative weight each is assigned; and the making of these decisions is essentially the first design stage.

Motivation of Designers. The objectives of the designer are significant, whether his concern is for providing the amenities which permit the inhabitants personal choice, or whether his vision is narrow and directed toward a minimum marketable solution or toward a static art form. The degree to which the designer is concerned with a high level of amenity of design frequently relates to whether design is his primary concern or whether design is merely a necessary service adjunct to more profitable matters such as construction, the marketing of products, or financial investment.

Technology of Construction. The rate at which the construction industry responds to known technologies will accelerate, following the newly established trend toward premanufactured, prefinished items such as hardware, plumbing fixtures, and windows and extending to larger packages like kitchens and bathrooms, then to entire dwelling units. For commercial construction, manufacturer-designed systems components for walls and ceilings, factory fabricated and prefitted and requiring only on-the-job assembly, will replace field-fabricated material systems.

The detailed environment will be highly responsive to "power accessories," small-scale transportation devices, communication systems, power appliances, artificial environments; all will be part of the minimum standard of living for all incomes. For larger-scale developments, structures will become less differentiated as to use, and construction will be planned to permit continued change for differing activities. The design and finish of the immediate environment will be controlled by its "accessories" and will become more temporal, frequently changing and more subject to current vogue and style. Large super-structures of building complexes will have public and private zones as in a city and will have both public amenities and spaces for private uses. These patterns are already clear in shopping centers and resort hotels and will extend to structures intermixed with working, residential, and institutional needs.

All of these factors will tend to make handcrafted finish and material systems more costly than their premanufactured counterparts, and the appearance of structures for commercial investment will have a more manufactured look. As a result, handcraft shall represent an even more desirable attribute and will still be in great demand as a personal expression of preference. Designers will be called upon to be more innovative in their manipulation of the material systems available to reduce the quality of sameness generated by manufactured systems. At the same time, the designer must become more understanding of the underlying psychological need of persons and create a

266

variety and choice of activity patterns to permit individual occupants greater opportunity for control of their own immediate environments.

Public Priorities

There is little reason to believe that there will be a significant change in the public's personal priorities for the physical environment, but continued increase of individual income will make personal choice more evident. The current trend for the "here and now" will continue, and the priority for one's immediate personal environment will be identified first with consumer goods and secondly with recreation. Expenditures in these areas will form the most prevalent uses of the increased distribution of a higher per capita national income. Automobiles as symbols of personal choice and sought-after mobility will continue to dominate and will be the personal choice for recreational transportation until the end of the century regardless of increased public transportation. As a result of these factors, the biggest proportionate increase in physical developments will be supported by individual expenditures for recreation-oriented facilities, participation sports like boating and golf, spectator sports, restaurants and hotels and other entertainment facilities, and for vacation-oriented second houses.

Following entertainment and recreation, one's personal place of residence will be the next level of concern. The investment for residences will continue to grow and will provide both increased size and amenity. The increase in per capita income will support the desire for more space per person, and this trend will continue for all but the post-childrearing families. The apartment will be a symbol of independence for the young, the single, and the urbane, and a place with less responsibility for the mature; but the individual family house will continue to be the ambition of the vast majority of childrearing, garden-loving, status-seeking Americans. Many of those who will pride themselves on living in the city "where the action is" will also have a condominium in the country or spend their weekends at vacation resorts or country clubs and thus commit space in two locations. We can anticipate that the differences between apartments and single-family homes will diminish, each assuming the desirable attributes of the other. The need and demand of sub-parity groups will be first for an adequate apartment in the central city, but we must anticipate that it will soon shift to the ambition for, and expectation of, suburban living and resort vacations.

Improvement of the public environment such as parks, seashores and other public recreation or open space reserves will hinge on the degree to which the individual relates the improvement to his own personal priorities and to the nature of the tax structure of support. Consequently, the public can be expected to be erratic in its support for a better public environment, assigning high priority to some projects and low priority to others. Level of support for national and regional improvements will tend to receive higher priority because the funds seem to be supplied by others, but local improvements will be more difficult to fund where the tax consequence is immediate, particularly when related to personal property tax.

The individual's concern for his place of work and for his immediately local public spaces will be at about the same level of concern, both considerably below those mentioned above. The current trends toward more space per capita in working environments can be expected to accelerate. A vastly larger percentage of persons will be involved in service-related business, and the rate of growth of office-type space will be far more rapid than the growth rate of the population itself. The needs of industry will become increasingly more like those of service businesses with the percentage of space for human information and decision activities expanding at a more rapid rate than that for equipment and manufacture. The level of amenity at the place of work will continue to rise; and the expectation of working spaces which provide a high quality of human comfort, and visual quality will become the standard rather than the exception. As a result, the most significant changes in working spaces will be in their relation to other activities and the addition of amenities for both recreation and education.

In spite of a relative low personal priority by the general public, it is expected that there will be a general increase in the quality of public spaces for institutions such as schools, hospitals, libraries, governmental buildings, and local parks and playgrounds. Educational facilities will continue to be the largest single patron of this sector, and although longer periods of education will be considered normal, much of the increased demand will be met through new institutional forms and through new communications media in one's home or place of work.

With the exception of development for popular recreation activities, the priority for public space can be expected to be about equal to that for the working environment. However, as the level of affluence of the country grows and as more persons achieve an acceptable level of amenity in their personal environment, they will seek out and be willing to support a higher quality public environment. The relative priority is important, however, for in times of social or economic stress these priorities will have a major effect on standards for development and for its relative importance in comparison with other personal or public expenditures. In the event of extreme social pressures, expenditures for the public environment will be the first to disappear.

There will be a general demand for increased space for habitation per capita and a further trend for redundancy of space due to the needs for both personal and public activities, often in several locations. There will also be a demand for higher level of amenity by all segments of the population which will make existing buildings outmoded more rapidly. As a result, in spite of the enormous quantity of construction projected due to population growth and replacement of substandard construction, these estimates may be too low as compared to anticipated public demand. It appears safe to conclude, therefore, that the demand may be greater than normally projected, that much of this demand will be built at what once was considered a luxury level, and that an increasingly larger proportion of the population will demand environments at the highest level of physical comfort and psychological satisfaction that the age of technology can provide.

As previously described, the public's priorities from the environment will be most influenced by the primary social issues of the day. The present struggle for economic parity and for equalization of the divergent economic standards of living will be exacerbated by a higher level of communication and education. Not only television and other communications media but increased mobility and direct contact with other sectors of the economy will make more clear the disparity between standards of living. Contact through these means will bring an increasing awareness of the variations which exist and will produce a sense of impatience, urgency, and demand for greater equalization. The demand for a comparable quality of living standard will be considered a threat, and it will most probably be resisted by a significant portion of the population, by those who have already achieved and by those who hold early hope for a standard of living which they deem satisfactory. The stresses between the disparate income groups will often be disguised under the names of urban crisis, law and order, or personal status, but the issue of economic parity and standard of living and search for personal values will form the overriding social context for the development of the physical environment.

The resolution of the primary social issues, and the degree to which it is by socially oriented improvement programs for achieving parity as opposed to repression of one social group by another, will have a profound effect upon the public's expectation from the environment and their ability to achieve their ambitions. One should expect that the physical environment, particularly the equality of housing and the neighborhood, will become a symbol for, and a major part of the more general struggle for a higher standard of living.

As stressed in the Ewald study, the challenge of the near future will be in creating new social rather than technological inventions. Institutions, both private and public, and professions will focus their attention on solving the problem of utilizing known technologies to bring a higher level of social and physical amenity to the substandard sectors of the population. The byword will be "involvement"; and new organizations representing the left, right, middle and every splinter group will emerge to extend communication, not from the top down to inform the people, but from the people up to make government and other institutions more directly responsible to public representation. The solutions to the problems of the physical environment will be developed in this same arena. Group action and decisions which attempt to reconcile differences between opposing factions will become the norm and will become a central concern for the planning and design professions.

PUBLIC EXPECTATIONS

The continued increase in standard of living of the majority of the population has permitted the majority a personal choice of place for both living and pleasure. Competition for patronage of this affluent public has significantly increased the standard of accommodation and thus correspondingly raised the level of expectation from the environment. All who are members of this increasingly larger middle class expect more technologically advanced goods and better quality apartments, houses, shopping centers, coffee shops, and motel rooms than in the past.

As a consequence of the rapid rise in the standard of living and the expectations of a large majority of the society, buildings which were considered of average or "minimum code" quality in the past and present more rapidly will be considered outmoded. Similarly, subsistence-level buildings, which are below-average environments, will soon be considered slums, regardless of age. In contrast to the privilege and affluence of the majority, there are pockets in the cities and rural areas which now reflect an even lower standard than these same conditions would have represented a generation ago. As previously mentioned, the expectation of these groups will first be for a minimum-subsistence level, but the expectation will gradually shift to the level of amenity enjoyed by the majority of the population. Persons of low income experiencing high quality public spaces for shopping and recreation and education will not be content with mere subsistence-level for their personal place of residence. Failure to recognize the inevitability of this evolution will have critical consequences for both the social and physical environment.

The high level of expectation for one's own selected environments has gradually produced a sense that something is wrong with the environment. The public has awakened to the highly detrimental series of conditions of the large-scale environment. Land exploitation, highways, water, air, and noise pollution have now created a crisis of the large-scale environment which will cause enough social stress that control mechanisms will be initiated. In contrast to the case of the substandard personal environments which will be faced as a national problem, the methods for responding to larger environmental problems are apt to be regional. However, both will be dealt with at the level of governmental policy and will have short- and long-range impact upon the form and quality of the environment and upon those persons working in the design professions.

The public need for more improvements per capita and the demand for higher land amenity are clearly established trends. The present construction industry need not fear that there will be insufficient market demand but, on the contrary, must recognize that the demand will be so great that there will be stronger efforts made to increase its efficiency by enticing new groups with new areas of expertise (and bias) into the effort. There is little doubt that the efforts of all who are now involved will be needed, but there are signs that the organizational structure may violently change and that the industry may be under new controls and new management.

The building industry is often accused of being the most antiquated of the major industries, that construction costs relatively more than it did in the past and the industry has failed to keep pace with the efficiency of other industries. It is implied that persons are being deprived of amenity of environment which is known but which the present industry cannot deliver. Because of these beliefs, some conclude that the present entanglement of unions, subcontractors, designers, fabricators, and supervising authorities is a hopeless mess and not worth saving. The evidence does not support these views, but these beliefs are so widely held that one can expect more public (through government) manipulation of the building industry in the future.

The public demands from the industry will be for greater speed and economy, more technological gadgetry, and better environments. The demand for greater economy and speed will affect the time sequence for planning and construction and will accelerate the development of premanufactured, off-the-shelf systems and will lead to an overlapping of the design-construct process. The demand for technology will focus on accessories but will include more sophisticated environmental controls and materials systems. The demand for a quality of environment which enhances life style will be less well articulated, but is most basic. It will be expressed by each segment of the population if they are permitted reasonable personal choice in the selection of living and working environments.

One possible system break could cause a major revolution in the building industry. The social crises of the near future may force major government involvement in the building industry. When the public decides to support a massive program of rebuilding the substandard parts of the environment, there is some consensus that the present construction industry will not be able to meet this challenge either in capacity or in inventiveness. Should civil disorder become sufficiently great, and when the Viet Nam war ends, the pressures to make this expenditure will be enormous. There are already signs that the public's choice between military and social expenditure may be equalizing.

In the event of a major program for rebuilding substandard neighborhoods, the government may have no choice but to take direct action to improve the capacity of the present industry. Should the domestic program come at the expense of the present military industries, then there may be a demand by that industry to take the additional load which the present building industry could not accommodate. Even if the program does not result in a cutback in military expenditures, but the action is made under duress, the government may also turn to its normal emergency partner, the military-industrial complex. The public and the government have faith in this group to do the impossible, atomic bombs or flights to the moon, so by contrast, a few hundred thousand homes seems a small order. One should expect more government-industry partnerships in the building industry, first for research and development and perhaps later for construction. These partnerships are most apt to be made with conglomerates or joint ventures where research, design, fabrication and assembly, and guaranteed delivery can be provided.

The importance of the methods devised for solving a problem of emergency will be out of proportion to its share of the total construction market. The pattern which might be followed under these circumstances would create a break in continuity of past practices and would eventually have a major effect upon all segments of the industry.

The possibility of major new alliances and the entry of new groups into the construction industry could have either beneficial or harmful effects. The long-term effect of any major program to improve substandard neighborhoods is bound to be beneficial if the improvements create a high, rather than minimum, level of amenity. The introduction of new biases, techniques, and methods for problem solving could also have a long term benefit on the construction industry. The present work force, whether technicians or professionals, may be regrouped into new organizations or new alliances, and many of the work force might benefit from the realignment and might welcome it. Many of those with commitment and investment in the current system might suffer if unable to cope with rapid change but equally as many would find increased challenge and opportunity for service.

The most important consideration in a drastic break from current methods is whether the new power structures would bring sufficiently high standards, whether they would view the problem as a need for providing meaningful environments, not just technologically advanced hardware. Any such major program must find a means for communicating with and understanding the needs of the people it will serve and must be administered with great sensitivity. Should a massive rebuilding program be undertaken with the objectives of creating minimum accommodations, it will prove retrogressive and we will have built a slum of colossal proportions. But should the objective be for providing the best environments which a socially and technically advanced society can provide, then the beneficial results should be overwhelming.

The Midwest Research Institute report states that the major new developments in the next fifteen years will not be new construction technology but new management science. Both Ewald and MRI stress that emphasis in the near future will be placed on developing methods for delivering known technology in order to raise the standard of living for all income groups. The meaning of both reports is clear; the action will be in the policy, strategy, planning, and design phases. The design professions will be in the midst of the most volatile areas of change and increased technology. The demand will be extreme for developing new theory and new techniques and practices for communication, and for developing design and delivery of known advanced technologies. The public may be expected to seek out and support the most capable persons and groups to perform these roles regardless of their professional affiliations or educational background.

The public expectation from the design professions is great. Implicitly, it expects an integrated social-economic-physical theory for the form of the environment. If the present design professions are unable to find the resources and unable to combine forces to work jointly to develop such a concept, then the public must seek another group to do this task. The charge may not be so clearly expressed, but the frustration at lack of action to date may precipitate an emotional rather than rational rejection of the present professions as being unable to meet this challenge.

At a similar level of concern, the public expects coordinated methods for dealing with problems of the environment but does not know how to articulate this need. The close interrelation of all of the factors which were listed earlier in influencing the large scale environment will require methods of simulating and modeling their interaction. Policy planning and design to meet individual crises has proven highly detrimental to the environment; the solution of a transportation problem without concern for settlement patterns, pollution, new development incentives, etc., should become a thing of the past. The public is seeking a more comprehensive solution for coordinated planning but is unable to articulate their wishes and should expect the design professions to perform this function.

The public will also look to the design professions to improve and extend methods of public participation in the planning process.

A stronger sense of public expression in the design process will not limit the profession's role to that of coordination and management, for the public will expect that the professional will have the greater understanding of the qualities of the environment which are meaningful. The public will also expect the design professions to guide their own participation and to generate new concepts to fulfill their ambitions. To fulfill the public's expectation in this role, the design profession must be equally well founded in the social sciences as in the physical sciences.

The public demand for greater efficiency and speed and for more advanced technology will be in addition to and not in lieu of its concern for character, style and the sense of personal fulfillment which can be gained from the physical environment. The design professions and others who can contribute to the process will not be asked to abandon their ideals for the environment but to raise the breadth of their objectives and to perform their roles more effectively for the benefit of all rather than a small segment of the society. Each person who plays a role in the design professions will be expected to be more knowledgeable and more effective than in the past.

EXPECTATIONS FROM THE ARCHITECT

Architects, too, must re-examine their objectives and their social role. Traditionally they have served as specialists who translate human need for shelter into a physical form which reflects the highest level of the art and science of the day. The profession is small and has never attempted to assume the responsibility for fulfilling this need for every structure; but it has provided the ideas, the models, or prototypes which set the standard and set an example of the highest achievement in the field. The professional must look closely at the changes which are projected for the future to determine where its efforts for setting the standard will be most effective.

3.

TOWARD A DEFINITION
OF THE PROFESSION OF ARCHITECTURE

THERE ARE MANY SIMPLIFIED DEFINITIONS for the field of architecture which refer to the art and/or science of building and describe the architect as the master builder or one who designs and supervises the construction of buildings, or one who is a student of the field; but none seems adequate. In any society of specialization, there are many persons who contribute to any complex problem area; appropriately, there are a large number of people who contribute to the art and science of building and many who make decisions which affect the design. All of them are not architects; but if not, what are the characteristics which distinguish the architect and his profession from the many others who contribute? A profession may not be defined by a commonality of the problem area alone, but perhaps an adequate definition can be framed by defining the commonality of the fields of knowledge that its members draw upon, the commonality of the methods of application of this knowledge, and the personal values that its members hold in common.

Mere association with a problem area is not an adequate definition for a profession, for there are few which do not require the services of several fields. "Health" for example, does not describe the medical profession nor does "physical environment" define that of architecture. A more definitive problem area such as "housing" is still inadequate, except that we may more easily define the individuals who are associated with it and may more easily name the field from which they might draw their knowledge. Considering all of the activities

276

involved in housing, for example — legislation, taxation, and finance at one end of the spectrum and construction, sales, and promotion at the other — no clear identity for a profession is implied. Working relationships and congruence of understanding may result between those persons and professions who long associate in a particular problem area, but the problem itself does not make a new profession. For example, economists, planners, architects, and financiers and realtors who are all experienced in housing will each have learned aspects of the other's field as it applies to this problem area, but this does not tend to make them part of the same profession. The economist working in housing remains an economist if his professional knowledge is sustained by the theories which originate in all of the areas of economics, not just those in housing alone. It is the ability to draw from the entire field which is one of the critical factors in identifying the professional, and the architect maintains his status as such when he draws his knowledge from the entire field of architecture regardless of the particular problem area in which he is engaged.

Professional architects are currently expanding and changing the emphasis of their traditional problem area. Rather than buildings alone, the architect seeks to use his knowledge and skill in the larger context of the environment. The concern for the finite spaces of buildings is not lost but is expanded to include an equal concern for the spaces of the site and their relation to the surrounding area and with the physical and social systems which integrate buildings into complexes, neighborhoods, and communities. This current trend for increased concern for buildings as part of the larger environment will eventually result in their spending a greater part of their energies to the programmatic and policy aspects of design and toward developing the configurations for larger scale building groups and "total" environment.

Should a profession be defined by delineating the knowledge that its members hold in common? Such a definition might suggest that one would limit its members to those with precisely the same knowledge; or even more limiting, that the knowledge associated with the profession could be no greater than that of each individual. Obviously, neither of these alternatives is acceptable. Better, then, is a definition which defines a profession by the knowledge which it holds as a group, for this description expands the knowledge associated to include that of its most advanced specialists as well as the more practical concerns of its average practitioners. By making explicit that the scope of knowledge of the profession is beyond the capability of any one individual, it follows that individuals must hold different areas of knowledge.

Parenthetically, it is important to distinguish between the sum of the knowledge in the field of architecture as compared to the knowledge of the individual professional. The knowledge of the discipline includes the total body of its history and all the known facts ever recorded about it. The professional presumably has the ability to retrieve and make use of this information but need not have current knowledge thereof. It is the awareness of its existence, the ability to call upon it and to apply and make value judgments using the knowledge of the field, rather than the limits of his personal ability to store knowledge, which defines the professional.

After arguing against commonality of knowledge as a basis for defining the profession, one must accept some degree of commonality, some part of the body of knowledge of the field which all of its members held in common, or there is no basis for a profession. It is important, therefore, to recognize some commonality of knowledge for each professional but not to consider this the total or even the major portion of the individual's knowledge. This consideration must have a strong influence on the policies which will influence the future of the profession, for we must now recognize that all professionals may hold some knowledge in common, but that their main areas of expertise may be quite different. This is an important concept to accept if the field is to grow in depth and in breadth.

One may also define a profession by the commonality of its methods for the application of knowledge. We visualize the profession in this model as groups of individuals who utilize certain sophisticated techniques to apply theoretical knowledge to specific real-life problems of society. In this construct, the profession functions as the delivery system between society and its bodies of knowledge. The medical internist practices his profession by applying appropriate theoretical knowledge in biochemistry and biophysics for the diagnosis of internal disorders; the mechanical engineer utilizes his knowledge of fluid mechanics and thermodynamics to design pumps. The architect uses his knowledge to define physical forms which will implement the activities and aspirations of the occupants. In each case, the primary role of the professional is to draw upon the useful information from various bodies of knowledge and by using the most appropriate techniques and methods, to make judgments and pose solutions to the problem at hand. The academic discipline must advance the theoretical horizon of its own domain, but the professional extracts the knowledge from these disciplines that relates directly to his practice.

It is the methodology for analysis and decision which may be the most fundamental characteristic of a profession and which contributes most to the value system of its professionals. Architecture, for example, depends heavily upon the empirical knowledge which its practitioners have gained through observation and experience. Solutions are neither encoded nor subject to mathematical or other precise methods of analysis but are measured by subjective values. It is the dependence upon personal judgment which is both the strength and weakness of the profession. The architect's strength lies in the fact that he must define his own problem and establish the factors against which he weighs alternative solutions; at the same time this characteristic forms his weakness, because his reliance on personal decision-making often causes him to function on an ad hoc basis, frequently not recording or systematically evaluating his work and disregarding more procedural analytical techniques operative in other fields but which may have applicability to the field of architecture.

This model is relevant to the study of the future of the profession for it represents the profession as the interface between bodies of knowledge of the field and the problem areas of society and indicates that any change in either the problem area or the available bodies of knowledge or in the techniques for its application must result in a change in the profession.

The public associates a profession, regardless of the personal differences of opinion and the conflicting political persuasion of its members, with the professional values which it represents as a social group and which subliminally influence its base of professional judgment. The belief systems, or biases, which a profession holds in common are partially a result of the behavioral traits and talents of those who are attracted into it, but they are also derived from the character of the bodies of knowledge and methodology in which its expertise lies. Regardless of how these beliefs are acquired, they consciously and subconsciously affect the professional's judgments and tend to make his actions predictable to a degree that the public can anticipate the effect of engaging his services.

The medical profession holds maintenance of life as a professional value above practicality, or cost, or other personal value judgments of the individual doctor. Similarly, the engineering profession is normally held to represent a value system of technological efficiency with design as a balance between economy and safety as derived from the laws of the physical sciences. The architectural profession likes to view itself, in contrast, as representing humane and social values through technological solutions and for dealing in the personal idiom of subjective decision in the reconciliation of both social and technical issues.

Historically the profession of architecture has been associated with a value bias in favor of artistic form as opposed to highest technology or minimum cost. It is revealing that one definition of the word architecture refers to the "style" or "character" of buildings. The difference in values is an important distinction, for it is upon aesthetic and social considerations that the public distinguishes between the services of architects and engineers. Both are design professions which deal with the art and science of building and have access to largely overlapping areas of knowledge. Recently, there is evidence that the profession is growing uncomfortable with the art values with which it has been traditionally associated. It now wishes to be identified with the science of problem solving and seeks a methodological base for the resolution of social and technical problems which relates to building and the larger question of habitation. Should this trend continue and should the public sense the profession's change of values and purpose, it would have a profound effect upon the responsibilities which it would entrust to the profession.

Using the models described above to define the profession, one can examine the relationship among all of the professions concerned with the man-made, or controlled, physical environment for habitation. There was a distinction made earlier between the immediate knowledge a professional can recall, as opposed to that which he knows exists and knows when and how to find and to use. The academic "discipline" was referred to as being the sum total of the knowledge of the "field" of architecture. Actually, the knowledge which is known, or which is an active resource to a professional, normally comes from several basic academic disciplines. Medicine, for example, draws its knowledge from the disciplines of chemistry, biology, and bacteriology, etc. It is important to note, however, that having command of knowledge from several different academic disciplines does not make the doctor "interdisciplinary."

One can construct a useful image of the relationships between academic disciplines by visualizing knowledge as being divided into a series of distinguishable bodies; these bodies being in a state of flux, always changing in form and expanding with each new hypothesis. As new knowledge is added to an existing body such that two sufficiently separate sets of theories begin to emerge, then that body may divide into two just as physics and chemistry emerged from the more general body of knowledge of physical science. In like manner, parts of two separate bodies may rejoin to spawn a new hybrid such as biochemistry, which now has a sufficiently separate set of theories and knowledge that it can be considered a separate discipline even though it still largely overlaps its two parents, biology and chemistry. On occasion, a technological advance in several fields permits the emergence of a new body of knowledge such as computer science, which affects existing relationships and makes new combinations.

If each body of knowledge is considered a discipline, then within each it is possible to distinguish separate "subdisciplines" which may be overlapping but with sufficiently different facts and working theories to be considered reasonably separate. A profession may draw upon the knowledge of one subdiscipline but not necessarily all of the discipline. Another profession may also draw upon another subdiscipline in the same field or upon the same one, but perhaps at a different level of mastery. For example, both the architect and structural engineer draw upon the subdiscipline of mechanics of materials but at different levels of depth in so far as their ability to make professional judgments.

Turning to the models posed earlier, one can examine the academic fields corresponding to the professions now operating within the rubric "environmental design." The fields of architecture, planning, and landscape architecture share certain areas of knowledge, some analysis or synthesis techniques, and many value systems. Each also draws upon some subdisciplines and methods which are peculiar unto it as compared to the others. It is through the areas of commonality that the linkages between the professions are made, but it is the areas of difference which give them sufficiently separate identity to remain separate professions. As the areas of linkage between them change, and as new linkages with separate bodies of knowledge emerge, new professions and subprofessions may appear. It is also possible, but perhaps less likely in an expanding area of knowledge, that several of the existing professions could merge and become one.

Both landscape architecture and architecture share concerns for the human use of space, for analysis of human needs, and for design syntheses for these needs. They do not totally share, however, the areas of technical knowledge which they utilize to fulfill their solutions; the architect draws upon the physical sciences, and the landscape architect also utilizes knowledge from the life sciences. Similarly, because of the lack of scientific evidence for human response to the environment, each of these professions often operates in an area of subjective decision-making. Their central concern for human response interacting with the physical form of the environment results in a set of personal values which are quite similar in each of these fields. The architect shares a different set of congruences with the city planner. Each has a concern for the interaction between the physical systems of individuals and those of the community at large; however, the planner extends his knowledge toward the social and governmental institutions which foster them and their quantifiable characteristics while the architect has been primarily concerned with their qualitive, social, and physical characteristics.

Similar areas of commonality can be made with other design professions, with the several branches of engineering, and to a lesser degree with sociology, and psychology, and law. The commonality is often small, however, and is frequently separated by ideological gulfs influenced primarily by their differences in methodology, whether subjective or objective. The emphasis on objective, quantitative decision-making by the engineering fields, for example, tends to create a significant difference between the value systems characterizing the engineering professions as compared to the generally qualitative areas of decision in architecture and landscape architecture. These differences in value systems are actually beneficial to the public, however, and should not be minimized, for it is the confrontation of these differences in value systems which make interdisciplinary design collaboration an effective instrument. At present, there are movements in architecture toward a more objective methodological base and discussions of a more qualitative concern in engineering. There may, therefore, be closer congruence between the disciplines in the future than at present.

The most difficult problems to assess in projecting the future of the profession of architecture are as follows:

What specific areas will emerge within the field of architecture, with sufficiently separate bodies of knowledge and related skills that they will be recognized as subdisciplines? (Programming is a candidate at the present time.)

Will sufficiently separate roles for professionals be generated by new subdisciplines that they shall begin to be recognized as a new profession? (Computer design applications might fall into this category.)

Will subdisciplines which develop in architecture combine with subdisciplines in other fields to create a new hybrid and a new profession? (Urban design as a combination of subdisciplines in architecture, planning, and landscape architecture is a likely candidate.)

Will the present field begin to polarize into different sectors such that their commonalities are more closely related to disciplining outside the field than to each other? (This appears to be happening in city and regional planning with the division between the socially oriented and physically oriented planners.)

Referring to the model of the design professions as the "delivery system" between society and known bodies of knowledge, one must conclude from the studies conducted by Ewald and MRI that these professions are in the area where one should expect the most dramatic future changes. The most significant changes which are anticipated in both society and the building industry are in social mechanisms, in communications systems, and in cybernetic and mechanized cognitive assists. These are precisely the areas in which the profession practices. As a result, one must expect the near future to be one of great change, an age of experimenting with new methods of analysis and synthesis which are developing in computer science operations research and systems engineering. The near future will also find a new thrust for exploration of the social and behavioral sciences for the development of theories which will attempt to bring the relationship between design theory and known science in this area more clearly in line with the relation between theory and practice in the physical sciences.

One must expect, therefore, that there will be a temporary fragmentation of effort, a probing by the field of architecture for applicable techniques from outside the field. Concurrently there will be an exploration in the problem areas associated with architecture by persons outside the field who believe they have knowledge or techniques which might be applicable. During this highly volatile period in the future, one must expect that there will be new subdivision and new combinations within the existing professions. The definition of any one profession will become more blurred, but the alignments which will ultimately be made in order to form the profession of the future will depend upon the value systems and objectives the individuals share as well as the knowledge, techniques, and problem areas they hold in common.

4.

THE PROFESSIONAL ARCHITECT,
HIS ENTERPRISES AND INSTITUTIONS

SOCIETY, THE CONSTRUCTION INDUSTRY, and the activities and responsibilities of each professional are now quite different from what they were only a generation ago. In this age of accelerated social and technological change, we must expect correspondingly rapid changes in the profession. The challenge posed is to understand, anticipate and to use change as an opportunity to further the values and objectives of the profession and to increase its skill and effectiveness. In looking into the future we must recognize that the nature of the service which the profession provides and the organizations most effective in its implementation must be continually changed in response to the knowledge and social structures of the day. At any point in time, the profession must be viewed as an integral part of the social context in which it functions.

If architecture is to persist as a social endeavor, then one may ask who will be considered architects and how their actions may influence the quality of the environment. The answer to these questions appears to be within the profession itself. Its viability will depend upon the ability of its individual members, the strength gained from the organizations they form, and the degree to which they exert influence at critical junctures. Similarly, their influence will depend upon the alliances which they make with other design professions, and whether these alliances prove to be the most effective social mechanisms for meeting the demands of the times. It may well be that the profession of architecture will become more diffuse, more difficult to define as an entity, as it combines its talents with the several other fields which must all be joined to create the man-made environment.

Let us broadly define the peculiar characteristics of the field of architecture. Below is a discussion of professional and certified architects, the enterprises in which they ply their service, and the institutions which they form.

The Field. The field of architecture has existed since man began to rationally build for his habitation at a reasonably high level of sophistication. It consists not only of the attendant body of knowledge but also of the ideals and objectives with which it is associated. The field includes all those who earn their livelihood helping to create architecture as professionals, technicians, or specialists, whether entrepreneurs or employees. Equally as important are those who are concerned with the theory and knowledge of the field, the researchers, students, and teachers.

Professional Architect. Distinguishable within the field is the professional architect whose role has long historic precedence. Emerging from the crafts and arts first as master builders and then later from the ranks of the gentlemen-scholars, professional architects have only recently been formally educated for their role. Regardless of the background or the nature of his education, it has been his objective to create the highest known level of environment for human habitation. His effectiveness in promoting this objective has distinguished him as a professional. In spite of the wide range of individual activities in which he may be engaged, or the nature of the public or private enterprise in which he works, the professional architect is distinguished by his command of a significant sector of the knowledge of the field and his use of this knowledge and experience to render professional judgments. These persons may be distinguished from the many who may contribute to the field but who are not called upon to make professional value judgments and are, therefore, not professionals.

Intern-Architect. As used herein, the use of the term "intern-architect" shall mean a student of architecture who has satisfactorily completed a course in academic study of architecture and has been awarded a professional degree in architecture by a college or university accredited by the NAAB. Presently, these persons are not considered professionals until they have received certification, but in the future, professional status may begin to be based upon the person's capabilities and actions as defined above rather than legal certification.

286

Certified Architects. From among the professional architects, there are those who seek registration as "certified architects." This registration, granted by each state, certifies that the individual may title himself "architect" and that he is qualified to engage in the commerce of architecture, to seek commissions and accept remuneration from the public for the professional practice of architecture, and to accept the legal responsibilities attendant therewith.

There is a wide variation and there are many vagaries among the individual registration laws as to what constitutes the practice of architecture and under what basis of public protection they should be certified. Consequently, there are many who, by avoiding the use of the title, engage in several of the roles which are herein termed "architecture." As most enterprises which offer architectural services need only one certified architect and because many architects engage in roles which are not covered under registration laws, the distinction between professional architects and those among them who are certified may have increasingly less meaning. Should the use of the title "architect" be denied to all those who are not certified, then the public image and impact of the profession will be greatly reduced.

Enterprises. Professional architects, including those who are certified, may be engaged in many different kinds of public and private organizations or firms which we shall refer to herein as "enterprises." The nature and structure of the enterprise must necessarily change through time in order to remain the most viable form for providing service at the highest known level and may vary depending upon the problem area or nature of the client being served.

As the field of knowledge and technology has advanced, the number of different individual professional roles has increased and the nature of the enterprises which utilize even a few of these roles has grown more complex. At the present time, most of the enterprises which utilize professional architects are "professional service firms" led by members of one of the design professions, but in the future one should expect professional architects in a far wider range of enterprises, both public and private.

Institutions. Individuals with a common need within the field of architecture have formed "institutions" to provide for these needs. Schools of architecture as institutions of society serve the public and the entire field of architecture as well as the profession. As such, the schools should have as their objective the offering of study in the knowledge and theory of the field and its associated objectives and values, regardless of the person's career objectives. The advanced graduate schools should also have as an objective the extension of the knowledge of the field.

The American Institute of Architects is an institution created by certified professional architects with objectives that go beyond the needs of these individuals alone. A professional society, its members are currently reexamining its relative priorities for service to the public, to the entire field of architecture, and to (noncertified) professional architects as compared to service for professional certified architects and to the business enterprises which they head.

The future of these institutions will depend upon the degree to which they serve the objectives of their constituents.

By distinguishing between the various segments, one can more easily assess the impact of future changes in society and the building industry upon the field as a whole and the individuals, enterprises, and institutions which are parts thereof. Returning to the conceptual model described in the introduction to Part III, the role of the individual is the most logical frame in which to examine these future trends.

The range of roles which is projected for the future may not sound significantly different from that which one can identify today, but each will be quite different. Each will have its own expanded knowledge and skills and its own tie to knowledge and specialists outside the field of architecture. In many instances, specialists will emerge to practice and develop these roles at a higher level of expertise than has been known in the past, and there will be a change in the proportionate number of persons who are engaged in each role. Most significant, there may be a change in the relative influence individual roles will exert on the form and character of the environment. The roles in which individual architects will seek responsibility will range from those which are primarily concerned with theory, policy, and social criteria to those where the concern is for determining the physical form and for creating the physical reality.

The ordering of the list reflects only their relative relation to those concerns and implies no hierarchy of values or importance. It may appear to coincide with the sequence in which these tasks have been performed traditionally, but this will be less true in the future when automated systems will permit the sequence of tasks to be interchanged, cycled, and performed simultaneously. In the past and for small projects today, the general-practitioner architect has played several of the necessary roles well. In the future, the scale and complexity of most projects will demand a higher level of expertise in each role, and collectively they will be performed at a level of theoretical knowledge and experience far beyond that of any one person. The list which follows suggests probable future roles and indicates those groups which are presently most closely identified with each role, the probable future new actors in each role, and by symbol indicates whether their activities are expected to increase ($<$), stay constant ($-$), or decrease ($>$). Hundreds of slightly different roles could be identified, and one could quarrel with the individual importance of several which are grouped together as compared to those which stand alone; however, the list has been kept short in order to make more specific comparisons. It is important to point out that the roles are not symmetrical, and in order to effect the entire process of creating the physical environment, it may require only a few persons in some roles as compared to a large number in others.

Role	Normal present actors	Additional future actors
1. policy	government $<$ material lobbies $-$ builders' lobbies $-$ finance lobbies $-$ industry lobbies $-$ labor lobbies $>$ planners $<$	citizens groups nonprofit corporations R & D firms industry-military complex lawyers conglomerates architects?
2. research	physical sciences $-$ engineering schools $-$ R & D firms $<$ planning schools $<$	nonprofit corporations social sciences architectural schools architectural firms?
3. design criteria & coordination (socio-political)	planners $-$ engineers (codes) $-$ local govt. (codes) $-$ state govt. (codes) $-$ federal govt. (finance & codes) $<$ financial institutions $<$	citizens groups nonprofit corporations architects?

(Continued)

289

Role	Normal present actors	Additional future actors
4. project initiation	project owners > developers < realtors — users > financial institutions < government <	citizens groups nonprofit corporations conglomerates industry-military complex mutual funds, employee funds architects?
5. control management (in broad sense)	package builders < real estate manage- ment <	investor management conglomerates engineers architects?
6. project feasibility & strategy	project initiators > developers < economists < financial institutions < builders —- programmers — government < planners —	nonprofit corporations conglomerates systems analysts architects?
7. programatic definition of needs, par- ticularly design, and advocacy planning (socio-political)	architects < project initiators > owners > programmers < social & physical planners <	citizens groups conglomerates nonprofit corporations users industry component mfgrs.

8.
master plan-
ning and
facilities
planning
	physical planners <
	engineers —
	architects &
	    landscape architects <
		conglomerates
		nonprofit organizations
		    (at regional levels)
		systems analysts

Role	Normal present actors	Additional future actors

9.
design concept & urban design
	architects & landscape
	    architects & designers —
	builders —
	engineers —
	physical planners —
		interdisciplinary design team
		conglomerates
		industry component
		    manufacturers

10.
design development & systems design integration (physical-technical)
	architects & landscape
	    architects & designers —
	structural designers —
	mechanical & electrical
	    designers —
	industry systems
	    designers <
		industry component
		    manufacturers
		conglomerates
		interdisciplinary team
		systems analysts
		industrial designers

11.
component & detail design, & applied materials science
	architects & structural
	    designers >
	industry component
	    manufacturers <
	industrial design engineers <
		conglomerates

12.
finishes, colors, interiors, space planning
	architects & landscape
	    architects & designers —
	interiors specialists
	    & decorators <
		conglomerates
		behavioral scientists
		industrial component
		    manufacturers

13.
communication documents
	architects & landscape
	    architects —
	engineers —
		machine retrieval & trans-
		    mission systems
		communications specialists
		industrial component
		    manufacturers

14.
estimates, cost control, scheduling, materials-ordering
	builders —
	industrial component
	    manufacturers <
	architects & engineers <
		designers and machine
		    orders

(Continued)

291

Role	Normal present actors	Additional future actors
15. observation of construction for design	architects > govt. inspection agencies < builders >	industry component manufacturers new specialist firms
16. direction of construction	builders —	industry component manufacturers architects?
17. construction	contractors — subcontractors —	conglomerates industry component manufacturers architects?
18. management of interdisciplinary professional services	design professionals —	conglomerates managers

Currently, the field of architecture already includes a few persons in this entire range of roles, but the profession is normally associated with levels 7 through 15. In order to assess the roles which professionals and nonprofessionals in the field of architecture will select for their futures, it is necessary to review the factors acting upon the person as an individual both from outside the profession and from within.

External forces which will act upon the profession as a whole are treated in detail in Parts I and II of the report. The following may be considered most significant:

Factors	Acting on
new social ideologies	public image of the profession
availability of public funds	government policies (all levels)
availability of private resources	government-industry partnership
scope of development needed	building component manufacturers
new management technology	research and development enterprises
new construction technology	building industry
political power	investors
capital power	design professions
profitability	

Almost more significant than the forces external to the profession are those acting within the profession and a part of the individual himself. Although no detailed study has been made of the character traits and motivations of architects and future architects, the main factors can be generalized as follows:

Factors	Acting on
opportunities	students
capabilities	persons attracted to study in the field
personality traits	present professionals
personal interests	architectural schools
ambitions	professional society (AIA)
responsibility	
liability	
capitalization	
competition	
level of income	
tax structure	

Based upon projected future trends of factors external to the profession and the Committee's knowledge of the existing professions, it is possible to speculate about which roles professional architects will select for their personal areas of involvement and the relative future importance of each role within the profession.

1. Policy: If the profession is to exert a major influence on the quality of the physical environment beyond the capacity to personally design an individual structure or project, then it must become more fully committed to a policy role in government at local, regional, and federal levels. Individual graduate architects, particularly those with backgrounds in architecture and planning or law, must be encouraged to enter government service as a highly respected form of professional practice; and the profession must use its political leverage to seek such appointments. The trend for student interest in this role is increasing, but students must acquire a different combination of professional skills than has been available in the past.

Equally as important as involvement by individuals is the involvement of the professional society (AIA) which can represent the collective strength of the profession. It is important that this involvement should not serve as a self-interest lobby. On the contrary, it should act as a selfless, informed contributor, offering constructive assistance in the initiation of legislation and providing information

293

regarding the issues, alternatives, and consequences of decisions regarding the physical environment. It must also seek legislation which will increase the standard of living and the quality of the environment, and in all cases take the position of serving the public regardless of the impact upon the architectural profession itself.

2. *Research:* Architectural schools, the professional society, individual professional firms, and nonprofit corporations organized by architects must all begin to build competence in this area. No other viable profession has such a poor history of scholarship and research, nor depends so totally upon other fields for the advancement of knowledge of its specialty. Few other fields are so inadequate in recording and transmitting the knowledge developed through its practice.

Whether the field of architecture can gain the competence in education, research, and development as quickly as is needed is one of the most critical factors affecting the future of the profession. Present trends indicate that there are capable student candidates in architecture who are now seeking depth of competence for service in this role, but until such time as the schools can develop stronger capability in this area, the professional society must take the lead. Until the schools can develop a sufficient number of graduates with advanced study and research experience, the profession must supplement the field's present capability by recruiting researchers from other disciplines.

Research in architecture should include three areas:

• *The environment,* human needs therefrom and response thereto, and the formulation of social and behavioral criteria and theoretical constructs for meaningful environments.

• *The design process,* including formulation of techniques for syntheses of both social and technological criteria through new communication and management techniques.

• *Design solutions,* technological and management techniques for greater economic efficiency for delivery of the nation's industrial capability to a larger percentage of the public.

Research, particularly in these areas, will become a necessary base for advancing the expertise of the individual professional architect and the level of achievement of the field as a whole. It will also serve as the necessary base to substantiate policy positions for governmental relations programs. Research could also become the most meaningful line of government-profession communication, an absolute necessity for the future. Professional capability in this area will be a major factor in determining whether the architectural profession will be a major contributor to the quality of the environment and whether it will share in the roles of leadership within the new building industry.

3. Design Criteria and Coordination: In the future, more graduate architects will head and serve as staff in redevelopment and planning agencies and in local and federal policy agencies which generate the objectives and general criteria for project design and implementation. Similarly, an increasing number of professional architects will serve in this role in private industry and public institutions like universities. Professional service firms will also develop this capability for clients who must contract for this specialty. In these roles, architects will have direct access to or be a part of the policy-making groups, thus having significant impact upon the quality of the environment. Architects will also have greater responsibility for preparation and enforcement of codes, ordinances, and design criteria. The increased trend for professionals to seek these roles is clearly established, and in the future, these architects will represent a more significant segment of the profession.

4. Project Initiation: An architect acting as a developer has been a fairly recent or undercover phenomenon, but it can be expected to increase in the future. The architect-financier partnership is the most likely first pattern to evolve, and this joint venture could bring meaningful innovation. This evolution should be encouraged by the profession as an effective method for architects to initiate unusual environmental experiments which otherwise could never appear. However, there will be a fine line of distinction between professional involvement in this area, which is for public benefit, and involvement for purely financial return, a problem which will cause much ethical controversy.

5. Control Management: Although most practicing professionals believe they offer management service, few offer the kind of broad control management which is intended at this level. (Most professional service firms now fulfill the role listed as activity 18, managing the services generally falling within Roles 9-15.) Control-management at this more theoretical level relates more closely to the interests of the project initiator rather than to the phyical effectuation. Perhaps the most critical new role in the entire range, it emerges as a pooling of knowledge gained from contractors, realtors, investment advisors, and developers and assumes the most influential responsibility for large-scale projects.

295

As discussed in the MRI study, this service, often offered by large conglomerates, will undertake the coordination of all of the client's interests and will include complete development based upon economic feasibility and cost control (and the guarantee thereof), direct control of design and construction, leasing, sales, and maintenance management. This type of management package may also be offered by the most advanced interdisciplinary professional service firms in association with construction firms and in competition with the emerging conglomerates. Only the largest and strongest of the existing firms can begin to acquire the capability for this kind of management, but they should be encouraged to develop their capabilities for these services. Professional architects with additional background in economics, business administration real estate, and systems management will be attracted to play a part in this role.

6. Project Feasibility and Strategy: Although normally included under the broader form of control management discussed above, this role warrants separate distinction in that it will exist as a specialty separate from the management-design-construct conglomerates, or as professional service firms. These specialists will act as developers and will provide their services to project initiators, both public and private and will be highly mobile, acting as brokers and forming joint ventures or subcontracting all of the other roles. Some of these groups will include architects, but the leaders are most apt to come from finance, real estate development or construction.

7. Programmatic Definition of Needs and Objectives, Participatory Design, and Advocacy Planning: The analysis of the users' needs, the definition of meaningful activity relationships, and the relating of physical facility to activity need is emerging as a distinguishable role. Based upon increased research related to the social and behavioral sciences, there are many who believe that this function will continue to grow as a more specialized contributor to the design process. This programmatic phase is most effective when conducted concurrently rather than sequentially with the development of the design concept, where both objectives and the formal consequences can be explored concurrently. However, in spite of sequential overlap, this role can still be identified as being separate from design.

An important need is emerging for techniques which permit participation by user groups in the design process. Both advocacy planning and participatory design will play important roles in communicating the needs of user groups for projects initiated by others. As in

Role 6, this role may often be performed by professional architects who are part of corporations and institutions; and as in Role 5, this role will often be performed by specialist firms, which include behavioral scientists, that serve as consultants to private management, professional service firms, or citizen groups. Architects, who have a strong background in the social and behavioral sciences, will be attracted to this role and their activities will have a significant impact on society and the profession.

8. Master Planning and Facilities Planning: Physical master planning is now performed almost equally as often by landscape architects whose bias favors the natural environment, architects whose bias traditionally has related to the building configuration, and physical planners whose primary concerns have been for land use and movement patterns; however, each considers all of these factors. Facilities planning is currently distinguishable as being separate and relates master planning to corporate and institutional planning, cash flow, personnel growth, maintenance policy and sequence of development. This role has often been the province of engineers. In the future, facility and master planning will merge including all the factors associated with both, and its importance will continue to grow. Many large public and private enterprises will have their own interdisciplinary staffs for this purpose, and architects will frequently be part of this team. Professional service firms will offer this capability for groups who contract for this service.

9. Design Concept and Urban Design: The exploration of formal alternatives for fulfilling programmatic need and the conceptual development of the physical solution is the central role associated with the field of architecture and should continue to so be in the future. Presently this role is normally a part of professional service enterprises which include Roles 9 to 15 and 18. This trend may continue to dominate in the near future, but one can expect to find this role in combination with other groupings and may expect the appearances of small specialized interdisciplinary teams who will perform only the design concept role for both buildings and urban design projects. These specialists will be skilled in new design synthesis techniques, systems analysis, and computer design techniques for relating user needs with physical configuration. They will work closely with the client, providing a personalized service, but they will not provide detailed design or be closely involved with construction. These specialist firms will have little in-house technical capability and will operate without the capital

297

investment and liabilities associated with detailed design development or involvement in construction. Several different combinations are worthy of specific mention. Concept design and urban design may be combined with the programmatic definition of needs and participating design. Development from this point would be undertaken by the traditional form of professional service firm or by a detail design, fabrication-construction group. Alternatively, persons specializing in this role may joint venture or subcontract with larger professional service firms with detail design and communication documents capability. All large professional service firms will continue to have their own capability for this activity. Personal identification and a small scale of operation will appeal to many young professional architects who may practice in this area in the future without the previous normal range of technical capabilities. Whether these teams will function under the rubric of architecture will greatly depend upon the registration examination for architecture. They might not be certified because of their lack of detailed technical design competence, though they may be important contributors in the field. A most critical professional role, it may be expected to have a different significance as it combines with newly emerging "upper" roles rather than with the more traditional "lower" roles associated with detailed design.

10. Design Development, Systems Design Integration, and Criteria Coordination: This phase forms the second phase of design synthesis, consisting of optimizing compatible physical and mechanical systems to implement the conceptual design. For the most sophisticated solutions, this phase should overlap and be cycled concurrently with the design concept phase. In spite of a preferred sequential overlap, the role draws upon sufficiently different sources of knowledge and skills to be identified as a separate activity. This role will continue to form the backbone of the technical service which has been associated with the field of architecture and, next to the management role, Role 18 requires the most technical experience and breadth of knowledge of all of the technological factors which relate to design solution. Grouped with this role and requiring an increasingly larger percentage of time is the coordination of the design development with the long list of code, ordinance and other statute-enforcing authorities and with criteria defined by government, planning, financial, and coordinating agencies.

Note for convenience, Roles 10 and 11 include the corresponding design activity for both the systems designed by architects and engineers although each has its own distinguishing characteristics and separate body of related knowledge.

11. Component and Detail Design and Applied Material Science: More liability continues to accrue to those professionals assuming responsibility for this, the third phase of design. Although the work must be performed and will continue to utilize a large number of technical designers, it will be performed in the future in fewer professional service firms with large capital bases, and by manufacturers and fabricators. Detailed design will occur more commonly with material and component development and testing programs and will, therefore, be able to utilize a higher level of materials technology. The slow move toward greater industrialization of the building process will find more professional service firms with this capability providing detailed design service and component research and development to contractors, material fabricators and manufacturers of industrialized building systems. However, there will be an increasing amount of design performed by industrial designers who will be part of the fabricator, manufacturer, and construction groups.

In the last two generations, architects have assumed an increasingly large responsibility in this area, slowly assuming it from the crafts themselves, until Roles 10 and 11 occupy about half of the normal professional services. One can expect this trend to reverse in the future and for the crafts (fabricators) to provide more in-house design. Professional service firms and individual architects will spend a proportionally larger part of their time in other roles. The majority will not preclude small specialist architectural firms with expertise in architectural design, structure, and industrial design from making an important contribution to the role.

12. Finishes, Materials, Colors, Interiors, Space Planning: The fine grain design decisions which have significant effect on the visual quality of design, long the province of the architect, will be more frequently performed by professional architects who are specialists in this role and by designers and decorators working in collaboration with architects. The most difficult problem faced by the profession is that of maintaining a high level of control of visual quality at each of the several identifiable levels of design as each includes more technical and administrative criteria controls. As the field of architecture becomes broader, it will become increasingly more difficult to find, educate, and train "renaissance men" who can be as effective in making detailed aesthetic decisions as they are in performing computerized design synthesis or assisting in government policy-making. As a result, this function will tend to become a recognizable specialty within the field.

13. Communication Documents: The promise that only a few persons will be required to prepare contract documents is still some time away. In the near future a large percentage of the effort of traditional architectural firms will be involved in this function. Although new communication systems will soon make possible direct design to fabrication communication, its general applicability is ten to fifteen years away for all but the largest firms and industrialized projects. The capital outlay for this equipment by a few large professional service firms will tend to give them a unique market. These production firms will provide this service for their own work and for smaller firms; thus, it will tend to become a specialty in itself. Although complete machine recording and transmission appears to be distant, the systems and component design approach to building design and construction will standardize and permit incorporation by reference of materials previously individually recorded. One can anticipate a slow but consistent proportionate reduction of time in this activity as compared to other professional roles.

14. Estimating, Cost Control, Scheduling, and Materials Ordering: Some of these functions are normally thought of as part of the construction phase, but in the future they will more often tend to become part of the detailed design phase. This will be particularly true on large-scale projects where there is greater need for maintaining current cost control and for leaving open the decisions regarding detailed systems until time for installation, all as part of the need for shortening construction time. It is important that present professional ethical limitations regarding involvement of architects in construction not prevent professional service firms headed by architects from including this role, otherwise the fabricators and builders will be forced to include all of the detail design role. The large professional service firms will be drawn into this activity not because of interest, but because it will become a routine and necessary part of detail design. Large-scale fabricators and industrial systems manufacturers will also be drawn into this work through their increasingly large role in detail design.

A portion of the general contractor's present function for bidding and making subcontracts will become part of both the systems design and the detailed design phase in the future. The larger and more detailed the predesigned and prefabricated components, the less it will be possible to maintain open competitive subbids. As a result, these Roles, 13 and 14, will both include the negotiation of contracts for subcontracts and the fixing of these subcontracts as part of the design phase. As is true today only on large projects, many design decisions will be made and systems contracts let after some of the systems are already under construction. This work will usually be performed within the professional service firm, or by a joint venture of designer and contractor or fabricators, and on large projects by the all-inclusive conglomerate.

15. Observation of Construction for Design: The role of project observation, or supervision-for-design, is also an area where the architect has assumed an increased necessary responsibility when he wishes to exert absolute control over the finished product. Because of the courts' interpretation of the extent of responsibility, this role also continues to incur increasing liability. General contractors have defaulted this responsibility in their move toward brokerage only, and architects may also be expected to do so when other alternatives appear. In the future, this service will begin to be recognized as a specialized service in its own right and will be provided by small specialized groups and by the large professional service firms who undertake detailed design, production and materials ordering, and construction supervision, both for themselves and for small design-concepts firms. The present lack of adequate on-site supervision by both the general contractors and subcontractors and the low quality service provided by most "professional inspectors" will eventually require breaking past trends in this area, with a new form of control mechanism evolving among detail designers, subcontractors, and systems fabricators. Where major prefabrication exists, the supervisory coordinating role will tend to be taken by the systems manufacturers, not by choice, but by necessity. In other cases, the systems integration designer will assume this role whether he be in industry or part of a design firm.

16. Direction of Construction: General contractors perform this function only for work which cannot be subcontracted; the majority of their effort here is expended upon bidding, scheduling, and directing sequence of operations. The methods for direction of construction will vary in the future with the general contractor tending to dominate for many years, although the current trend toward off-site fabrication will accelerate with less and less field direction being required. The trend for off-site fabrication will continue its present development toward preassembled or prefitted component systems with the majority of the direction being performed in the factory.

17. Construction: On-site construction will continue to be performed by individual subcontractors. However, the trend will continue toward subcontractors who are systems installers who will include coordination and installation of component systems by several trades in lieu of traditional subcontractor structure which primarily related to individual trade union organizations and types of raw materials.

18. Management of Interdisciplinary Professional Service: This activity coordinates the work of all of the roles which are grouped within one organization. It coordinates this work with that performed outside of the organization by subcontractors, joint ventures, and consultants. It requires a person with both knowledge and experience in all of the individual roles or activities which must be related; it includes the responsibilities of the job captain, project manager or principal-in-charge. This role will be filled by the most competent generalist with the capability for responsibility, considered professional judgment, and management leadership. Many will say that this is the only true "architect" role; but it will be filled by the most qualified professional, regardless of his background, and he may not always be from any of the traditional design professions.

NATURE OF THE PROFESSION

It is important to note that although professional architects will be involved in the full range of roles which has been described, it does not follow that this range describes the profession of architecture. Many persons from other design professions and from other fields will participate in these roles. The ability to perform in any one of them will in itself not constitute professional status. Returning to the argument put forth earlier, the definition of the professional architect will be both his ability to draw from the entire field and his capability in any particular specialty area. It will be necessary, however, for the field of architecture to review the range of possible roles and identify those in which it should train skilled professionals, as well as those which should be offered by professional service firms. Although the field may not normally encompass the entire range, the professional society and the registration boards would be ill-advised to set artificial barriers which prevent architects from engaging in any of these activities. The AIA should encourage, and the NCARB should not prevent, involvement by professionals in the full range of roles, for it is difficult to predict which may prove most effective for fulfilling the objectives of the profession.

The professional institutions may recognize the full range, but the schools have a different problem. None can hope to offer meaningful education for the knowledge and skills associated with all of these roles, many of which will require work in architecture plus other professions such as law, business administration, planning, or operations research or will require work in architecture plus another discipline in either the physical or behavioral sciences. Each school will be forced to limit its own offerings at the graduate level to those areas where its faculty has a depth of advanced expertise and where there is a strength and willingness to cooperate in the related fields outside of architecture. The limitation of the schools own offerings should not prevent the encouragement of students to work outside of the department in joint degree programs. The professional society should cooperate with the schools in helping them to establish the full range of programs in all the schools collectively, since none can attain this objective individually.

There will be disagreement within the profession as to which is the most important role for effecting significant improvement in the physical environment, but each will be important in varying degrees depending upon the nature of the problem. Historically, the important decisions in architecture were associated with construction itself and later with more finite design description. Recently, however, many of the important decision areas have related to policy, theory, and strategy. It is perhaps a truism to say that the most important contribution will come from those few who can effectively integrate the entire range.

Until recently, the field of architecture has had very little impact upon the "upper" more theoretical roles which involve policy, finance, research, and management. The natural selection process represented by architectural education and registration has tended to eliminate persons who are more interested in criteria for improvement, or strategy of implementation than in defining the precise physical form. In the future one can anticipate that the capabilities of the field will increase in the more theoretical areas and that many more professional architects will seek involvement at these levels.

In a similar manner, architecture has screened from it persons who might make a contribution at the more finite end of the diagram. In recent years the field has made little contribution for advancing the

303

technology of building construction. The capital demands for involvement in construction itself and the AIA ban on direct construction activity have helped to conspire against the architect's active engagement in the construction process, thus reducing the profession's contributions for technological advance. In the future, the merging of the detailed design activity, scheduling, material ordering, and the brokerage aspects of contracting will bring a closer relationship between design and construction and should result in better feedback into the theoretical and conceptual design activities.

Those professions which are most qualified, or whom the public believes most qualified, will be identified with a particular activity and may dominate it, but this should not restrict the activity of architects who are also qualified. In the near future, the opportunities will remain open and a number of different professional and business enterprises will seek primacy in each role. There will be strong competition from the professional as well as from the new actors identified in the diagram, particularly from program-planning research and development firms, the computer-based soft sciences and management-finance related fields, and industrial design. The most critical factor will not be the nature of the competition, but the qualifications of those enterprises which offer architectural services.

Specific trends for change of emphasis by individual professionals and in the nature of their enterprises can be summarized as follows:

1. The policy and theory roles will find all of the design professions more involved as individuals and through their professional societies. Following the example of the city and regional planners, the fields of architecture and landscape architecture will seek to have greater impact upon the formation of public policy and must plan to combine forces for this effort. The engineering profession will follow later, hopefully to join with the design professions rather than as separate advocates. Activity will be channeled primarily through the professional societies and the largest firms. Professionals engaged full time in these roles will be few in number but critical to the profession's impact upon the physical environment.

2. The remaining more theoretical roles in research, project feasibility, design criteria, programming, advocacy planning, master planning, and design concept will be highly volatile levels in the next fifteen years. Many professional architects will act in these roles in nondesign based enterprises, in particular nonprofit foundations and corporations; others will practice in small professional service firms.

304

New graduates in all the design professions will have new skills in these areas and will ignore tradition in their professional alignments. These groups will form alliances with disciplines not previously associated with the design processes including the physical and behavioral sciences, law, as well as the other design professions.

These new firms will seek specialist commissions and will avoid the traditional areas of architectural involvement where competition from existing firms will be strong and where many years of technological experience is required. Instead, they will seek new kinds of commissions at the programmatic conceptual levels, most at the urban and large-project scale, primarily for clients like neighborhood groups, government, civic organizations, and industry. The nature of the commissions will tend to be more advisory and consultative, thus avoiding the need for production capability. Their areas of practice will thereby also avoid those professional services with the highest liability.

Professional service firms in these activities may be more like the traditional concept of architecture, with persons providing personal professional consultation, operating individually or in small groups; the difference will be in the nature of their activity. It is important to note that these small architectural or interdisciplinary firms may not choose to align themselves with any existing profession, since these areas of professional service tend to fall outside of existing registration laws in most fields.

There may be a tendency to seek identification which suggests a broader range of capability than that of any one field, such as "environmental designer" rather than association with any one of the existing professions. If persons in these firms are graduates from architectural schools, yet not considered architects, it would be a serious setback for the profession, for this may be the most viable group in the field and they may have the greatest conceptual impact upon the physical environment. These small specialized firms may play vital policy-formulating roles.

3. The roles relating to physical development may be equally as active as those mentioned above, but with a different set of actors. These activists will become more closely related to large enterprises, usually interdisciplinary, which can offer a full range of specialists and technicians. Many of the persons in this phase of work will be from industrial design and, as mentioned earlier, much of the work will be done in joint venture with, under contract for, or by the fabricators, manufacturers, and contractors themselves. One exception to

305

this pattern will be those architects who will emerge as specialists in the design of systems and who may practice in enterprises of the small scale suggested for the more theoretical roles. These persons will have expertise in the physical and engineering services and be knowledgeable in industrial production technology, and they will offer their services to the large, full service field and to industry and contractors rather than to the general public.

As suggested earlier, some of the small firms, who now provide service primarily for these roles, will move their activities generally "up" the scale and into professional activity with less liability and need for production capability. Most of these firms will continue their present practice in the near future, for the amount of construction which will be needed is so large that there is little threat of their not finding sufficient work to keep busy. Most of these firms will slowly evolve, however, and a larger percentage of their time will be spent in consultative, coordinative, and management roles with government agencies and direct representative groups at the upper end of the scale and with predesigned construction systems at the lower end. This evolution will be continuous, but gradual enough to be unnoticed.

4. The full range of role will be attempted only by the very large existing professional service firms, combining all the design professions and containing or in joint venture with other specialties including contracting. These groups will tend to become less "architectural" even when headed by architects, and most will be headed by representatives from several fields. Some of these large firms will be merged into other business organizations to form conglomerates to give a stronger capital base and to obtain better access to the financial community, thus enabling them to provide broad management control. All of these firms will have the full complement of interdisciplinary teams to provide service in the full range of activities. The primary differences in their character will remain the motives, ambitions, and values of their top management.

The multi-discipline firms will tend to merge persons from different educational backgrounds into the total process depending upon their personal skills. One's professional title or registration will have little bearing on the scope of his activities. Most of the professional employees will not have need for personal registration except as a personal gratification, and thus a significant number will have less identity with any profession. Those firms who are strong in several of the roles and who do not form permanent alliances for a wider base of service will tend to joint venture more often in order to bring together for a specific project all the activities into one coordinated effort.

In the more distant future, one can predict that the nature of professional enterprises will tend to divide into several groups: a large group of individuals, nonprofit corporations, small professional service firms in the upper roles, a small group of skilled specialists in the middle and lower roles who act as consultants to the rest of the profession, and a few giants in the full range. The present emphasis on detail design and production will slowly diminish until the number of professionals who practice primarily in this area are the exception to prove the rule. The increased levels of responsibility and liability and low profitability will tend to make this lower middle range of roles increasingly more difficult in which to practice. This work will be more often an adjunct to manufacturing than to other professional service roles.

SUMMARY

Returning to the distinction made at the beginning of this chapter, one can speculate about the future for the field of architecture, individual professionals, the enterprises which include or offer professional services and their institutions. In general one can characterize the future as being related to higher levels of expertise in both social relationships and technical process, with less emphasis on the craft of architecture.

No detailed evaluation has been made of the existing profession as part of this study, but there are indications that the field of architecture through its institutions for education and research is beginning to educate and train persons with better capability for the full range of roles associated with controlling and creating the physical environment. Many of the most able are combining study in architecture with work in other fields and will select a role or activity not traditionally associated with the profession. The demand for these persons will be far greater than their numbers can provide, however, and many will be attracted into government and industry rather than professional service firms. However, the majority of the present graduates are not unlike those of a generation ago and do not bring new or more advanced skills or knowledge into the profession. In particular, most architectural students are behind other related fields in their involvement in the cybernetic revolution of our era.

The institutions for education and research are not strong when compared with other professional or academic fields. They have an unproductive record of scholarship, research, and development, particularly when compared to engineering. Most schools lag behind the practicing profession both in quality of personnel, development of new theory and method, and as a training ground for professional practice. There is an indication that this condition is beginning to change, but a significant leap must be accomplished before the schools can provide the profession with new skills and abilities beyond that of present experienced professionals.

It will be necessary to revise the definition of a professional. Traditionally, only those persons who sought and secured professional certification (registration) were considered professionals. In the future, this definition must be changed, for the most valued contributors and original theorists may not need nor seek certification. An increasingly large number of professionals will work as employees in professional service firms where registration for the individual will have no particular significance. Others will practice in areas which do not include design development or detailed physical design and, as such, will not be subject to registration laws. These persons will be professionals in every sense of the true definition but may by law be prohibited from calling themselves architects. Failure to permit these persons to identify with the profession, some of whom may be on the leading edge of the field, would seriously erode the public view of the profession.

Individual architects will find a role for rewarding professional practice in many forms of public and private enterprise. Some will be in nonprofit research foundations or research and development firms, others in the aerospace industries, and many will continue in firms whose primary activity is providing professional design service. Many will be part of in-house design consultation for development or manufacturing or construction and some will be in institutions and in local, regional, and federal government agencies, in contrast to the present where the majority are employed in professional service firms. By the year 2000, no one of these enterprises may dominate the entire field.

Many of these architects will be in enterprises which will be in direct competition with existing professional service firms. Some of these new forms of enterprises will grow out of present firms in the fragmenting and rejoining which will take place in the next few years.

308

In twenty years, there will be few professional service firms which represent only one design profession, for most will represent several fields or disciplines even if they specialize in only one or two roles. It will be more difficult to distinguish "architectural" firms from the professional service firms headed by other design professions — the landscape architects and physical planners at the upper level roles and the industrial designers and engineers at lower roles. It is clear that the nature of the enterprise will change and the existence of the profession of architecture should not be thought to depend upon its identification with a particular form of business enterprise which is solely architectural.

The profession of architecture will be more diffuse; it will no longer be possible to identify it with only one or two roles or with a particular type of professional enterprise. Individual professionals will practice in the full range of roles described earlier — some as specialists in one or two activities, others as broader generalists with a wider range of capabilities, but none will be master of all. Among these professionals there will be those who are certified for personal public practice but many who are not. One must reaffirm, therefore, that it is the professional architects as individuals, both generalists and specialists, certified and uncertified, who constitute the profession of architecture. The professional status must be considered as being independent of certification, independent of the particular roles they select in their specialty, and independent of the nature of the enterprise — public or private — in which they practice their profession.

To serve the rapidly changing field and profession, several different kinds of professional societies could emerge. A professional society could come forward to represent the entire field of architecture with its full range of student, professional, and nonprofessional roles. This society would represent the strongest voice for the field as a spokesman for environmental quality and, as such, it would have as its primary obligation a responsibility to the public and to the field as a whole. It would use its leverage politically to improve the environment. Such a society would offer individual personal identification and association for the heterogenous members who make up the field. It would require great effort to establish a common ground for joint effort.

A second kind of professional society could emerge which would represent professional architects in all of the roles described earlier.

The granting of a professional degree and completion of a stipulated internship period from an accredited architectural school would be sufficient credential for full participation. Certification would hold no particular status. This society would offer a broad base of support for entrepreneurs and employees, certified and noncertified, and would be limited to those with reasonably similar educational backgrounds, objectives, and maturity.

If neither of the first two types of professional societies emerge, one should expect much more fragmentation of the field. A society would appear to represent each of the subdisciplines like architectural, programming, specifications, etc., and each of the hybrid fields like urban design or interdisciplinary groups. In addition, there would be separate organizations to represent entrepreneurs and employees; or there would be separate organizations related to the kind of public or private enterprise in which the individual practiced. This kind of fragmentation would be highly detrimental to public orientation with the field and would negate its potential effectiveness as a collective advocate for better environments.

The response of the AIA to these eventualities will in large measure determine the profession's future role in American society.

5.

RECOMMENDATIONS
FOR THE PROFESSION OF ARCHITECTURE

THE PROFESSION must recognize that we are now entering a critical period in history, a period of social realignment and reorganization which will have profound effect on all public and private institutions and enterprises. The extent of these changes may be revolutionary, and the greatest demand for innovation will be in communication and delivery systems to provide technological solutions for social problems. The profession will be in the center of this revolution by choice or default and must see its actions in the near future as critical to its viability in the more distant future. Therefore, we must establish the following policies:

Definition and Objective. The profession must reaffirm its belief in the traditional breadth of the field of architecture as the art and science which bridges both humanistic and scientific values to effect man's habitation. It must also reaffirm its primary objective for fulfilling its social responsibility for developing programs and facilities which will enhance the life style of all of society.

The profession must reaffirm its pride in the fact that its objective is virtually impossible; to bridge the subjective and objective. It should continue to seek to establish itself with the other leaders in this world of extra-rationality, for society is in desperate need for leadership in this regard.

Social Context. The profession must recognize that it is an integral part of its social environment and that, increasingly, it will be the worldwide society rather than the U.S. society alone, to which it must relate. As a social mechanism, the profession must recognize the importance of active involvement in current social issues as they relate to the physical environment and must seek to constantly change the profession to maintain the most viable form for performing its service to society.

Technological Context. The profession must recognize that we are in a technological age and that society needs and will demand the highest achievable social and technological solution for its habitation. The profession must seek to improve its own technological ability and to join with those in other fields to bring to bear the most advanced knowledge of both the social and physical sciences.

Interdisciplinary Effort. The profession must reaffirm that it will require the knowledge and skills of many industries, professions, and disciplines to create the highest achievable quality of the environment and must pledge itself to develop more productive relationships of equal status with these fields and whenever possible to promote joint effort. The profession must recognize the mutual dependence of all of the design professions and should seek to aid in the improvement of the individuals and institutions of all of these fields.

Maximum Effectiveness. The profession must accept that it is small in numbers and can be most effective in achieving its objectives at two levels: policy and research for the large-scale environment and innovative prototypical solutions for the small scale environment. Both are equally valid objectives. Creating unique, standard-setting solutions for individual problems must be achieved, as well as providing the best solutions for the repetitive sector of the environment which affects a larger percentage of the population.

Breadth of Profession. The profession must recognize that there will be an increase in the knowledge and methodological skills pertaining to the field and a broadening of the range of roles which architects will assume. Architects will have differing capabilities and individual specialities and therefore will conduct the practice of the profession by providing new combinations of service in a wide variety of public and private enterprises.

Growth and Development. The profession must recognize that for its continued growth and development it is dependent upon attracting the most creative persons to join in its efforts. Attracting the most innovative minds to study, teach, practice, and participate in the professional society is crucial to the field. Equally important is the solicitation of the most able persons outside the field to participate in professional services and collaborations.

THE AMERICAN INSTITUTE OF ARCHITECTS

As the most viable institution of professional architects, the American Institute of Architects must clarify its objectives and must seek effective cooperation with other institutions within the field to provide leadership. The institute should initiate program planning policies for short- and long-run implementation. Many of the recommendations which follow are not new, and progress has been made in several of the programs recommended; but the Committee believes that they must be restated to illustrate the overall commitment which is required to prepare for the future.

Objective. The professional society must have as its primary objective the implementation of the objectives of the profession as stated above. It must recognize as a prime responsibility service to the public as it relates to the profession and service to the entire field of architecture as well as service to professionals.

Resource Development. The institute must develop programs to increase its inventory of human talents, time, and funds through growth of membership within the field of architecture, alliances with other professions, industry, and nonprofit public and private institutions which will support programs related to improving the quality of the man-made physical environment.

Policy Development. The institute must more actively involve itself in current issues and to that end should establish special study groups related to the major problems of the environment of habitation and of the building industry. They should be charged with the responsibility of collecting data, proposing strategies and developing institute policies therefor.

Government Relations. The institute must, as one of its primary roles, provide vigorous representation for the field and profession of

313

architecture to the public and to government at all levels. It must provide legislative assistance and act as advocates to implement the institute's policy programs related to improvement of the physical environment.

Public Relations. The institute should expand its public relations program as a means of informing the public about the issues concerning the environment and for making known the policies and positions of the AIA regarding these issues. This program should be seen as an adjunct to the legislative assistance program and should help attract issue-oriented young architects to become members of the institute.

Research and Development Brokerage. The architectural profession must develop a network of research and development capability combining the resources of the Institute's and the schools' individual practices. The institute must seek the establishment of a research and development center or expand the existing Urban Design Development Corporation to work with other existing research groups. The center must actively seek research contracts to develop knowledge about man's habitation, and must publish it for the benefit of all the design professions and the schools and to serve as a data base for the institute's policy and legislative programs.

Data Utility. The institute must find appropriate partners and seek the establishment of a data bank relative to the habitation of the environment and the building industry; it must act as an information utility for the benefit of all of the design professions, school and institute research, policy and legislative programs. The total expenditure for this will be staggering and it will require the cooperation of many; but the need is evident, and the AIA must take the initiative.

Improvement of the Profession. As its primary internal service, the institute must initiate an intensive program of continuing education for the improvement of both the professionals and nonprofessionals who are now in the field of architecture. The AIA must seek new and imaginative means to convince the profession of this need and to provide incentive for several different kinds of programs, beginning by funding the preparation of a monograph series, films, and correspondence courses. In addition, the institute should encourage a rapid and broader improvement of its professional firms by encouraging them to seek graduates from other fields with advanced expertise to improve the level of professional service.

The profession must increase its program for attracting and providing support for members of minority races to study in the field and enter the profession of architecture. The major thrust for improving the central city must involve participation by those who will be most effective, i.e., architects who are members of these communities.

Improvement of the Schools. The profession must join in a cooperative effort with the architectural schools and provide assistance in improving these capabilities. This help must come through a massive program of education and advocacy with universities and college administrations, their trustees, and state legislatures, seeking a higher commitment of funds for better faculties. The building industry must be pressed for student fellowships to assist in producing more highly qualified architectural graduates. Additionally, the profession must support better educational programs in the related design professions in order to strengthen the design professions as a whole and to produce more capable collaborators.

Service to the Community. The institute must initiate a program by chapters and individual architectural firms to provide free professional service to neighborhood groups and to underprivileged individuals through direct assistance, community design workshops, participatory design and advocacy planning programs. These programs will not only further the objectives of the profession for improving both the physical and social environment, but will provide valuable professional training in developing improved communication techniques.

Scope of Professional Service. The institute must establish policies which encourage rather than restrict change and innovation in the methods for providing and in the scope of professional service. Restrictions and prohibitions regarding the nature of roles and the nature of the public and private enterprises in which a professional may complete his internship and may practice should be eliminated and new innovations should be encouraged and publicized. Graduate architects should be encouraged to serve in any of the wide range of roles which will contribute to bettering the quality of habitation. The standards for practice and internship and the professional ethics should be positive rather than negative in stating the objectives for professional service.

The profession must recognize that the traditional scope of services does not include the wider range of roles offered by the most progressive professional service firms. The institute should not suggest any "normal" scope of service except that each organization should limit itself to those roles for which it is qualified professionally and for which there is adequate fee to provide a high quality of service.

Constituency. The institute should immediately broaden its base of representatives to include, with a full and equal status, certified architects, professional architects, intern architects, and teachers of architecture. In addition, the institute should consider a form of bonafide representation in the institute for all others in the field of architecture including students. The institute must recognize that a smaller percentage of architects will be individual entrepreneur-practitioners in the future, and it must not direct the majority of its efforts toward this minority. Special programs should be initiated such as minimal dues obligations to attract young members of the field into an active role in the institute.

As a first step toward closer, long-range cooperative efforts with all of the other design professions, the institute should admit to full, equal, and indistinguishable membership status those related design professionals whose objectives, knowledge and methodology are closest to that of architects.

The institute should study possible reorganization of its structure to provide more direct communication from the chapter level, stronger national-local communication and cooperation with related design professions on issue oriented programs. Consideration must also be given to AIA Board representation on a uniform per capita basis.

Continuing Study. The Committee strongly urges that the institute continue to sponsor further studies of the factors which will most influence the future of the physical environment and the profession. Some of these studies can be conducted by the policy study groups proposed above, others by the appropriate standing committees. The AIA should be the continuing source for the most relevant material pertaining to these concerns. The areas of study which should receive the next highest priority are as follows:

316

1. the design professions in the United States including architecture;

2. international influence on the physical environment, the building industry, and design professions;

3. the micro-environment;

4. the new conglomerate, macro-operators;

5. family pattern and life style.

THE COMMITTEE MEMBERSHIP OF 1969
Rex W. Allen
Robert W. Cutler
Samuel T. Hurst
George E. Kassabaum
Gerald McCue, Chairman
David A. McKinley, Jr.
Louis De Moll
William H. Scheick

NOTES

PART I. *Reconnaissance of the Future*

INTRODUCTION

1. Donald N. Michael, "Urban Policy in the Rationalized Society," *Journal of the American Institute of Planners* (November 1965): 285.

2. Dwight David Eisenhower, attributed to him in reflecting on his boyhood.

3. William R. Ewald, Jr., *Environment for Man, The Next Fifty Years* (1967); *Environment and Change, The Next Fifty Years* (1968); *Environment and Policy, The Next Fifty Years* (1968) (Bloomington: Indiana University Press). Commissioned and edited as part of the $1 million, four-year consultation, "The Next Fifty Years, the Future Environment of a Democracy," Ewald organized and directed for the American Institute of Planners marking their fiftieth year as the nation's professional society of state, city, and regional planners.

4. Zbigniew Brzezinski, "The Search for Meaning Amid Change," *New York Times National Economic Review* (January 6, 1969): C-141.

5. Jacques Ellul, *The Technological Society* (New York: Alfred A. Knopf, 1964). Originally published in France, 1954.

6. John Kenneth Galbraith, *The New Industrial State* (New York: Signet Books, New American Library, 1967).

7. Daniel Bell, "The Post Industrial Society," in Eli Ginzberg, ed., *Technology and Social Change* (New York: Columbia University Press, 1964), pp. 44-59.

8. Peter F. Drucker, *The Age of Discontinuity: Guidelines to Our Changing Society* (New York: Harper & Row, 1968, 1969).

9. Herman Kahn and Anthony J. Wiener, *The Year 2000. A Framework for Speculation on the Next Thirty-Three Years* (New York: The Macmillan Co., 1967), p. 39; from Pitirium A. Sorokin, *Social and Cultural Dynamics* (Boston: Sargent, Porter, 1962).

10. John A. T. Robinson, *Honest to God* (London: Westminster, 1963); Gabriel Vahanian, *God is Dead Debate* (New York: The McGraw-Hill Book Company, 1969).

11. John R. Platt, *The Step to Man* (New York: John Wiley & Sons, 1966), p. 196.

12. Harrison Brown, James Bonner, John Weir, *The Next Hundred Years* (New York: Viking Press, 1957), p. 67.

13. Donald J. Bogue, "The End of the Population Explosion," *The Public Interest* (Spring 1967), p. 11.

319

14. Edward Schillebeeckx, O.P., *God the Future of Man* (New York: Sheed & Ward, 1968), p. 63.

15. President's Commission on Urban Housing (Kaiser Commission), *A Decent Home* (Washington, D.C.: Government Printing Office, 1968); see also *National Commission on Urban Problems* (Douglas Commission).

16. Charles W. Moore, "The Project at New Zion: Interaction and Building," *Eye* (Magazine of the Yale Arts Association), No. 2 (1968), p. 19.

CHAPTER I: *Two Perspectives into the Future*

1. *What about the Year 2000?* (Prepared by the Joint Committee on Bases of Sound Land Policy composed of the American Civic Association, American Institute of Park Executives, American Park Society, National Conference on City Planning, National Conference on State Parks), (Harrisburg, Pa.: Mount Pleasant Press, 1929).

2. Martin Van Buren, quoted in *Armco Today,* published at Middletown, Ohio, December 1968.

3. William R. Ewald, Jr., from conversation with Mr. Lilienthal while investigating potential of Appalachian development for President John F. Kennedy, 1964.

4. *Farm Population Estimates 1920-1967,* Economic Research Service, United States Department of Agriculture (Washington, D.C.: Government Printing Office).

5. Nancy T. Gamarra, *The Library of Congress Legislative Reference Service,* "Erroneous Predictions and Negative Comments Concerning Exploration, Territorial Expansion, Scientific and Technological Development" (Selected statements prepared at the request of the Senate Committee on Aeronautical and Space Sciences) (Washington, D.C.: Government Printing Office, 1967).

6. Kenneth G. Slocum, "The Dying Lake," *The Wall Street Journal* (February 10, 1969), 1.

7. Herman Kahn, "World Futures," *Science Journal* (October 1967), 122.

8. Kenneth E. Boulding, "Expecting the Unexpected: The Uncertain Futures of Knowledge and Technology," in Edgar L. Morphet and Charles O. Ryan, eds., "Prospective Changes in Society by 1980," *Designing Education for the Future No. 1* (New York: Citation Press, 1967), p. 203.

9. Ibid., p. 211.

10. F. L. Polak, *The Image of the Future,* vol. 2 (New York: Oceana Publications, 1961).

11. Pierre Bertaux, "The Future of Man," in Ewald, ed., *Environment and Change, The Next Fifty Years* (Bloomington: Indiana University Press, 1968), p. 19.

12. Roger L. Shinn, "Human Responsibility in the Emerging Society," in *Designing Education for the Future, No. 1,* p. 254.

13. Raymond A. Bauer, ed., *Social Indicators* (Cambridge, Mass.: MIT Press, 1966); also Eleanor Bernet Sheldon and William E. Moore, eds., *Indicators of Social Change* (New York: Russell Sage Foundation, 1968).

14. Ewald, *Environment and Policy, The Next Fifty Years* (Bloomington: Indiana University Press, 1968), p. 448.

15. Gladwin Hill, "Scientist Decries Rising Population," *The New York Times* (March 6, 1969).

16. Ewald, *Environment and Policy,* p. 446.

17. Ibid.

18. Ibid., p. 452.

19. Associated Press, "Conflicts Between Business, Society Continue to Grow," *The Hot Springs New Era* (February 27, 1969).

20. Leonard J. Duhl, "The Parameters of Urban Planning" in Stanford Anderson,

ed., *Planning for Diversity and Choice, Possible Futures and Their Relations to the Man-Controlled Environment* (Cambridge, Mass.: MIT Press, 1968), p. 73.

21. Clyde Kluckhohn, *Mirror for Man* (New York: Fawcett World Library, A Premier Book, 1960), p. 197.

22. Roger J. Williams, in *Planning Versus or For the Individual* (Austin: University of Texas Press, 1969).

23. H. Mewhinney, "The Architects at Mid-Century," in Francis R. Bellamy, ed., *Conversations Across the Nation* (New York: Reinhold Publishing Corp., 1954), p. 73.

24. Ewald, *Report of the Appalachian Institute Committee to the Conference of Appalachian Governors and The President's Appalachian Regional Commission,* Area Redevelopment Administration Technical Assistance Project (Washington, D.C.: Department of Commerce, October 1964) and *Appalachian Institute Prospectus/Budget/Funding* for The Appalachian Regional Commission (Washington, D.C.: Department of Commerce, September 1966).

CHAPTER 2: *The Dimensions of the Future*

1. Harris Survey, "Public Finds Cities Worth Saving," *Arkansas Gazette* (January 29, 1969).

2. William James, "The Moral Equivalent of War," in Staughton Lynd, ed., *Nonviolence in America: A Documentary History* (Indianapolis: Bobbs-Merrill Co., 1966), p. 142. ". . . The transition to a 'pleasure-economy' may be fatal to a being wielding no powers against its disintegrative forces. If we speak of the *fear of emancipation from the fear-regime,* we put the whole situation into a single phrase; fear regarding ourselves now taking the place of the ancient fear of the enemy."

3. William R. Ewald, Jr., and staff of Office for Regional Development and consultants, *Change/Challenge/Response,* A Development Policy for New York State (Albany: Office for Regional Development, 1964).

4. For total year 2000 U.S. population, U.S. Census "C," see Table I-2 of this chapter, extracted from Economic Associates, Inc. (see Projections Table 1, p. 109 in this volume). Urbanized area populations in year 2000 derived from Jerome P. Pickard, *Appendixes to Dimensions of Metropolitanization,* Research Monograph 14A (Washington, D.C.: Urban Land Institute, 1967). Regional distribution in year 2000 from Pickard, *Appendixes,* p. 8; from Pickard, "If Present Trends Continue," in Ewald, ed., *Building the Future Environment (An Atlantic Region Perspective to the Year 2020),* to be published by Indiana University Press, 1970; and from Ewald et al., *Change/Challenge/Response,* p. 42-45.

5. Pickard, *Appendixes,* p. 8; also Ewald, *Building the Future Environment* (Great Lakes Region including Canada), p. 42.

6. Eliel Saarinen taught that understanding the character of the next largest context was fundamental to successful design; at Cranbrook design that was practiced from the sponsor to the regional plan. Constantine Doxiadis speaks of the hierarchy of spaces. Corporations may relate products to world markets, etc.

7. Ewald, *Environment and Policy, The Next Fifty Years* (Bloomington: Indiana University Press, 1968), p. 450.

8. Economic Associates, Inc., from Projections Tables 1, 2, 4, pp. 109, 114, 119.

9. Lyle C. Fitch, "National Development and National Policy," in Ewald, *Environment and Policy,* p. 297.

10. Economic Associates, Inc. and Ewald (derived from U.S. Labor Department figures), in unpublished report "Community Development and New Residential Systems," General Electric Study Team Report (April 1965).

11. Harris Survey.

12. Report of the National Advisory Commission on Civil Disorders (New York: Bantam Books, 1968), pp. 390-91.

13. Economic Associates, Inc., from Projections Table 1, p. 109.

14. Economic Associates, Inc.

15. Herman Kahn and Anthony J. Wiener, *The Year 2000. A Framework for Speculation on the Next Thirty-Three Years* (New York: The Macmillan Co., 1967), p. 125.

16. Donald N. Michael, "Urban Policy in the Rationalized Society," *Journal of the American Institute of Planners* (November 1965): 123.

17. Economic Associates, Inc., from Projections Table 5, p. 120.

18. Ibid., Tables 10, 11, pp. 139, 141.

19. Ibid., Table 7, p. 126.

20. Associated Press, "Moving: Way of Life for Many in U.S.," *Chicago Tribune* (February 8, 1969). A recent study by Robert E. Marsh, "Geographic Labor Mobility in the United States, Recent Funding," *Social Security Bulletin,* No. 30 (March 1967), pp. 14-20 indicates that 15 per cent of U.S. family heads moved between labor markets in the 5-year period, 1958-1963. More than two-thirds of the family heads in the United States are living in labor market areas other than the one in which they were born (both the latter from C. E. Bishop, University of North Carolina).

21. Eldridge Lovelace, "Commuters for a New Generation," *The Post Industrial City,* in the *New Mexico Quarterly* (Fall 1968), 52.

CHAPTER 3: *Basic Alternative Paths to the Future*

1. Rockefeller Panel Reports, *Prospect for America* (Garden City, N.Y.: Doubleday & Co., 1961).

2. Leonard A. Lecht, *Goals, Priorities and Dollars* (New York: The Free Press, 1966), p. 42.

3. Sir Geoffrey Vickers, "Individuals in a Collective Society," in William R. Ewald, Jr., ed., *Environment and Change, The Next Fifty Years* (Bloomington: Indiana University Press, 1968), p. 301.

4. Dr. Seymour L. Halleck, "This Week," *The Chicago Daily News* (March 16, 1965), p. 5.

5. Dr. Bruno Bettelheim, "The Perils of Overexposing Youth to College," *Washington Post* (March 23, 1965), p. C4.

6. John Leo, "Small-Business Men Called Obstacle to Reform," *New York Times* (November 24, 1968).

7. National Commission on Technology, Automation and Economic Progress, *Technology and the American Economy,* vol. 1 (Washington, D.C.: Government Printing Office, 1966), p. 16.

8. Rene Dubos, "There's Some Stone Age in Our Modern Bodies," *Washington Post* (April 20, 1969), p. B5.

9. Leon H. Keyserling, "The Problem of Problems," *Social Policies for America in the Seventies, Nine Divergent Views,* ed. Robert Theobald (New York: Doubleday & Co., 1969), p. 13.

10. Ibid., p. 11.

11. Herman Kahn and Anthony J. Wiener, *The Year 2000;* reference cited in Ewald Appendix Table 1, Authority "F," p. 112.

12. Ewald. See estimates in Chapter 4 under low birth rate section, p. 45.

13. James P. Sterba, "Student Unity Crumbles Over Tactics," *New York Times* (March 31, 1965).

14. Tod Peck, "Apartment Survey Speech" (unpublished), Owens-Corning Fiberglas, undated (circa 1968).

15. Ewald. See estimates in Chapter 4 under Better Homes, p. 58.

16. Ewald, "Signs and the City," *Washington Post,* Magazine Section (May 22, 1966) p. 21.

17. "Science, Forecast on Weather Forecasting: Cloudy," *New York Times* (April 27, 1969); Frederick Sargent, ed., "Weather Modification and the Biosphere," *Technology Review* (MIT), March 1969, p. 43; Thomas F. Malme, "Tinkering with our Atmospheric Environment," *Technology Review* (MIT), May 1968, p. 41; U.S. Department of Commerce, *Man's Geophysical Environment, Its Study from Space,* Environmental Science Services Administration, March 1968; National Academy of Sciences — National Research Council, *An Outline of International Programs in the Atmospheric Sciences,* Publication 1085, 1963.

18. Ewald, staff of Office for Regional Development and consultants, *Change/Challenge/Response,* A Development Policy for New York State (Albany: Office for Regional Development, 1964).

19. Edmund K. Faltermayer, "We Can Afford a Better America," *Fortune* (March 1969), p. 90; Charles L. Shultz, "Budget Alternatives after Vietnam," *Agenda for the Nation,* ed. Kermit Gordon (Washington, D.C.: The Brookings Institution, 1968), p. 47; Edwin L. Dale, Jr., "What Will We Do with All That Extra Money," *New York Times Magazine* (February 16, 1969), p. 32.

CHAPTER 4: *Shifting Factors of Greatest Importance*

1. *U.S. Bureau of Census,* through 1968.

2. Population Reference Bureau, Inc., *Population Profile* (July 1968), p. 5.

3. Population Reference Bureau, Inc., *World Population Data Sheet — 1968.*

4. "Gallup Poll, 'Family-Size' View of Nations Varies," *New York Times* (Nov. 13, 1968).

5. American Public Health Association, "Public Health Group Advocates Abortions Even to Plan Families," *Wall Street Journal,* circa Nov. 11-16, 1968.

6. In discussion with leading gerontologists, statistical projectors of Metropolitan Life Insurance, and discussion with Dr. Paul Jacobson there; see also testimony in U.S., Senate, Special Committee on Aging, *Developments in Aging: Hearing,* pursuant to S. Res. 20, 91st Cong., 2d Sess., 17 February 1967. (Committee Report 1098, April 29, 1968.)

7. Rene Dubos, *Man Adapting* (New Haven: Yale University Press, 1965), p. 230.

8. Special Committee on Aging, *Developments in Aging.*

9. Ibid., p. 11. "The National Institute of Child Health and Human Development — assigned the mission of improving 'the quality of life for persons of all ages, principally by providing scientific information regarding development throughout the lifespan' — turned its attention to research on retirement in 1967."

1969 budget of NICHD:	
Research grants	$3,549,331
Training grants, fellowships and research career development awards	2,177,491
Research contracts	48,241
NICHD Adult Development and Aging Information Center	41,160
Direct extramural operations and conferences	139,577
Direct research (Gerontology Research Center)	1,742,179
Total	$7,697,979

CREATING THE HUMAN ENVIRONMENT

10. Ibid., p. 150.

11. Ibid., p. xiv.

12. Ibid., p. 151. Testimony of Dr. Harold Sheppard, W. E. Upjohn Institute for Employment Research; see also Robert W. Kleemeier, ed., *Aging and Leisure* (New York: Oxford University Press, 1961), p. 239.

13. Sir George Thompson, *The Foreseeable Future* (Cambridge: The University Press, 1962), p. 118.

14. Dubos, *Man Adapting,* p. 21.

15. Robert W. Prehoda, *Extended Youth* (New York: G. P. Putnam's Sons, 1968), p. 86.

16. Ralph G. H. Siu, "Role of Technology in Creating the Environment Fifty Years Hence," in William R. Ewald, Jr., *Environment and Change, The Next Fifty Years* (Bloomington: Indiana University Press, 1968), p. 95.

17. Margaret Mead has discussed the desirability of an early trial marriage through the college years, then another marriage to raise the children. But she was thinking in terms of 70 to 80 years of life. In Sweden the experiment to emancipate women, to bring them to equal status with men, goes forth especially with efforts for child day-care centers, job opportunities, sharing of housework with husbands, new legal and social status and finally, communal marriages of six or so couples, married or not. Karl E. Meyer, "Sweden Redefines the Family," *Washington Post* (April 13, 1969); see also Swedish Institute, *Sweden Today — The Status of Women in Sweden* (Stockholm, 1968).

18. Carl Berstein, "Housing Opposition Seen as 'Age-ism,' Not Racism," *Washington Post* (March 7, 1969). Interview with psychiatrist Dr. Robert Butler.

19. U.S. Department of Commerce, "Summary of Demographic Projections," *Population Estimates* (March 14, 1960), p. 11.

20. Canadian Embassy, Research Librarian, Washington, D.C.

21. Donald N. Michael, *The Next Generation* (New York: Vintage Books, 1965), p. 121.

22. Gallup Poll, "Assured Income Opposed in Poll," *New York Times* (January 5, 1969).

23. U.S. Department of Commerce, *Population Estimates,* p. 12.

24. Yankelovich Survey, "What They Believe," *Fortune* (January 1969), p. 70.

25. Harris Survey, "What People Think about Their High Schools," *Life* (May 16, 1969), p. 24.

26. Anthony B. Oettinger, "Education and Technology," *Toward the Year 2018* (New York: Foreign Policy Association, Cowles Education Corporation, 1968), p. 77.

27. Outdoor Recreation Resources Review Commission, *Outdoor Recreation for America: A Report to the President and the Congress* (Washington, D.C.: Government Printing Office, January 1962), p. 35.

28. Sebastian de Grazia, *Of Time, Work and Leisure* (New York: The Twentieth Century Fund, 1962), p. 88.

29. ORRRC, *Outdoor Recreation for America,* p. 31.

30. ORRRC, *Participation in Outdoor Recreation: Factors Affecting Recreation Among American Adults,* Study Report 20, p. 35.

31. Ibid., Table 47, p. 47.

32. Ibid., Table 5.46, p. 272.

33. Ibid., Table 27, p. 32.

34. Henry Clark, "Responsible Use of Free Time," *AAUW Journal* (May 1966), p. 181.

35. Michael, *The Next Generation,* p. 143.

36. President's Commission on Urban Housing (Kaiser Commission), *A Decent Home* (Washington, D.C.: Government Printing Office, 1969).

324

37. William K. Hausch, "Housing as a Consumer Product: An Emerging New Industry," unpublished paper for Task Force on Economic Growth and Opportunity, Chamber of Commerce of the United States, 1968, p. 13; Mitre Corporation study of HUD, *An Analysis of Twelve Experimental Housing Projects* (Washington, D.C., December 1968), p. 77.

38. Jacob Bakema, comments at session "Creating a New Standard of Life, with Man as the Measure," at American Institute of Planners' conference "The Next Fifty Years, The Future Environment of a Democracy" (Washington, D.C., October 1-5, 1967).

39. "Housing Boom: How Big?" *U.S. News and World Report* (March 17, 1969), pp. 86-88.

40. Paul Rudolph, "Twentieth Century Brick," Urban Futures Conference, Rice University (Houston, March 28, 1969).

41. "Worried About Your Budget? An Official Guide to Costs," *U.S. News and World Report* (March 24, 1969), p. 58.

42. Ibid.; also U.S. Department of Housing and Urban Development, FHA, Division of Research and Statistics, Statistics Section, April 1967.

43. "Market Study of the Mobile Homes Industry," *Mobile Home* (Recreational Vehicle Dealer Magazine), January 1969.

44. Tri-State Transportation Commission, "Regional Forecast 1985, the Future Size and Needs of the Tri-State Region" (New York, December 1967), p. 10.

45. *U.S. News and World Report,* Economic Unit based on data from FHA, U.S. Department of Housing and Urban Development, U.S. Dept. of Commerce.

46. William Michelson, "Most People Don't Want What Architects Want," *Transaction* (July/Aug. 1968), pp. 37-43.

47. Colin Clark, "The Economic Functions of a City in Relation to Its Size," *Econometrica,* Journal of the Econometric Society, University of Chicago (Menasha, Wisc.: Banta Publishing Company, April 1945), p. 113; also Werner Hirsch in *Urban and Rural America, Policies for Future Growth,* Advisory Commission on Intergovernmental Relations (Washington, D.C.: Government Printing Office, April 1968), pp. 47, 56.

48. Muriel Allen, ed., "New Communities' Challenge for Today," *American Institute of Planners Background Papers No. 2* (Washington, D.C.: American Institute of Planners, October 1968).

49. "Welfare Payments Vary Greatly," *New York Times* (April 27, 1969).

50. John T. Howard, "The Crisis of the Cities," in Robert A. Goldwin, *A Nation of Cities: Essays on America's Urban Problems* (Chicago: Rand McNally & Co., 1966), p. 83.

51. Jonathon Lindley, EDA, U.S. Dept. of Commerce, "The Economic Environment and Urban Development," in National Planning Association, *Basic Policy Assumptions for Viewing the Future,* Proceedings: Eighth Annual Conference of the Center for Economic Projections (Washington, D.C., July 1967), Table I, p. 63.

52. Ibid., Table II, p. 65.

53. President's Advisory Commission on Rural Poverty, *The People Left Behind* (Washington, D.C.: Government Printing Office, September 1967), p. x.

54. Ibid, p. 75.

55. Ibid., p. xiii, 4.

56. Ibid.

57. Ibid., p. 11.

58. Ibid., p. 13.

59. U.S. Census Survey, 1967.

60. Ibid.

61. Gunnar Myrdal, "The Necessity and the Difficulty of Planning the Future

Society," in Ewald, *Environment and Policy, The Next Fifty Years* (Bloomington: Indiana University Press, 1968), p. 256.

62. Advisory Commission on Intergovernmental Relations, *Urban and Rural America: Policies for Future Growth* (Washington, D.C.: Government Printing Office, 1968), p. 131.

63. Ibid.

64. Chamber of Commerce of the United States, *Rural Poverty and Regional Progress in an Urban Society,* Task Force in Economic Growth and Opportunity, Fourth Report, 1969.

65. Allen, "New Communities' Challenge for Today."

66. Ewald, *National Policy Statement,* derived from the AIP/Arkansas conference on "Deciding the Future — A New Perspective for the Developing States" (Hot Springs, Arkansas, July 1968), mimeograph, January 30, 1969.

67. Ewald, "The Dimension of Change," opening statement at Arkansas/AIP conference, see note 66.

68. Marion Clawson, "Urban Renewal in 2000," *Journal of the American Institute of Planners,* 34 (May 1968), 3:173-179.

69. National Commission on Technology, Automation and Economic Progress, *Technology and the American Economy,* vol. 1 (Washington, D.C.: Government Printing Office, 1966), p. 11.

70. "Unemployment Rate Gap for Teenagers by Color," *Washington Post* (February 23, 1969).

71. Walter W. Heller, *New Dimensions of Political Economy* (New York: W. W. Norton & Co., Inc., 1966), p. 53.

72. Leon H. Keyserling, "The Problem of Problems," in Robert Theobald, ed., *Social Policies for America in the Seventies: Nine Divergent Views* (Garden City, N.Y.: Doubleday & Co., 1968), p. 13.

73. Heller, *New Dimensions of Political Economy,* p. 9.

74. Herbert Stein, "Unemployment, Inflation and Economic Stability," in Kermit Gordon, ed., *Agenda for the Nation* (New York: The Brookings Institution, 1968), p. 278.

75. Edmund K. Faltermayer, "A Way Out of the Welfare Mess," *Fortune* (July 1968), p. 62.

76. Gallup Poll, "Assured Income Opposed in Poll," *New York Times* (January 5, 1969).

77. James C. Vadakin, "A Critique on the Guaranteed Annual Income," *The Public Interest* (Spring 1968), p. 53.

78. Editors of Fortune, *Markets of the Seventies, The Unwinding U.S. Economy* (New York: The Viking Press, 1968), p. 3.

79. Keyserling, "The Problem of Problems," p. 21.

80. Heller, *New Dimensions of Political Economy,* p. 105.

81. National Commission on Technology, Automation and Economic Progress, *Technology and the American Economy,* p. 16.

82. Gerhard Colm, "Introduction: On Goals Research," in Leonard A. Lecht, *Goals, Priorities and Dollars* (New York: The Free Press, 1966), p. 8.

83. National Commission on Technology, Automation and Economic Progress, *Technology and the American Economy,* p. 16.

84. William T. Butler and Robert A. Kavesh, *How Business Economists Forecast* (Englewood Cliffs, N.J.: Prentice-Hall, 1966), p. 143.

85. Editors of Fortune, *Markets of the Seventies,* p. 8.

86. Arnold B. Barach, *The New Europe and Its Economic Future,* A Twentieth Century Fund Survey (New York: The Macmillan Co., 1964), p. 121.

87. National Association of Manufacturers, "Statement" in National Commission on

Technology, Automation and Economic Progress, *Technology and the American Economy,* Table 1, p. 192.

88. Lyle C. Fitch, "National Development and National Policy," in Ewald, *Environment and Policy.*

89. Spencer Klaw, "The Nationalization of Science," *Fortune* (September, 1964), p. 159.

90. U.S. Committee on Science and Astronautics, "Hearing on Science, Technology and Public Policy," January 1965–December 1966 (Washington, D.C.: Government Printing Office, 1967), p. 53; Daniel Bell used terms *extern* and *intern* challenge in his essay "The Measurement of Knowledge and Technology," in Eleanor B. Sheldon and Wilbert E. Moore, eds., *Indicators of Social Change* (New York: Russell Sage Foundation, 1968), p. 232.

91. Bell, "Measurement of Knowledge and Technology," p. 235.

92. Ibid., p. 233.

93. Robert A. Charpie, "Technological Innovation and Economic Growth," in *Applied Science and Technological Progress,* a Report to the U.S. Committee on Science and Astronautics, p. 257.

94. Lester B. Lake, *Technological Change: Its Conception and Measurement* (Englewood Cliffs, N.J.: Prentice-Hall, 1966), p. 4.

95. Charpie, "Technological Innovation and Economic Growth," p. 359.

96. Klaw, "The Nationalization of Science," p. 158.

97. Gene Bylinsky, "U.S. Science Enters a Not-So-Golden Era," *Fortune* (November 1968), p. 199.

98. Ibid.

99. Ann D. Walton and Marianna O. Lewis, eds., *The Foundation Directory,* Edition 2, The Foundation Library Center (New York: Russell Sage Foundation, 1964), p. 39.

100. J. C. R. Licklider, Robert W. Taylor and Evan Herbert, "The Computer as a Communication Device," *Science and Technology* (April 1968), p. 21.

101. U.S. Dept. of Commerce, Bureau of International Trade.

102. Paul Armer, "Computer Aspects of Technological Change, Automation, and Economic Progress," *The Outlook for Technological Change and Employment,* Report for the National Commission on Technology, Automation and Economic Progress (February 1966), p. 229.

103. Ithiel de Sola Pool, "Social Trends," *Science and Technology* (April 1968), p. 101.

104. Department of Housing and Urban Development, *Tomorrow's Transportation* (Washington, D.C.: Government Printing Office, 1968), p. 82.

105. Lyle Fitch and Associates, *Urban Transportation and Public Policy* (San Francisco: Chandler Publishing Company, 1964), p. 15.

106. Ibid., p. 42.

107. Christopher Lydon, "Trust Fund Asked for Mass Transit," *New York Times* (April 25, 1969).

108. "An Electric Solution to the Traffic Problem," *Esquire* (February 1969), p. 63; see also Highway Research Board, National Research Council, "Urban Mass Transportation Planning" (7 reports), No. 25 (Highway Research Record), 1968.

109. Rufus C. Phillips III, "Is Your City's Airport Ready for the Air Travel Explosion?" *Nation's Cities* (May 1969), p. 14; Tom Alexander, "Wheels-Up Time for STOL," *Fortune* (March 1968), p. 160.

110. Garth Keith, "Transportation: An Equal Opportunity for Access, Appendix B," in Ewald, ed., *Environment and Policy, The Next Fifty Years,* p. 196.

111. Ibid.

112. Federal Power Commission, Advisory Committee on Underground Transmission, "Underground Power Transmission" (Washington, D.C.: Government Printing Office, April 1966), p. 4.

113. U.S. Bureau of the Census, *Pocket Data Book, USA 1967* (Washington, D.C.: Government Printing Office, 1967), p. 63.

114. Gerard Piel, "The Public Stake in an 'Accelerated Program of Applying Biomedical Knowledge'," *Research in the Science of Men: Biomedical Knowledge, Development and Use,* conference sponsored by the Subcommittee on Government Research, and the Frontiers of Science Foundation for the Committee on Government Operations, U.S. Senate (Washington, D.C.: Government Printing Office, 1967), p. 20.

115. Department of Health, Education and Welfare, budget, 1968.

116. James E. Birren, "Research on Aging: A Frontier of Science and Social Gain," in Piel, *Research in the Science of Men,* p. 50.

117. Private correspondence with Dr. John Olwin.

118. Piel, *Research in the Science of Men,* pp. 18, 19.

119. Ewald, "Introduction" and "Appendix A," *Environment for Man, The Next Fifty Years* (Bloomington: Indiana University Press, 1968), pp. 3, 280.

120. U.S. Public Health Service, HEW, An Interim Report, 1968, *Survey of Community Solid Waste Practices;* Consumer Production and Environmental Health Service, Environmental Control Administration, 1968; also Atomic Energy Commission; see also Report to the Secretary of Health, Education and Welfare by the Task Force on Environmental Health and Related Problems, *A Strategy for a Liveable Environment,* 1967.

CHAPTER 5: *Organizing Knowledge to Create a Human Future Environment*

1. American Institute of Architects, "Where Is Architecture Going Today?" *AIA Journal* (March 1968).

2. E. Schillebeeckx, O.P., *God the Future of Man* (New York: Sheed & Ward, 1968), pp. 193, 176.

3. William R. Ewald, Jr., *Environment for Man, The Next Fifty Years* (Bloomington: Indiana University Press, 1968), p. 7; also *Environment and Change, The Next Fifty Years* (Bloomington: Indiana University Press, 1968), p. 3.

4. "COSATI Subject Category List," *Federal Council for Science and Technology* (December 1964), p. iii.

5. Ewald, *Bibliography of Studies of Future Technology, Change and Philosophies of Life,* for American Institute of Planners (Washington, D.C., December 1967; updated January 1969).

6. Ibid.

7. K. Lundberg-Holm, and C. D. Larson, *Development Index* (Ann Arbor: University of Michigan, 1958).

8. Robert L. Geddes, and Bernard P. Spring, *A Study of Education for Environmental Design,* sponsored by the American Institute of Architects, December 1961, pp. 24-26. Recognizes the process, scope and scale of design and was not intended to integrate this with science and humanities.

9. Ewald, *Environment for Man, The Next Fifty Years,* p. 7 and Appendix.

10. John B. Calhoun, *On Environment,* mimeographed paped for Unit of Research and Behavioral Science, National Institute for Mental Health (March 1968).

11. United Press International, "Study Finds Protests Widespread," *Washington Post* (March 3, 1969).

12. "American Youth: It's Outlook Is Changing the World," *Fortune* (Special issue: January 1969), pp. 1-202.

13. Israel Stenker, "Scholars' Debate: 'Think' vs. 'Feel'," *New York Times* (March 4, 1969).

14. P. B. Medawar, *The Future of Man* (New York: Mentor Books, 1961), p. 61.

15. Victor C. Ferkiss, *Technological Man: The Myth and the Reality* (New York: George Brazuller, 1969), p. 128.

16. J. Bronowski, in "The Third Millenium," *Progressive Architecture* (December 1966), p. 109.

17. Robert Oppenheimer, in William R. Cozart, ed., *Dialogue in Science* (Indianapolis: Bobbs-Merrill Company, 1967), p. 3.

18. Barry Commoner, "To Survive on Earth," *Population Bulletin,* 23 (December 1967), 5:143-147.

19. Lamont C. Cole, "Man and the Air," *Population Bulletin,* 24 (December 1968), 5:112.

20. Rene Dubos, *So Human an Animal* (New York: Charles Scribner's Sons, 1968), p. 216.

Afterword and Recommendations

1. Roderick Seidenberg, *Anatomy of the Future* (Chapel Hill: University of North Carolina Press, 1961), p. 30.

2. Ibid.

3. President's Commission on National Goals, *Goals for Americans* (Englewood Cliffs, N.J.: Prentice-Hall, 1960).

4. Rockefeller Panel Reports, *Prospect for America* (Garden City, N.Y.: Doubleday & Co., 1961).

5. Daniel Bell, ed., *Toward the Year 2000: Work in Progress* (Boston: Houghton Mifflin Co., 1968).

6. *Next Fifty Years, 1967-2017, The Future Environment of a Democracy,* The American Institute of Planners' fiftieth year consultation, 1965-1969.

7. Committee for Economic Development, *Budgeting for National Objectives, Executive and Congressional Roles in Program Planning and Performance,* a Statement on National Policy by the Research and Policy Committee (January 1966), and other papers.

8. Hans H. Landsberg, Leonard L. Fischman and Joseph L. Fisher, *Resources in America's Future* (Baltimore: The Johns Hopkins Press, 1963); and other publications.

9. National Planning Association, Center for Economic Projections, *Basic Policy Assumptions for Viewing the Future,* 1967 conference papers, and other publications; Chamber of Commerce of the United States, *Rural Poverty and Regional Progress in an Urban Society,* Fourth Regional Task Force on Economic Growth and Opportunity, 1969.

10. John Gardner, *Excelling, Can We Be Equal and Excellent Too?* (New York: Harper & Row, 1963); also Gardner, *Self Renewal; the Individual and the Innovative Society* (New York: Harper & Row, 1963).

11. Bayard Rustin, "Minority Groups, Development of the Individual," in William R. Ewald, Jr., ed., *Environment and Policy, The Next Fifty Years* (Bloomington: Indiana University Press, 1968).

12. R. Buckminster Fuller, "An Operating Manual for Spaceship Earth," in Ewald, ed., *Environment and Change, The Next Fifty Years* (Bloomington: Indiana University Press, 1968).

13. Paul Goodman, *Like a Conquered Province, The Moral Ambiguity of America* (New York: Random House, 1966); others, *Growing Up Absurd, Communitas* (with

Percival Goodman), *People or Personnel, Computerizing Mis-Education, The Society I Live In Is Mine.*

14. Ewald, "Introduction," *Environment and Change, The Next Fifty Years,* p. 3.

15. Ibid., p. 8.

16. Ewald, "Introduction," *Environment and Policy, The Next Fifty Years,* p. 5.

17. Daniel P. Moynihan, *Maximum Feasible Misunderstanding, Community Action on the War a Priority* (New York: Free Press, 1969).

18. Advisory Commission on Intergovernmental Relations, *Urban and Rural America, Policies for Future Growth* (Washington, D.C.: Government Printing Office, August 1968); and many others.

19. William James, "Moral Equivalent of War," in Staughton Lynd, *Nonviolence in America, A Documentary History* (Indianapolis: Bobbs-Merrill Company, 1966), p. 147.

20. Henry David Thoreau, "Court Disobedience," in Lynd, *Nonviolence in America,* p. 82.

21. Sir Geoffrey Vickers, taped comments at *The Next Fifty Years Conference,* on Individual and Society (Washington, D.C., October 1969).

22. Ibid.

23. Alexis de Tocqueville, in J. P. Mayer and Max Lerner, eds., *Democracy in America* (New York: Harper & Row, 1966), p. 485.

24. Bruce L. B. Smith, *The Future of the Not for Profit Corporations* (Santa Monica: Rand Corp., 1966), distributed by Clearinghouse for Federal Scientific and Technical Information, AD 633257; Nake M. Kamrany and John E. Elliott, *A Heuristic Investment Model for Nonprofit Research* (Santa Monica: System Development Corp., 1966).

25. Committee on Science and Astronautics, 1969.

26. Ewald, *Environment and Policy, The Next Fifty Years,* p. 446.

27. Richard C. Cornuelle and Robert H. Finch, *The New Conservative Liberal Manifesto* (San Diego: Viewpoint Books, 1968).

PART II. *The Building Industry: Concepts of Change*

CHAPTER 1: *Today: Building Industry Actors and Characteristics*

1. Donald A. Schon, *Technology and Change* (New York: Dell Publishing Co., 1967).

2. Sources for data on the nature of the building industry: Interview with E. Taylor Gregg, editor of *Construction Magazine;* U.S. Census Bureau, *County Business Patterns, U.S. Summary,* Table A-1; "Top 500 Record Billings Push," *Engineering News Record* (May 23, 1968); "Here Come the Giants," Professional Builder (August 1968); "The 400 Largest Contractors' U.S. Awards," *Engineering News Record* (April 23, 1968).

CHAPTER 2: *Tomorrow: Shifts in Structure, Characteristics, and Markets*

1. President's Commission on Urban Housing, *A Decent Home* (Washington, D.C.: Government Printing Office, 1968).

2. *Report of the National Commission on Urban Problems,* 1969.

3. *Automated Specifications: A Research Survey* (Prepared by Stanford Research Institute for the Construction Specifications Institute), November 1967.

Chapter 3: *Financing Construction*

1. U.S. Statistical Abstract, 1969, p. 336.
2. Joint Economic Committee Reports, February 1969.
3. U.S. Department of Commerce.
4. U.S. Office of Education (HEW).
5. Harvard Business Review, July-August 1967.

Chapter 4: *Land and Land Use*

1. President's Commission on Urban Housing, *A Decent Home* (Washington, D.C.: Government Printing Office, 1968).
2. *Report of the National Commission on Urban Standards, No. 12,* October 1968.
3. National Commission on Urban Problems, *Building the American Economy,* Part III (Washington, D.C.: Government Printing Office, 1968).

Chapter 5: *Construction Technology: Change and Implications*

1. The term *systems building* is here restricted to the open, or components', approach as distinguished from various proprietary building systems.
2. See "Industrial Housing," U.S. Congress, Joint Economic Committee, April 1969. Median values derived from various comparisons.
3. R. Buckminster Fuller, "The Age of Astro-Architecture," *Saturday Review* (July 13, 1968), pp. 17-20.
4. See Britton, "Can Architects Live Without Computers," *AIA Vital Questions.*